COBRA

A Jessica James Mystery

BY KELLY OLIVER

COBRA

A JESSICA JAMES MYSTERY

(Book 7)

By Kelly Oliver

____

Chapter 1

____

Squashed against the wall, Jessica James stared out the open window of the cloister. *Who else has looked out this same window over the last two hundred years?* Women who'd given up their families and worldly possessions to become nuns? Women who'd become nuns because they had no family and the world offered them nothing?

The stone wall above her head was cool. It had finally cooled off overnight. Soon, it would be hot again. The sun was already high in the sky over the verdant fields of North Umbria. Unlike the rugged Rocky Mountains where she'd grown up, the saturated blues and golds of the hilly landscape were soft and wistful.

Burrowing between the cool wall and Adrián's warm body, she fell back against the pillow and closed her eyes. She still couldn't believe she'd made it to Italy. Her first trip off the continent. *Thank you, pocket rockets.* A winning hand in a high-stakes Texas Hold 'Em had been enough to pay for her plane ticket—and the tuition for the best Art Crime Certificate Program in the world. One more week and she'd be certified to consult on art crime investigations.

Opening just one eye, she glanced over at the mop of

brown hair nestled in the pillow next to her and cringed. The medieval monks who'd built the cloister of San Francesco most certainly never spent the night like she had… unless maybe they were characters in an Umberto Eco novel.

She never should have let Adrián pass out in her bed. No matter if he'd hashed over the crime scene with her into the wee hours. She should have given him the boot the minute he mentioned her teeth. *What kind of guy admires a woman's teeth? Maybe he's a dentist back home in Madrid.* Or maybe, her three painful years in braces as a teenager had actually paid off.

At least, he was enough of a gentleman to keep his paws to himself after she removed them from her midriff with an "over my dead body."

Adrián Garcia had stuck to her like a magnet since the very first day of the forgery seminar. After doing their homework together for the last five weeks, they were a team. A darn good team. And he came in handy at the cafés since he was fluent in Italian.

The other students thought they were an item. She had to admit, Adrián had a certain charm—being a sexy nerd who cared more about winning a chess game or coming in first in the class than getting another notch on his belt. But she already had a boyfriend back in Chicago. She didn't need another. In fact, one was more than enough. She sat up in the twin bed and inhaled the fresh morning breeze coming from the hills. She could stare out this open window all day. *Sigh.*

You're burning daylight. That's what her aunt Mary would say when she came to get her out of bed at the crack of dawn to feed the horses.

With the jagged nail of her index finger, she poked the blanket in the vicinity of Adrián's shoulder. "Wake up, sleepy head."

"Don't people sleep back in *la montaña?*" Adrián yawned. As he stretched his smooth tanned arms above his head, his forearms flexed into well-formed muscles.

From the backwoods of Montana to the heart of Italy. If it weren't for Adrián's grumbling, she would have had to pinch herself to make sure she wasn't dreaming.

"Not if they want to get all the chores done before lunch."

The sun penetrated the open window like a laser beam. *What time is it?* There was no clock in the room. *It must be late.* She grabbed her cell phone off the nightstand. *Holy crap.* It was one in the afternoon already. And they still hadn't solved the case.

Adrián pulled the covers up over his head and his stockinged feet poked out the other end. She slid off the bed and then yanked the blanket clean off him. "We still don't have the evidence to prove the painting is a forgery."

"Relax, *linda*. It's Sunday." Adrián sat up, ran his hands through his mess of hair and then adjusted the St. Christopher's medal he always wore around his neck. "It's not due until tomorrow." He swung his long legs over the side of the bed and slipped his argyle stockinged feet into his espadrilles. "First, *un caffè e panino*." He waved his hand in the air. "What do they say? When in Rome." He stood up and tucked his linen shirt into his trendy distressed jeans.

"We're not in Rome." Jessica blew at her bangs. "We're in Amelia."

She'd taken two planes, a train, and a bus to get there. And she'd spent nearly every penny she had. She wasn't about to waste her time drinking coffee and eating prosciutto sandwiches with Adrián… not any more time than she already had, anyway.

"Let's examine the provenance again." She'd learned that art is authenticated through provenance, namely the paper trail of receipts leading back to the original artist. "There's something bugging me about it."

"Bugging?" Adrián came around the bed and stood next to her at the window. A bit too close for comfort. *He isn't going to put his arms around me again, is he?* "Want one?" He held out a colorful lollipop.

She scowled. "A sucker for breakfast?"

He shrugged, unwrapped the candy, and popped it into his mouth. "How about compromise?" His dark eyes sparked. "Let's take the provenance folder to Caffè Roma and sort it out over coffee." He grabbed his fedora from the bedpost and tipped it onto his head.

She gathered up the folder from the small wooden desk in the corner of the room. Like everything else in the small room, the desk looked like it was a thirteenth century original. *How many hands have crossed this roughhewn surface?* She lingered at the desk, running her finger across the top, imagining monks with halos for hair using feathers for pens, blood for ink, and parchment for paper.

A modest stone room with only a desk, a bed, and a sink. No air conditioning. Only a large, shuttered window that opened wide to let in fresh air. *Yeah.* She could get used to living like a monk. Especially since the food in Italy was so good it made her want to cry.

Maybe Adrián was right. Some coffee and bread would give her sustenance and help her think. Although she'd only just learned the word, *provenance,* she knew there was something wrong with this one. She tucked the folder under her arm.

Adrián waited for her at the door. "After you, *linda.*" He stopped her before she crossed the wooden threshold. "Wait a second." He straightened the collar of her blouse and smiled in admiration. "Perfect."

Caffè Roma was only a few blocks from the cloister. But the intense summer sun made it seem further. By the time they arrived, Jessica had stripped down to her T-shirt and was using her snap-front blouse as a handkerchief to wipe sweat from her forehead. Her face was hot, evidence that her "peaches-and-cream" complexion had become tomatoes-and-cottage-cheese.

The waitress seated them at a café table under an umbrella. *Thank goodness.* Jessica plopped into a wire chair—sigh—and took in the sights.

Whereas everything in her hometown of Whitefish, Montana was made of wood from local trees, everything in Amelia was made of stone. Even the narrow streets were cobblestone and were lined with short caramel-colored houses with brown and green wooden shutters and flowerpots out front. The town looked ancient. Tile roofs and stone arches accented the village charm.

The aroma of rich coffee and freshly baked bread coming from the café made her mouth water. *Yes. I could get used to this.*

While they waited for their breakfast, Jessica opened the folder and examined the documents, including receipts for a small black and white painting by the American abstract impressionist Willem de Kooning, which had been sold by an art dealer in Michigan to a collector in New York seven years ago, but had recently come under investigation by the FBI.

The assignment was to determine whether the painting was real or fake and provide evidence. This was the last test in the Amelia Workshop Art Crimes Institute, the best intensive art crimes seminar in the world. The top two students in the class had a shot at an internship with the FBI art crime team.

This was her chance. If she could solve the case first, she had a foot in the door for a job… a big job. If she didn't solve the case, she'd be just another unemployed philosopher.

Now that she'd finally graduated and gotten her Ph.D., it was high time she got a real job. She'd miss teaching, but she wouldn't miss the measly paychecks that barely kept her in books and whiskey. If she got a job working in art crime, she might be able to graduate from whiskey to champagne.

Nah. She'd stick to whiskey. Jack Daniels was more reliable than any boyfriend she'd ever had.

But if she didn't get a job in art crimes, and couldn't get one in philosophy, then she'd have to move back in with her mother. She cringed. Alpine Vista Trailer Park seemed a lifetime away… a lifetime she'd just as soon forget. Growing up below the poverty line with an alcoholic mother was no picnic.

Jessica had worked her backside off to get the grades necessary for a fancy scholarship to escape that pit of despair. She'd do just about anything to keep from going back.

Unfortunately, she was just one paycheck away from dragging her sorry butt back to her mom's sad-sack doublewide with its freezer full of cheap vodka and rancid orange sherbet.

"We already established the signatories are real," Adrián said. "Too bad they're all dead."

"Conveniently, they're all dead." The documents dated back decades. She turned over a receipt that had been witnessed by a lawyer, a now *dead* lawyer. It looked old and authentic.

"We have confirmed the art galleries and law firms exist." Adrián was lively when he talked, using his hands, his head, and his whole body. He could get quite a workout just holding up his end of a conversation. *No wonder he is so skinny.*

"Still, something isn't right." She sifted through the papers. "I can feel it in my gut."

"And a nice gut it is." He smiled.

She glared at him.

He held out his manicured hand and wiggled his fingers. "Let me see the file again."

She passed him the folder. How many times could they go over these same documents?

Adrián shuffled the papers. Even when the waitress delivered his coffee and sandwich, he didn't look up. He spread seven pieces of paper—letters, receipts, bills of sale—across the table. "Look." He pointed. "What do these all have in common?"

She shrugged. "They're all related to the de Kooning painting?"

"Look at the type."

"It looks old."

"But isn't it odd that the type is exactly the same on all of them?"

She grabbed one of the receipts and took a closer look. "Holy cow. You're right. They were all typed on the same old typewriter."

"I think we are closing in on our proof." He took a big bite out of the middle of his fancy ham sandwich. A piece of arugula stuck to his upper lip and wagged when he talked.

She reached over and plucked the leafy mustache off his face.

"Want half?" he asked. "What is mine is yours." He pushed his plate toward her.

Five minutes ago, she would have gobbled it up. Now, she was too distracted by their find. If all the receipts and letters were typed on the same typewriter, that pointed to forgery. But they needed more to prove it conclusively.

She dumped a couple tablespoons of sugar into her Americano and stirred. Even sugared up and watered down, the first sip jolted her tongue with a zap of burnt bitterness. She pushed the coffee aside, picked up a letter from de Kooning's lawyer, and examined it for the umpteenth time.

Wait. A firecracker exploded in her brain. She grabbed her phone and started tapping. *Come on stupid internet. No wonder they called it the World-Wide-Wait.*

Finally. "I've got it." She beamed over at Adrián.

"Got what?" he asked with his mouth full and his cheeks bulging out like a chipmunk's.

"Look at the date on this letter from de Kooning's lawyer." She held up the letter.

"July 14, 1947." Adrián shrugged. "So what? That fits with de Kooning's black and white period."

"Now look at the address."

"525 Park Avenue, New York, New York, 10065." He squinted at her. "What is wrong with it?"

"Zip codes weren't used in the U.S. until 1963." She pumped the air with her fist. "Yes. Gotcha."

"Aren't you clever." He put up his hand for a high five. No one had done that to her in years. "This calls for a Grappa."

Five weeks in Italy and she still hadn't gotten used to the stuff. She'd take a Jack-n-Coke over that firewater any day. "Shouldn't we write up our report?"

"After a toast to our success," Adrián said, jumping up and heading inside to the bar. A minute later, he returned with two tulip glasses half-full of golden liquid. He handed her a glass and then sat down and lifted his own. "To a great art crime solving team."

"To catching the bad guys." After clinking glasses, she took a sip and grimaced. *Yucko*. It never got any better. Cloyingly sweet and acidic at the same time.

"To us, the best students in the class." Adrián raised his glass again. It was true. Every week they'd solved the case first and gotten points for the best job. She was ahead in the point count. But Adrián was a close second. And then there was that snobby Louvre woman, Simone Bernard in third.

Whenever Simone did stoop to talk to Jessica, she always managed to zing her with some lefthanded compliment. "You must be the cleverest little cowgirl in those barren plains." "You're a dear, but not really cut out for serious crime work." "I bet your mommy will be glad to have you back at the ranch." Jessica wanted to pop the stuck-up beatch right in the kisser.

"To us," Jessica said, taking another drink. This must be an especially bad year. In addition to the sweet battery acid, there was a hint of salty sea water.

"Pretty good for leftovers," Adrián said.

She gave him a quizzical look.

"Grappa. It's made from the leftover skins and stems from making red wine." He took a sip. "A lot stronger than wine, too."

"No wonder it tastes like crap." Must be the heat. She was getting tipsy after just a few sips. She wiped her forehead with her shirt. "Bourbon is more my speed."

"Would you like me to get you a whiskey?" he asked, jumping up again.

"Isn't it a little early for whiskey?" She shook her head. "Maybe after we write our report."

"To you, my beautiful American friend." Adrián drained his glass. "I will settle up. After you finish your grappa, we will go back to your room and write a killer report." He sauntered off to the bar.

By the time he returned a few minutes later, her head was spinning. How strong was that stuff? Usually, she could hold her own. *Could it be the altitude? Nah.* She grew up at seven thousand feet, for crap's sake.

"Shall we?" Adrián held out his hand.

Reluctantly, she took it… and then clung to him. *What is going on?* Had she contracted some travel bug? All she could think about was lying down. Leaning against Adrián's shoulder, she stumbled along the cobblestones until they reached the cloister. Good thing it was only a few blocks away.

The ancient stone building lurked in the shadows of a new bank building, giving it an ominous vibe. The gargoyles staring down at her from the battlements didn't help. One particularly grotesque stone monster with its large mouth gaping reminded her of Edvard Munch's *The Scream*.

She tripped over the threshold and Adrián caught her before she did a faceplant. Without his help, she never would have made it back to her room. He ushered her to bed.

"But the report…" She wiped sweat from her forehead. "The internship… I have to—" Her head fell back against the pillow.

"Don't worry," he said. "I will type it up. Then I'll come back and wake you up before class. We will turn it in together." He smiled down at her.

As he drew the blanket up over her body, she whispered, "I owe you one."

"What are friends for?" Adrián tucked her in. "I'll be back soon. Rest up, *linda*. At the doorway, he turned back and blew her a kiss. "Our hour of triumph is near."

She forced a weak smile and then allowed her brain to follow her body into the black pool of nothingness—calling out to her from beyond consciousness.

As she felt herself falling into the darkness, a strange question echoed through her head. *Did I jump or was I pushed?*

Chapter 2

Jessica felt like she was floating on an ocean of dread. She didn't know why. Mayhem, her black gelding. Stoli, her mom's cat. Nick Schilling, her former lover. Jack Grove, her boyfriend back in Chicago. Kandinsky's painting, The Blue Rider. *Wait.* Someone was tearing the precious painting. A man. He looked familiar. Was it Adrián?

She opened her eyes and clawed at the covers trying to escape the chaos of her dreams. Through the haze in her head, the streetlight seeped through the open window. *Where am I?* Her pulse quickened. There was something uncanny about waking up and not knowing where you were.

Right. The cloister. Amelia, Italy. Art Crimes Institute. The report! It was due. She thrashed around in the bed. Her sweaty shirt was sticking to her back.

Had Adrián come and gone already? *Did we write the report?* Why couldn't she remember? She struggled to wake up. It was no use. She fell back into the pit of a recurring nightmare of quicksand sucking her down. No matter how hard she tried to claw her way out, she continued to go down. The more she struggled, the deeper she sank.

When she opened her eyes again, the sun was barreling

into the room. Her hair stuck to her forehead, and her mouth tasted like the floor of a barn. She rolled over and searched the nightstand for her cell phone. Her palm touched the cool surface of the nightstand. Where is it? She propped herself up on her elbows and scanned the room. *How long have I been sleeping?* Without her phone, she had no idea. She could have been asleep for an hour or twenty-four hours. She had no idea.

Wait. The report. The forgery class. She had to get out of bed.

The events of yesterday afternoon came flooding back. The de Kooning case. Adrián's smile. Evil grappa.

Where is Adrián? She had to thank him for dragging her home, putting her to bed, and taking care of the report. At least she hoped he'd taken care of it.

She rubbed her temples. She was feeling a bit better… except for the lingering headache. Whatever bug had taken her down had been stealthy and fierce. The grappa bug. She slid out of bed, went to the little sink in the corner of her cell, and splashed water on her face. Somewhat revived, she padded over to the window and looked out.

The sun was already high in the sky and the cafés were full of diners. How late was it? *Crapulence.* She had to get to class.

Luckily, she was still wearing her clothes from yesterday. Unluckily, they stunk of grappa induced nightmares. She ripped off her shirt and threw on a clean T-shirt, and then stuffed her feet into her canvas All-Stars. At a gallop, she bolted from the room, and took off down the stairs, slipping and sliding to the bottom.

"Crap, crap crap." She was late for class. And the assignment was due first thing. "Adrián, please, please, please, tell me you turned it in already." Speed walking, she mumbled to herself all the way across the courtyard. If only she had time to get a cup of coffee. *Caffeine. I need caffeine.* Her head was pounding. There would be time for coffee later… after she averted the disaster.

If she didn't stay at the top of the class, there would go her chance at a job. *Hello, life imprisonment in a trailer park in the back-woods of Montana.* You'd think she could fall back on her Ph.D. *Ha!* Academic jobs were as scarce as hen's teeth. *So, it's make this art crime thing work, or go back home with my tail between my legs.*

Her bootcut jeans swished as she broke into a trot. It was tricky zipping across the courtyard cobblestones without twisting an ankle. Good thing she was wearing sneakers.

Her head was spinning, and the high stone walls of the courtyard seemed to close in on her. The shadows they cast danced ominously as if taunting her.

The arch that led to the education wing was just up ahead. Picking up her pace, she sprinted down the corridor to the heavy wooden door at the end. When she yanked it open, the bright dry outside of the cloister gave way to the dark dank inside.

She trotted down the hallway to the door of the class-room, skidded to a stop outside the door, and peeked inside through a tiny window. Sitting at the small desks, the other nineteen adult students looked like Gulliver visiting Lilliput.

Adrián was in the front row, his rapt attention focused on the front of the room. *Why didn't he come back to wake me up? Has he turned in our report already?*

She strained her neck, but couldn't see the teacher, famed art historian and forensic scientist, Hans Brubeck. Her cheeks burned as she cracked the door open and slid inside. At times like this, she wished she was invisible.

"Dr. James, so good of you to join us." In his early fifties, Hans Brubeck already had graying hair and the hard features of an athlete living on nothing but bean sprouts.

Out of the corner of her eye, she saw Simone Bernard smirking. *Irritating woman.* With her oversized eyeglasses and exaggerated jewelry, bright red lipstick, and thick, blue eyeshadow, she looked like a cartoon character. Jessica felt like sticking her tongue out. Instead, she headed for the only vacant seat at the back of the classroom.

As she passed by, Adrián looked up at her and whispered. "What happened to you?"

She stopped in her tracks. "What happened to *you*?" Why hadn't he come back last night so they could write up the report together? She only hoped he'd done it on their behalf.

"This might be a good time to take a ten-minute break before we discuss art crimes during wartime." Hans Brubeck opened his hands, as if by waving an invisible magic wand, he'd just imparted enlightenment.

"You don't look so good." Adrián stood up from his desk and took her elbow. "Let's get you a cup of coffee and some food."

She shook him loose. "Why didn't you come back and wake me up in time for class?"

"Let's talk about it outside." Adrián's lashes were blinking a mile a minute.

Jessica tightened her lips and followed him down the hall and out into the courtyard. Once outside, under the glare of the morning sun, she interrogated him. "Why didn't you come back and wake me up?" She stood with her hands on her hips.

"I did come back." He ran his fingers through his thick hair. "You didn't answer. I thought you'd gone out."

She narrowed her eyes. Usually, she was a light sleeper. Then again, she'd been under the influence of that evil grappa and some mysterious Italian bug. She took a deep breath. "Did you turn in our report?"

"I tried." He looked down at her with pleading eyes. "But Hans insisted that since you weren't there, your name couldn't be on it." He fingered his St. Christopher's Medal.

"What?" Her heart sunk. "But I solved the case."

"Hans thought I was cheating for you." Adrián blushed. "Anyway, we solved the case together. Partners? Right?"

"If we were partners, you would have put my name on that report." She paced back and forth in front of him. "Now what?" *Now, I'll fall to the back of the class and be doomed to spend the rest of my life changing dirty diapers and fetching some lumberjack his beer… that's what.*

Adrián shrugged and gave her a sheepish grin. "We can run to Kinkos and you can photocopy my report."

"There's a Kinkos in Amelia?" *An Italian village in the middle of nowhere. Yeah, right.*

He fiddled with his St. Christopher's medal again. "I can print it at my hotel but with your name on it." Adrián was staying at some fancy hotel across town.

"And prove Hans right that I'm a cheater?" She shook her head. "No way." The only thing she hated worse than cheaters was chickenshit men who didn't say what they meant. "I'll just have to hustle and write it up myself." With that she turned on her heels and strode out of the courtyard.

Adrián ran after her. "I can help, if you want."

"I've had all your help I can bear," she said over her shoulder without slowing her pace.

"Wait," Adrián yelled after her. "Your phone. You forgot it at the café yesterday." He caught up to her and held out her cellphone.

She snatched it out of his hand. "Thanks."

"I'm really sorry about everything…" His voice trailed off.

"Me too." She forced a smile. "It isn't really your fault." She reached out and patted his arm. "I guess I should thank you for getting me home." Then she punched his arm. "But no thanks for that deadly grappa. What was in that stuff?"

"Strong, eh?" He laughed. "Even for a cowgirl from Montana."

"I'm never touching that poison again."

"You just need more practice."

"Forget it." She waved him off. "I know when a horse is too much for me to handle."

"Horse?"

"Never mind. I've gotta run and write my report. I hope old stick-up-the-butt Hans will let me turn it in."

"Peace offering?" Adrián held out a *Chupa Chups.*

Sigh. She took the lollipop and left him on the street corner unwrapping one of his own. She dashed back to her room, ran up the stairs, and flung the door open. As quickly as she could, she yanked her laptop from her bookbag, slapped it down on the desk, and plopped into the chair.

It took all her patience to go through the evidence step-by-step rather than just cutting to the chase. *Argggh!* Her brain was faster than her fingers. If only she could plug her brain directly into the computer.

Forty minutes later, she did a quick spellcheck and then sent the document to a printshop up the street. *Dang.* She could use a coffee. If only she had time… As it was, she'd be lucky if stickler-for-rules Hans Brubeck would accept her report since it was a couple hours late.

What's a couple of hours? She thought of those long drives across Montana with her dad. He drove a logging truck. One time she rode with him up to Flathead National Forest. On those windy, narrow, dirt roads, the distance from the cloister to the train station could have taken two hours.

She hightailed it to the printshop to pick up her report. Of course, there was a line. *Crapulence.* Pulling her phone from her pocket, she glanced at the time. *Shoot.* In fifteen minutes, the class would break for lunch. With each passing minute, there was less chance that Hans would accept her late report. She moved from foot to foot, willing the line to move faster.

After she snagged the printout, she sprinted back to the classroom. Just her luck. It was empty. Sure enough, everyone had gone to lunch. She knew where to find them. At one o'clock, the class took a two-hour lunch at Café Apollo, a local pasta and pizza joint around the corner on Via del Monte.

Clutching her report, she zipped back outside, through the courtyard, and onto the street. Via del Monte was on the edge of the city and overlooked the rolling hills of Umbria, which were dotted with the terra cotta roofs of neighboring villages.

The chaos in her soul was at odds with the tranquil scene. If only she could disappear into the landscape instead of face Hans Brubeck.

She found the class seated around three long tables. They were yucking it up, eating pizza and drinking vino. Hans was seated at the center table, surrounded by his disciples. He was waving his hands in the air and holding forth as usual. *What a blowhard.* He absorbed adoration like a dry, brittle sponge soaking up sea water. She could practically see his chest expanding with every fluttered eyelash from one of the female students. Adrián sat next to him, slapping him on the back. *Teacher's pet.*

Jessica waved, trying to get Adrián's attention. But he was too busy brown-nosing to look her way. Either that or he didn't want to acknowledge her in front of the others. Simone made eye-contact for a second, pulled a sour face like she smelled something foul, and then looked away.

Skirting tables and other diners, Jessica made her way to the group, and then stood next to Hans's table, waiting for someone to acknowledge her. Finally, Hans looked up at her. "Dr. James, you've come back to us."

"My report." She held out the papers. "Sorry it's late, but I got really sick last night and overslept." She glared at Adrián, who was unusually quiet.

"Since you were sick, I'll accept it." Hans reached out and took her report. "But I'll have to deduct points for being late."

She nodded. Being a teacher herself, she knew what it was like when students made excuses. Then again, being a decent human being, she would never deduct points when a student was sick.

Hans stood up and did a three-sixty, making quite a show of gathering his leather briefcase. "Can I have your atten-tion?" He tapped a fork on the side of his wine glass. "Twenty minutes and then back to the classroom." He slid Jessica's report into his briefcase. "Then, I'll announce this year's internship winners." He bowed his head slightly as if he'd just received a standing ovation and strode out of the café.

Jessica's breath caught at the mere mention of the internship. Did she still have a chance? *Please, please, please.* This could be a defining moment of her life.

Not in the mood to chitchat—even with Adrián—she scooted out of the café just after Hans. She spent the next twenty minutes mindlessly walking up and down the hallway next to the classroom.

When Hans appeared in the corridor, she zipped into the classroom and slid into a desk in the back of the room. She considered moving up to the front, but she was trying to curb her expectations.

The rest of the students filed in, laughing and chatting. After they'd taken their seats, Hans leaned over and put his hands on the desk at the front of the room. He looked like a runner beginning a race. "What makes a good art crime detective?" He stared out at the class.

"Deduction," one student said.

"Deduction," Hans repeated. "What else?"

"Intelligence," another student said.

"Intelligence. What else?"

"Research."

"Research. What else?"

The class was silent. "Nothing?" He straightened up. "Dedication. It takes dedication to be a good art crime detective." He paced back and forth in front of the class. "What makes a *great* art crime detective?"

No one said anything. Obviously, everyone was tired of playing this game.

He stopped pacing and sat on top of the desk. "Experience. To become a truly great art crime detective, you need experience." He paused for effect. "The highest score on our assignments over the last three weeks will earn someone an internship where they will gain valuable experience. Street smarts. What can't be taught in a classroom."

Jessica bit her nail. The moment of truth. Had she scored high enough even with the point deduction to keep her lead?

"The person who has shown the necessary intelligence, research, and dedication over the last three weeks is…" Hans drummed his fingers on the desk. "Adrián Garcia. Adrián had the highest score. And he will be going to America to work with the FBI."

The class broke out in applause. Reluctantly, Jessica joined in. She felt like barfing. It wasn't fair. She was the one who had solved the last assignment, not him. And she was ahead in the point count until he fed her grappa and made her sleep late. Right now, she hated Adrián Garcia.

"The second internship goes to…"

Jessica held her breath.

"Simone Bernard." Hans jumped off the desk. "Congratulations."

No way she would clap for Simone Bernard, the stuck-up museum curator from the Louvre. How did Simone come in second?

Stupid Hans must have deducted a lot of points for turning in the report late.

"And the alternate is…" Hans opened his palm as if a tiny hologram alternate would appear standing on his hand like the projection of Princess Leah in Star Wars. "Dr. Jessica James."

Crapulence. Now I'm officially unemployed.

Chapter 3

Bang. Bang. Bang.

Wiping sweat from her brow, Jessica rolled over and grabbed her phone. Seven o'clock. Her taxi to the airport wasn't due until this afternoon.

Bang. Bang. Bang. Who was knocking so dang early?

Should she answer or just ignore it and go back to sleep? No brainer. She put the pillow over her head to block the sound and the light.

Bang. Bang. Bang.

Grrr. The knocking got louder.

"Jessica, are you in there?" *Adrián. What does he want?*

She sat up on her elbows. *Sigh.* "Just a minute." She crawled out of bed, threw on her jacket over her undies, and padded to the door in her bare feet.

Adrián had a crazed look in his eyes and a lollipop in his mouth. "You'll never guess what happened."

"It had better be good since you woke me up." She leaned on the door frame.

"Sorry about that." He shrugged.

She yawned and rubbed the sleep out of her eyes.

"You look worse for wear." He held out a lollipop with a

bright pink and yellow wrapper, a *Chupa Chups.* "Here. This will help."

She waved it away. "If you wanted bright-eyed and bushy-tailed, you should have caught a squirrel." She put her hand on her hip. "And hidden the grappa."

"Sorry about that too." He peeked inside her room. "Can I come in?"

She stepped aside to let him pass. "What's so important that it can't wait until after coffee?"

His eyes lit up. "You know Simone Bernard?"

"Yes." Jessica blew at her bangs. Of course, she knew Simone Bernard. The snobby Louvre curator who loved nothing better than to insult her. "The stuck-up so-and-so who got my internship."

"That's just it." Adrián's hands were flying like he was conducting Beethoven's fifth. "Hit and run. Late last night."

"Whaaat?" Jessica's mouth fell open. "Is she okay?"

Adrián quit flapping his arms. "She's in a coma in the ICU."

She just stood there, blinking at him, filled with a torrent of emotions. *Even if the arrogant so-and-so had it coming, I shouldn't gloat.* "Poor Simone."

"You know what that means?" His voice cracked. "You get the internship." He grinned. "We're both going to Washington. Maybe we'll be working together."

She couldn't think about that now. "Poor woman." She didn't want to profit from someone else's injury—a coma in the ICU. *What if she dies?* A tidal wave of guilty nausea hit her. She went to the window and looked out.

The girl selling flowers on the corner was handing a bouquet to an older gentleman. *Are they for his wife or his lover?* The baker across the street was standing in front of his shop smoking a cigarette; he had blotches of flour on his apron. A dove sat on the branch of an Aleppo pine tree singing a melancholy song.

Simone Bernard was unconscious. And the world was going on without her. Somewhere, someone must be worrying about her. Somewhere, someone's world had just been turned upside down. No matter how mean she was, Simone didn't deserve a hit-and-run.

Jessica would never forget the day she found out her dad had been in a fatal wreck. The fresh snow. Hiding in the barn. Her mother crying in the kitchen. Jessica was only twelve. It was still the worst day of her life.

"Aren't you happy?" Adrián asked, fingering his St. Christopher's Medal.

She stared at him. *Who is this guy?* She shook her head, unable to say a word.

Chapter 4

Boston, Massachusetts. *How in the world did I end up here?*

Federal Marshal, Lexington Colt dropped a sixpack of diet Mountain Dew onto the passenger-side floor next to the diaper bag. It was going to be a long night. The stupid babysitter had called in sick at the last minute, so baby Sammy was going to be riding shotgun. *If the director finds out I'm investigating a robbery with my kid in tow, I'll be canned immediately.*

She'd already been demoted from the Witness Protection Program for screwing up. A couple of witnesses had gotten killed. She grimaced. Was it her fault the flipping Taliban had messed with her head? The army psychologist called it PTSD and gave her a bottle of pills, as if that was some sort of compensation.

Sometimes she wished she hadn't enlisted. But what else could she have done? Married Travis jackass Dawson and worked her fingers to the bone scrubbing floors at Walmart? No. The army had been her ticket out of the humid hollers of Tennessee.

Lexi slapped the blue light on top of her car but left the siren off. She didn't want to wake the baby, who had finally fallen asleep. *Thank the Lord.*

Why did thieves always have to strike after dark? Things would change if they had to take their kids with them on a heist. She chuckled to herself.

She backed the Charger out of the parking spot and headed down Humboldt Street toward the expressway. At least at this time of night the traffic shouldn't be so bad.

At two-thirty in the morning, there were still a few people on the streets in her Roxbury neighborhood, mostly drunks, thugs, and partiers stopping off at the corner bodega on their way home. Even in the dead of night in Roxbury, you could pick up fresh pizza, falafel, or a bouquet of roses after a lover's quarrel.

She sipped her pop as she drove past block after block of triple-decker apartment buildings sitting shoulder-to-shoulder. Three thousand dollars a month for a six hundred-square-foot shoebox. *I've seen closets bigger than my apartment… okay, closets in the mansions of drug kingpins.*

The expressway had more traffic than it should have in the middle of the night. She kept her eyes peeled for the Cambridge exit. Who would have thought she was on her way to Harvard?

Just after midnight, a groundskeeper at Harvard had called the local cops about a robbery on campus. Some dummy had stolen a Gutenberg bible from the university library and was lying on his back like a bug below the library window.

Sometime after one o'clock, the Cambridge cops called the FBI, and now she was speeding across Boston with a half-empty can of Dew in one cupholder and a pacifier in the other… just in case Samantha woke up.

I wonder if Mountain Dew is transmitted through breast milk. She smiled. Never too early to get started on the Dew. *Okay. Okay. I need to cut down on the Dew.* Tomorrow. *I'll go cold turkey, tomorrow.*

By the time she crossed the Charles River, it was almost

three in the flipping morning. Since the precious bible wasn't *actually* missing, why did they need the FBI?

She sighed. She'd gone from taking down the most dangerous criminals in the country to investigating college pranks in the middle of the night. What was next? Meter-maid in Nebraska?

Lordie. There were no parking spots on campus. Were these college kids vampires, or what? Did every rich kid have his own car? She slid the Charger into an open spot in front of the administration building reserved for the vice chancellor for academic affairs. Hopefully the vice chancellor was home in bed.

Lexi hated to wake the baby. But she couldn't very well just leave her in the car by herself. As carefully as she could, she scooped Sammy out of the car-seat and tucked her into the Baby Bjorn. Slipping her arms through the straps, Lexi cinched the baby around her own body like a lifejacket. *Yes. Baby Samantha, you saved my life.*

She shut the car door, trying not to make a sound. *Sammy's binky.* She opened the door again, bent in, and grabbed the pacifier out of the cup holder, clipping it onto the front pocket of her shirt.

Waaaaaaa. Sammy started wailing. *Dammit.* Lexi might as well slap a blue light on her back. Good thing she didn't have to sneak up on any bad guys. They'd hear her coming a mile away.

"Shhhh." She jostled the Baby Bjorn. Tapping her phone awake, she asked it for directions to the library. She'd never been on Harvard's campus before. Holding her phone out in front of her like a Geiger-counter, she started walking, keeping her eyes glued to the screen. As she made her way across campus, she sang softly, "Robed in garlands soaked in brine… you are gone and lost forever, oh my darlin' Sammy mine."

A screaming grenade was easier to dodge than a screaming child, especially when it was your own. She'd rather tear her own heart out than listen to Sammy cry. In Afghanistan, Lexi had defused landmines, fired AK47s, and gone without water for nearly forty-eight hours, but nothing prepared her for motherhood.

One nail takes out the other, as her daddy used to say.

The black streetlamps along the sidewalks were cute, but they didn't put out a lot of light. She could barely see where she was going.

Aside from the eerie hoot of an owl and the rustling of leaves, the campus was quiet. The co-eds were probably sleeping it off after a night of hitting the books… either that or hitting the bars.

Who knows what these smarty pants rich kids do late at night? Not her, that's for sure. She hadn't made it past high school.

Dammit. The wet grass was getting her slippers wet. She'd been in such a hurry that she'd left her apartment in sweatpants and slippers. She wished she'd taken the time to put on some proper clothes.

The library was easy to spot… and not just because of the crime scene tape and local cops milling around. It was the only building fully illuminated by flood lights in its portico. Lit from behind, giant columns in front of the library looked like the bars of a jail cell. And the windows on either side of the entrance shone like the huge eyes of whatever creature was locked inside.

Lexi shivered. She should have grabbed a jacket. The June breeze was cool against her bare arms.

Still, it was a far cry from the Wyoming winters that seemed to last forever. Then again, from what she'd heard, Boston winters laughed and said, "Hold my beer." She'd frozen her behind off in the Cowboy State, why not in Beantown too?

The bureau had it in for her. They knew she was from Tennessee and couldn't take the cold, so they purposefully were trying to freeze her to death.

"Hey boys," she said when she got within earshot of the locals. "What have we got?"

The two uniformed cops stared at her. When she stepped under the crime scene tape, one of them held his hand up. "Can we help you Ma'am?"

Ever since she'd had a kid, strangers called her *ma'am* instead of *miss*. And every time, it felt like a punch in the gut. She'd grown up with a bunch of dickhead men who used *ma'am* like a put down.

"Colt." She pulled her badge out of her back pocket. "FBI."

One of the cops had the nerve to grab her badge and examine it. As he handed it back to her, he looked her up and down and scoffed. "Marshal Mamma," he said under his breath.

"What did you say?" *Ignore them, Lex. They're only campus rent-a-cops.*

He just shook his head.

Now she really wished she'd put on proper clothes. These arseholes weren't going to take her seriously. "Haven't you seen an FBI agent with a binky clipped to her shirt before?"

He turned and walked away. *Jerk.*

"Who tried to steal the Gutenberg?" She ignored jerkface and addressed his partner.

"The kid is in the hospital," the partner said. "He fell from the second-floor window trying to make off with the bible."

She looked up at the window. There was a rope hanging from the roof down to the window. Stupid thief. He didn't bring enough rope to get to the ground. "Was the bible hurt?" she asked.

"Not too bad considering the kid fell on top of it." The partner pointed to a large divot in the grass. "He had the book in his backpack and fell backwards."

Idiot kid underestimated the weight of that bad boy. She smiled. Taken down by a bible. How appropriate.

"Can you show me where it was taken from?" Lexi asked. Sammy gurgled and instinctively she kissed her daughter's little, fuzzy head.

"Sure," the partner said. "Follow me, Marshal Colt."

Jerkface had disappeared. He'd rather sit in the squad car eating donuts than work with a woman… and worse, a mamma. *Let him try to push a nine-pound baby out of a nine-millimeter hole and then see who's the toughest.*

She followed the partner to the wrought iron gates protecting the front entrance. He pushed them open.

"Not locked?"

"They were. But the head librarian unlocked them for us." She nodded.

Stepping through the interior glass doors, the foyer looked like the entrance to a bank, complete with marble columns and floor buffed to a shine. A corridor led to a rotunda that screamed money and privilege. The entire domed cavern was ivory, except for the black veins in the marble and black and white tiles on the floor. A brass chandelier hung from the center of the dome.

"Whew," she whistled as they walked up a grand marble staircase. *I wonder how much those suckers pay to go to Harvard?* Sammy squirmed. Climbing the stairs must have woken her up again. Lexi unclipped the pacifier from her shirt and popped it into the baby's mouth.

The crime scene was a wood-paneled room with built-in bookcases and carved moldings. With its oriental rug, tiffany lamps, and fresh cut flowers, the room looked like a fancy study out of a movie. In the center of the room was a glass-covered wooden case where the bible had been on display.

"The glass isn't broken," she said, examining the case.

"It wasn't locked." The partner shook his head. "If that bible is so valuable, they should have better security."

"They should." She knelt next to the case. No easy feat with Sammy strapped to her chest. At least Sammy was sleeping again. "Something worth over five million dollars sitting in an open case." She sucked her teeth.

"Five mil. No way!" The partner came over and stood staring down into the empty case to see what all the fuss was about.

She stood up, deadlifting the baby as she went, and then checked out the broken window. *Clever.* The thief had used masking tape to keep pieces of broken glass from falling all over the walkway below. Maybe he wasn't so dumb, after all. "What did you find on him?"

"Kid had a backpack full of stuff." The partner joined her at the window. "Ball-peen hammer, screwdriver, chisel, masking tape, rope, crowbar, and electricians' gloves."

"Hmmm." Clutching Sammy, she leaned out the window, careful not to touch anything. "Whew," she whistled. *A good thirty-foot drop.* "Kid is lucky to be alive."

"Bible broke his fall."

"I guess God was looking out for him." Lexi said with a smile. She adjusted the Baby Bjorn and did a slow lap around the room, scanning the area as she went.

"Guess so." The partner followed in her footsteps, step-for-step.

She whipped around. "Quit tailgating."

He stopped in his tracks. Sammy's pacifier flew out of her mouth and bounced off his chest. "Sorry, Marshal Colt," he said as he picked up the binky from the oriental carpet and then wiped it on his pant leg.

Lexi snatched it away from him and clipped it back onto her shirt pocket. *Why isn't Sammy squirming?* All that jostling should have woken her up. *Is she still breathing?* Lexi put both hands on the Baby Bjorn. Her heart was racing. *Thank the Lord. She's still alive.* Lexi had a recurring nightmare that the baby quit breathing. *Terrifying.*

"Are you okay?" the partner asked.

Her terror must have been written across her face. She

adjusted the baby carrier. "Can I talk to the perp? I have to find out whether he was working alone or with some criminal group."

Through the broken window, a pinkish haze had replaced the darkness. She pulled her phone from her pocket and glanced at the time. *Lord have mercy.* No wonder dawn was breaking. It was nearly five o'clock. She'd been wandering around the library with this yahoo campus cop for over two hours.

Her mouth was dry. She needed another pop. "I think I've seen everything for now." How would she get through this day without any sleep? In less than three hours, she would be meeting the new kid. Gawd, she hated training those twerps. She already had one kid to take care of. She didn't need another nose to wipe.

"The librarian is around somewhere if you want to talk to him. He's fussing over that bible."

Interviewing a librarian. A good job for the new kid. Anyway, that sixpack of Dew was calling to her. "I'll catch him tomorrow." She shook her head. Demoted from gangsters to librarians.

One thing hadn't changed. The paperwork. She had to get her report written and turned in before meeting the newbie at headquarters.

The sun was coming up over Harvard green. Wispy clouds swirled orange and gray. Birds sang an upbeat tune. As she marched back to her car, Lexi felt like she was on the set of some British upstairs-downstairs kind of show… the upstairs part.

If only she could interview the library perp over the phone. Then she could do it while she drove home. *Dammit.* How was she going to get Sammy back home, write up the report, *and* get to headquarters in time for the meeting? Hang it. She turned on the light and the siren. *Here's hoping it screams louder than the baby.*

Lexi kept the baby in her peripheral vision as she sped

through the streets of Boston, siren blaring. Sammy's mouth was open. Her eyes were tearful slits. And her face was beet red. *Poor little thing. When we get home, I'll give her some applesauce. Her favorite.*

When they got home, Lexi barely had time to take the dog out to pee and then deposit Sammy—and a jar of baby applesauce—at Mrs. Faheem's apartment next door. Suffering from a recently emptied nest, Mrs. Faheem said she enjoyed looking after Sammy. Lexi was in no position to argue.

After a quick shower, Lexi pulled on a skirt, blouse, and blazer and slid her feet into a pair of pumps. She didn't have time to dry her hair. These days, it was so long it wouldn't be dry before lunchtime. After the baby was born, self-care had fallen by the wayside.

"Camo, keep an eye on the place." She patted the golden lab on the head. "Good boy."

After the WitSec mess, the bureau had insisted she take medical leave and get her head screwed on right. Along with those yellow pills, the army counselor prescribed a therapy dog. On her own in the big city with a tiny baby, *she* liked to think of Camo as a guard dog. *Who ever heard of a therapy dog?*

She tossed a dog biscuit into the living room. On high alert, Camo waited for the command and then went for it, tail wagging all the way. Technically, she was supposed to take Camo to work with her... and everywhere she went. No way. She'd never hear the end of it if the guys new she needed a therapy dog. "Be a good boy." She tossed him another biscuit.

She had exactly one hour to get across town to headquarters and then type up her report. It was going to be a short one, especially since she hadn't interviewed the perp yet. *Preliminary report. That's what I'll call it.*

Bang. Lexi hit the sidewalk. Her heart was pounding so hard her blazer was heaving. Terror. Sheer terror. Laying on her belly, she scanned the area, up and down. All clear. No snipers. *Good grief. Pull yourself together, Lex.* Just a freaking car backfiring.

Tears sprouted in her eyes. What the— She scraped herself off the sidewalk. The knees of her hose were torn to shreds. *PTSD. Would it ever go away? For pity's sake.* She had to snap out of it.

She limped to her car. Once inside, she pulled off the ruined hose and slipped her feet back into her pumps. Both knees stung, and road-rash blossomed bright red. She gritted her teeth, revved the engine, and took off.

Siren. Lights. The Charger tore from lane to lane. She hoped she would hit something. It would serve her right. *Headcase.* She was a hopeless headcase.

Two Mountain Dews later, she pulled into the parking lot in Chelsea, parked, jumped out of the car, and marched to the back entrance.

The headquarters building was a giant checkers board with alternating squares of glass and steel, eight stories high. Inside, there were more computer screens than agents. The central hub looked like a Vegas sportsbook, only instead of races on the television screens, there were surveillance grids.

Not making eye contact, Lexi took the elevator to the fourth floor. She kept her head down as she hustled down the hallway to her office. She was met with the pile of unfinished paperwork from last week. She dropped into her office chair, pulled off her blazer, booted up the computer, and got to work on the report.

What was there to say? Dumbass tried to scale the building with sixty pounds of Gutenberg on his back and fell to the ground like a rock. Next time, the wimp should hit the gym first.

Absentmindedly, she opened the top desk drawer and pulled out a Snickers bar, unwrapped it, and took a bite.

Ring. The desk phone. *Dammit.* The newbie was here already, waiting for her downstairs at the reception desk.

"I'll be right down." She saved her report, such as it was, and then wriggled into her blazer. Had it gotten tighter? Ever since the baby came, nothing fit right anymore. Everything was too small… including her life.

Her heels clicked on the tile as she made her way to the elevator. *Time to take the chick under my wings and teach her to fly… to fly out from under my wings… Whatever.*

From across the room, she sensed something vaguely familiar about the young woman waiting at the reception desk. Slender boyish build. Long blonde hair pulled back in a ponytail. Fringe jacket. *Where have I seen her before?*

As she got closer, Lexi recognized her. *Good Lord.* The girlfriend. Nick Schilling's girlfriend from Chicago. Lexi stopped in her tracks.

Nick Schilling was the last witness Lexi had been assigned to protect. He was the reason she'd been demoted to the "shoplifting" division. And, unbeknownst to him, he was Sammy's daddy.

Chapter 5

Jessica had never been in an earthquake. But when she saw Federal Marshal Lexington Colt from across the lobby, her knees went weak. *Crapulence. What's she doing here?* In her matching navy skirt, blazer, and pumps, the marshal looked more like a buttoned-down banker than an FBI agent.

The last time Jessica saw the marshal was in Wyoming when she'd gone looking for Nick. And she'd found him in the arms of Federal Marshal Lexington Colt. Jessica had been in love with Nick. Or so she thought. Now she didn't know.

Maybe Jack was right. He said, "Love is the result of compatible neuroses." And that's why he loved her. *Good old Jack.* Her stoner buddy and sort-of-boyfriend. A twinge of guilt stabbed her gut. She hadn't called him since she'd got back from Italy.

The marshal's hips danced as she walked across the lobby. Mouth open, Jessica stood there staring. Was it possible that the marshal was even prettier now? Motherhood obviously agreed with her. Yup. Last time she saw the marshal, there was a big ole bun in the oven… presumably Nick's bun.

Jessica still couldn't believe it. Nick and the marshal had a baby.

Did they get married? Where is Nick? Is he still in witness protection? And why is Marshal Colt in Boston? As the questions whirled through her head, knots twirled in her stomach.

Jessica turned back to the receptionist. She couldn't face the marshal. Not now. She was waiting for an important interview with the art crimes division. She couldn't blow it. Her future career was at stake. She'd lucked into this internship—if you counted someone else's coma as luck—and she wasn't about to mess it up.

She heard her mom's voice in her head: *If you stay back east, you'll be dealt a bum hand and come home with your tail between your legs.* Never mind the mixed metaphors, Jessica wasn't about to give her mom the satisfaction. *Twenty-five years old and Mom still treats me like a child.*

Jessica could feel the presence of Marshal Colt behind her, but she didn't turn around.

"Janet," the marshal said. "Where is my intern?"

Holy crap. Marshal Hottie is my new boss. How could that be? The marshal was an FBI agent, but she worked for Witness Protection and not art crimes. What would it be like working with the woman who stole Nick's heart away from her? Before he went into witness protection, he intended to propose to her... or so it seemed.

"She's right here," the receptionist answered, pointing.

Jessica's face burned. As she turned around to face the marshal, the image of Marshal Hottie out cold in a parking lot flashed through her head. Yup. Her friend Vanya had cold-cocked the marshal with his gun.

"Hello, Marshal Colt. Good to see you again." She held out her hand as a peace offering. After all, the marshal had stolen her boyfriend... possibly even fiancé. Not that it mattered now.

The marshal took it, but not without slicing her to bits with that steely stare of hers. "If it isn't Bonnie," the marshal said. "Where's your sidekick, Clyde?"

Very funny. Marshal Colt had taken to calling Jessica and Jack, Bonnie and Clyde. Back in Wyoming, she'd threatened to have them arrested. Heck. She *had* arrested Jessica. That's when Vanya wacked her with his gun. Jessica cringed.

"So, you're my new intern." The marshal sighed. "Small world." She looked Jessica up and down. "What's with the get-up?"

Jessica frowned. "What do you mean?"

"The fringe jacket and cowboy boots. Where's your ten-gallon hat?" The marshal snorted. "Or couldn't you get it on over your bedhead hair?"

Haha. Very funny. "I left it in the car." Jessica smirked. "What about you? Why the business suit? Are you working in accounting now?"

"Art Crimes." The marshal tightened her lips.

"I thought you worked for WITSEC. What are you doing in art crime?"

"I could ask you the same question."

"I took a certificate course in Italy." Jessica returned the marshal's stare. If they were playing chicken, the marshal had better watch out.

"You're not the only one who took a course in art crimes." The marshal put her hands on her hips. "Anyway, some things they can't teach in school." She looked Jessica up and down and shook her head. "The most important things."

"That's why I'm here." Jessica bit her lip. "I want to learn."

"Great." The marshal turned on her heels. "I have the perfect job for you." She marched back across the lobby, and Jessica scurried to catch up.

Jessica followed the marshal's swinging behind across the lobby and to the elevators. *Awkward.* Of all the FBI agents in the country, why did she have to be assigned to Marshal Colt? She blew at her bangs. This was going to be the internship from hell.

THE MARSHAL'S office looked like something out of a magazine. All white and black, glass and steel, and neat and orderly. Talk about anal-retentive. Probably a control freak, too. But she did have a great view of the back parking lot and dumpster from the fourth-floor window.

"Get down to Central Hospital." The marshal picked up a file folder off her desk and opened it. "Interview a guy called Edward Dean Braugh. Goes by Dean."

"Never trust a guy with two first names." Jessica smiled.

The marshal scowled. "He stole a Gutenberg bible from Harvard library last night."

"Let me guess. You shot him in the back while he was running away." She chuckled.

"Look, cowgirl. You don't have to like me." The marshal glared at her. "But don't disrespect me."

Whoops. "No… I mean… I respect any woman who has made it in a man's world." Jessica stuttered. Dang. The marshal didn't have much of a sense of humor. Jessica fiddled with the fringe on her jacket. "I'm really sorry." She meant it. Having survived five years in a philosophy doctoral program, she knew a thing or two about male-dominated professions. Any woman FBI agent had to be kickass.

"Good." The marshal nodded and handed her the folder. "Review this. Interview the perp. Write up a report. And be back here by noon."

"Aye, aye, boss." Jessica grabbed the folder. Her first assignment as an FBI intern. *So exciting!*

"Remember to stop at HR and get your ID badge before you go."

"Aye, aye, boss." Jessica opened the folder and was met by a grainy photograph of a guy in a sweatshirt lying on the ground.

"Quit calling me boss."

"Aye, aye… Marshal Colt." Jessica examined the photo. "Is this him?"

"The bible was too heavy." The marshal smirked. "He fell off his rope."

"If you reach the end of your rope, tie a knot, and hold on. That's what my mom always says."

"He held on for as long as he could. But eventually had to let go." The marshal sat at her desk, typing on her computer.

"There's a lesson in that."

"Plan ahead," the marshal said absentmindedly. She looked up from her computer. "And know the weight of your booty."

"Take the elevator." Jessica smiled.

Was that a tiny smile on the marshal's face? This marshal was a hard nut to crack.

"Speaking of elevators." The marshal waved toward the door. "Hadn't you better run along?"

Yes. It was. A glimmer of a smile on the marshal's face. Whatever had happened in the past, Jessica had to make a good impression on the marshal if she hoped to have a future in art crime investigation. If she played her cards right, she might even land a job with the FBI. Now that would be cool.

JESSICA FLASHED her brand-spanking-new FBI ID-badge at the uniformed officer outside Dean Braugh's hospital room. The chance to use her new badge almost made the visit to the hospital bearable. She'd spent too many nights inhaling the smells of bleach and tragedy, worrying about people she'd loved.

Not to mention her own trips to the hospital. She shuddered.

The policeman opened the door to the room. Jessica knocked on it anyway.

"Come in." It was a woman's voice.

Is this the right room? She glanced at the cop, and he nodded. She pulled aside the curtain.

The glare from the window was blinding. She shielded her eyes. The hospital bed, oxygen hose coming from the wall, corner sink, boxes of exam gloves… her head was spinning. *Come on, Jess, you can do this. It's only a hospital room.*

A thin-faced dude with a bandage on his head was lying in the bed with the blankets down around his hips and his concave tattooed chest exposed. She flinched and looked away.

Sitting next to the bed in an oversized hospital chair was a young woman dressed in all black with streaks of blue in her hair, sporting a nose ring and a neck tattoo…. And did she have a bun in the oven? A baby bump the size of a small basketball poked out from her small frame.

"Do I know you?" the young man asked.

Jessica shook her head. "No."

"Didn't think so," he said. "I hit my head pretty bad, but I'm sure I'd remember a face like yours."

She wasn't sure what he meant by that and didn't care to know. "I'm with the FBI—"

"Yeah right," he interrupted. "And I'm with the CIA."

She tightened her lips and inhaled through her nose. *Weird.* She smelled her grandmother's medicine cabinet— eucalyptus and camphor. *Breathe. Just breathe.* "I'm an intern with the FBI Art Crimes Division." She moved closer to the bed. The strange leafy smell got stronger. "I'm here to ask you some questions." She glanced at Goth-Girl.

"About time," he said. "Gloria, honey, could you go get me a Baby Ruth from the vending machine?"

Goth-Girl scowled. "Okay." She pulled a pack of Marl-boro Lights out of her shoulder bag. *Should she be smoking?* Her baby bump was more prominent when she stood up. "Dean wouldn't do anything wrong," she said as she walked past.

"He's incapable of… that." She tapped out a cigarette, propped it between her lips, and disappeared into the hallway.

Incapable of what? Jessica watched as Goth-Girl sulked out of the room, her Doc Martin boots scuffing the shiny floor as she went. After she was gone, Jessica pointed at the vacant chair. "Mind if I…?"

"*Mi casa es tu casa.*" Dean made a grand gesture with his free hand. The other one was cuffed to the bedframe.

"Tell me about last night." *Why didn't I bring a notepad?* She'd have to take notes on her phone. She pulled it out of her pocket and tapped it awake. She still preferred good old-fashioned pen and paper to screens.

At twenty-five, she was already an old lady when it came to the latest technology. Now, kids were practically born with an iPad in their little curled fingers. And the three-dimensional world had been flattened into two, and along with it, so had the soul… the flattening of psychic space.

"What's there to tell? I screwed up." Dean shrugged.

"What was your plan? How did you carry it out? Did you act alone? Why did you do it?" She shot off her questions rapid fire.

"Whoa there. Hold up. One at a time."

"Sorry." She twisted the fringe on her jacket. *Come on, Jess. Don't apologize to the perp.*

"My *plan* was to *borrow* the Gutenberg bible—"

"Borrow?" She had to get tough if she wanted to be a real FBI agent.

"Yes, borrow." He waited a few seconds as if trying to build suspense. "I hid in the john and then strolled into the reading room just after midnight. Piece of cake."

"The security guards didn't stop you?"

"What security guards?" He chuckled.

"I opened the case, took the bible, and then headed for the window—"

"I thought you went down a rope into the reading room."

He shook his boney finger at her. "Do you want me to tell you what happened or not?"

"Yes. I do." She nodded. *Sorry.* She stopped herself from saying it out loud.

"Well, quit interrupting." He sighed. "Earlier, I'd taken the stairs up to the roof and attached a rope to a drainpipe. Measured it exactly to hang just to the reading room window." He stared down at the blanket. "I put the bible in my backpack and was going to climb up the rope to the roof to stash it there for later." He closed his eyes. "I hung from that rotten rope for over an hour. I couldn't climb up. I couldn't swing back into the window." His eyes popped open. He took a drink from a pink plastic cup on the bedside table. "Finally, I had to let go." He shook his head and grinned. "The rest, as they say, is history."

"What were you going to do with the bible?" She tapped her phone, waiting to take down his answer. "Sell it on the black market?"

"No. Of course not." He tightened his lips. "I wanted to study it. To learn the truth." He kicked his feet under the covers as if for emphasis.

Okay. Either this guy is pulling my leg, or he's completely bonkers. "The truth about what?"

"Everything. Life, death, the afterlife. Infinity. Immortality." When he pulled the blanket up over his tattooed torso, the image of a bloody Christ on the cross disappeared from view. *Thank goodness.*

She'd had a hard time looking at him with so much of his skin exposed. "Couldn't you learn just as much from your run-of-the-mill King James?"

He scoffed. "Do you really trust those translators? Come on." He looked at her like she'd just suggested that he learn the truth about the universe from the back of a cereal box. "Cut out the middleman. That's what I say."

"So, you read Latin?" she asked. Did this nutjob know the Gutenberg Bible was not the original?

"Duh."

"You do know the bible was originally written in Hebrew and Greek, right?"

"What of it?"

"Just curious about that middleman you wanted out of the picture." She rolled her mind's eye. *Definitely a nutcase.* "Who helped you?"

"No one."

"You didn't have an accomplice?"

"No."

"Did you have a buyer lined up?"

"I told you. I wanted to study it, not sell it." His eyes flashed.

Either he was a darn good liar, or he was telling the truth. Either way, he was a creepy dude. Somehow, she had to get more information out of him. The marshal would not be impressed if she reported that the dude was some bible freak who wanted just a closer look. "Why would the Gutenberg bible give you the truth?"

"Because it's the word of God. God says, 'when you will know the truth, and the truth will set you free.'" Dean stared at her with unblinking bloodshot eyes.

Unnerving. Dean wasn't the only one who'd studied the bible.

"John 8:32." She recognized the verse. Her mom had made her go to Sunday school every week for her entire childhood. "Actually, it's the word of Saint Jerome of Stridon, who translated it into Latin." Saint Jerome, famous for instructing noble virgins on how to maintain their chastity by defiling them.

Dean's pale face flushed. "I knew you were a devil when you first walked in here with those red boots." He was so worked up that spit flew as he spoke.

Dang. Good thing he's cuffed to the bed. She decided to change the subject. "Are you a student at Harvard?"

"Do I look like one of those stuck-up snobs?"

"I wouldn't know. I've never met anyone from Harvard." At least they must be smart snobs. Arrogance was one thing. She could tolerate arrogance. She'd seen enough of it in graduate school. But arrogance combined with ignorance was insufferable. She could suffer fools, just not arrogant jerks.

"My mom couldn't afford Harvard." He relaxed back into his pillow. "I'm at MMC."

She wracked her brain. "MMC?"

"Middlestate Mortuary College."

Say what? Mortuary College? She raised her eyebrows.

"Funeral industry training." He narrowed his eyes as if throwing down the gauntlet.

She nodded. *Seriously weird dude.*

Goth-Girl returned with a handful of candy bars and smelling of cigarette smoke. She skulked around the room like a fox. Instead of handing Dean a Baby Ruth, she perched on the windowsill and then threw one to him.

Now what? Maybe the candy toss was her cue that the interview was over.

Silence.

More silence.

Goth-Girl sat on the sill nibbling on a candy bar. With her buck teeth she looked like a little squirrel… a pregnant little squirrel.

Jessica dropped her phone into the pocket of her jacket and stood up. "Well thanks." *Geez.* Now she was thanking the perp.

"Gloria is top of her class at MMC," Dean said, beaming. "Aren't you, honey?"

She's a mortician too? Jessica glanced over at the little blue-haired squirrel.

Goth-Girl shrugged.

"I *was* studying philosophy at Boston Community College," Dean said. "But I dropped out to do something more practical."

"Like steal bibles?" Jessica couldn't resist.

"No." He chuckled. "I didn't want to end up an unemployed egghead with more degrees than sense."

Touché. He'd nailed her without even trying.

<hr>

Chapter 6

<hr>

Adrián Garcia paced the floor of his new office. *America. Washington D.C. FBI Art Crimes Division.* He'd imagined the great J. Edgar Hoover building as grander and more elegant than the dirty, dilapidated concrete box he'd arrived at two weeks ago.

The carpet in his tiny office was as bald as Dr. Bunsen Honeydew… and it was the same fuzzy mustard yellow as the Muppet too. The small metal desk had a gash on one corner. Maybe from gun play? Boy, would he love to carry a gun. He pantomimed a quick draw like he'd seen in old American westerns.

His office was the size of a *menorquinas* shoebox, but it had a nice view of Pennsylvania Avenue from its sixth-floor window. He stopped in front of the small window and looked out at the capital in the distance.

Below, ant-sized pedestrians scurried up and down the sidewalks. How many of them were criminals? White-collar criminals like his father? And to think, his father wanted him to come work with him. Adrián shook his head. *No way.*

Adrián always did know how to push his old man's buttons. To piss him off, Adrián had studied art at the University of Madrid. And instead of becoming a "real" FBI agent, he was working in Art Crimes. His father didn't consider art crimes "real." Adrián exhaled.

His father scoffed at the Art Crimes Division. "Art is for finishing-school girls, not men." That's what he'd said. *Forget about him.*

Adrián rubbed his hands together. Only one worthy adversary. And it wasn't his father. It was the irresistibly clever Jessica James. Sometimes, he wished he'd never met her. She haunted his dreams and tormented his nightmares. Where is she now? He had hoped they'd be working together in Washington… after Simone Bernard's *unfortunate* accident.

He couldn't get the pretty American out of his head.

TOC. That's what his mother called him. What in America they call OCD. Obsessive Compulsive Disorder. It was true that when he fell for a girl, he fell hard. Was that a disorder? Or passion? True love wasn't by halves. *Todo o nada. All or nothing.*

"Garcia." The voice at the door jolted him out of his daydream.

He turned around to see his new boss, Agent Dan Stevenson, standing in the threshold. Stevenson was heavyset with graying hair that was just a tad too long to be fashionable. Stevenson wore a short camel leather jacket and khaki pants. Not a good combination, especially when his belly was sandwiched in between the two. Stevenson was in charge of the Art Crimes Division for the entire country.

"We've been called to a robbery in Boston." Stevenson chewed on a toothpick like a tough guy in some Hollywood flick. "Flight leaves in two hours. So, you'd better shake a leg."

"Shake a leg?" Some of these weird American expressions still baffled him. He'd learned English from watching American television. Gunsmoke reruns. CSI, and of course, Sesame Street and The Muppets. Grover was his favorite character. Unlike the simpering Big Bird or melancholy Kermit-the-Frog, Grover didn't overthink. He rose to every challenge.

"Flight leaves in two hours." Stevenson kicked the door frame. "Let's go."

Caray! Had to be a big heist for the FBI to call in the Division Head. "What did they steal?" Adrián grabbed his wool jacket and fedora from the coat rack. He had clearly confused North and South America. He'd thought it would be cold in New England. He should have packed his linens instead.

"A Rembrandt and a Bouguereau," Stevenson said. "And who knows what else. That's why they called us. This one could be big. Really big."

"*Dios Mío.*" Adrián's pulse quickened. *Finally, a chance to prove myself.* "Where?" He slipped his arms into his coat.

"Albertina Carpenter Museum." Stevenson buttoned his jacket. "Ready?"

Adrián rubbed his hands together. "Let's hit it." He flipped his fedora onto his head. He was eager to show the boss what he could do with a crime scene.

THE ALBERTINA CARPENTER MUSEUM was only a few miles from the airport. But with traffic, it took over half an hour to get there... almost as long as the flight.

On the quick trip, he'd only managed to get through half the words beginning with I in the English dictionary. Every day, he memorized new words and tried to use them in a sentence. *Today's word is inimitable. Matchless, peerless, incomparable.*

Adrián was excited to see another American city. He'd traveled all over Europe and Asia with his parents. But this was his first trip to America. *Boston. The city of brotherly love and the seat of liberty... and Rocky Balboa running up the steps to that art museum.*

On the drive from the airport, he kept expecting the scenery to get more interesting. But it looked just like the outskirts of Washington. Car dealers. Strip malls. As the taxi entered Boston proper, buildings got closer together and taller… but not as tall as the ones in downtown Washington.

The nondescript neighborhood with its dowdy brownstone buildings didn't seem appropriate for a museum that housed such valuable art. American cities lacked the charm of those in Europe. They all looked alike. No character. So far, Boston wasn't the charming city he'd imagined.

Even the museum was an ugly, four-story boxy red-brick building. The only thing distinctive about it was a giant letter "A" formed by contrasting white bricks running from the foundation to the roof. *Is it a sports team or an art museum?*

Adrián ducked under the yellow crime scene tape and followed Stevenson to the back entrance. This was where the robbers had entered shortly after midnight.

Inside, a flock of local police officers were milling around, a couple of them taking pictures and bagging evidence. The rest just jabbering.

Stevenson stopped to talk to one of them.

"Most of the stuff was taken from the Blue Room upstairs," the cop said. "Want me to take you up?"

"That would be great," Stevenson said.

"Super," Adrián said. He followed as close as he could without treading on Stevenson's heels.

The Blue Room looked like a tornado had ripped through it. Shattered glass was strewn across the floor. Wooden frames were busted and thrown here and there. Portraits had been taken off the walls and lay face up, their painted subjects staring off into space.

Weird. The robbers took the time to make this colossal mess, but took very few, if any of the paintings. The paintings were ripped from frames, but left lying on the floor.

"To pull this off, they had to be professionals," Stevenson said.

"Professional thieves maybe, but not professional *art* thieves." Adrián pulled a pair of latex gloves from his pocket, snapped them on, and picked up a broken set of stretcher bars. "The thieves didn't care about preserving the art." He put the broken wood back where he'd found it. "They skinned the canvases off their frames and left the wooden bars behind like piles of bones picked over by carrion birds."

"Weren't there security guards?" Stevenson asked.

"The robber tied him up," the officer said.

"Him?" Stevenson asked. "Only one?"

"Guards or robbers?"

"Both," Adrián said.

"One guard. Not sure on the robbers… one or two." The officer made peace signs with both hands.

"How did the thieves get into the museum?" Adrián asked. "Did they break a window or dynamite a door lock?"

"The security guard buzzed them in," the officer said with a chuckle. "I bet he'll be looking for another job."

"I hope so," Adrián said. "Can we talk to him?"

"Poor kid was pretty shaken up." The officer shrugged. "Sarge questioned him and then let him go home."

"You let him go home?" Adrián didn't mean to raise his voice. But he couldn't believe it. *A security guard buzzes in one or two thieves who take millions of dollars-worth of art and they just let him go?*

The cop furrowed his brows. "We know where he lives." He turned to Stevenson. "I'll leave you to it then." He left mumbling to himself. No doubt cursing the FBI.

"Go easy on the locals," Stevenson said. "They do a good job. Anyway, we need them."

From what Adrián had seen so far, the locals loitered around the crime scene and let the prime suspects go. He wasn't impressed. *The locals should leave it to the experts.* He kept his mouth shut.

Click. Click. Click. Adrián turned around to see a well-dressed, middle-aged woman walking toward them, her high heels clicking on the marble floor.

"Can I help you?" she asked. With her short, spiked white hair and barely-there makeup, she reminded Adrián of the ladies in his mother's bridge group—elegant, cultured, and all business.

"We're with the FBI." Stevenson extended his hand. "And you are?"

"The museum director." Her voice cracked. Her eyes were red and puffy.

Adrián wondered if she'd been crying.

"I just can't believe it." She sniffled. "How could this happen?"

"Poor security," Adrián said.

Stevenson scowled at him.

"We just installed our security system a month ago." She shook her head. "We spent a fortune on it."

"What kind of system do you have?" Adrián asked. He'd seen a couple of CCTV cameras outside and in the entrance. "Who installed it?" It wouldn't be the first time a security outfit collaborated with high level thieves.

"Black Cat Security," she said. "I can show you the paperwork. It outlines everything. Security cameras, heat sensors, printouts from motion detectors."

"Can we see the CCTV footage?" Stevenson asked.

"And the printouts," Adrián added.

"The robbers took them." Her mouth twisted into a grimace.

"Who is your insurer?" Adrián asked. Surely the insurance company would be sending someone to investigate… *someone to interfere with the investigation.*

"We weren't insured," she whispered and then covered her face with her hands. "Not yet."

"You weren't insured?" Adrián couldn't believe it. *What kind of museum is this? No insurance and security guards in cahoots with thieves.*

"After the new security system, we couldn't afford it." She stared at her shoes… designer flats with tiny gold buckles.

Millions of dollars-worth of art and no insurance. *Who are these people?*

"Let's go back to the robbery," Stevenson said. "Miss… Miss… I'm sorry I didn't catch your name."

"Ms. Finch, Eliza Finch." She peeked out from behind her hands. "I just started two months ago. How could this happen?" With a hand on each side of her head as if holding it in place, she paced back and forth in front of them.

"We'll do everything in our power to recover your paintings," Stevenson said. "How about you show us where you keep the surveillance equipment and walk us through the new security system?"

She nodded.

"Are you okay?" Stevenson asked. He put his hand on her shoulder.

She nodded again and gave him a weak smile.

With lax security, she was asking to be robbed. Why was Stevenson kowtowing to this woman? Adrián bit his tongue.

Ms. Finch led them to the elevator and pressed a button.

If one guard buzzed in the robbers, another must have been down here manning the surveillance system. He just couldn't believe there was only one guard. Why wasn't anyone patrolling the galleries? "How many security guards do you have?" Adrián asked. The cop had told him only one was on duty. *No way.* Not possible. Or was it?

"Only one on duty at a time," Ms. Finch answered. "We can't afford more."

One guard. No insurance. A rinky-dink security system. No wonder the place was robbed. It was an easy target. The guard wasn't manning the CCTV screens. Either that, or he wasn't patrolling the galleries. He couldn't very well be doing both at once.

The elevator door opened. Outside the elevator, two police officers were chatting.

Adrián held the door open.

"Sorry, this is the basement." Ms. Finch pointed across the hall. "That's where they tied up the guard." Her hand was shaking.

"We'll examine it later," Stevenson said. "Let's see the security system first."

Flustered, Ms. Finch punched another button.

When they reached the first floor, she led them to a suite of offices at the far end of the museum. The head of security's office was a cubicle not bigger than a walk-in closet.

Windowless and stuffy, the room had the acidic gamey smell of *Torta del Casar*. Adrián's father absolutely adored the funky cheese and had it delivered by the case fresh from a sheep farm in Extremadura. Adrián wouldn't touch the foul stuff.

Crammed into the small room were a swivel chair, a desk with three surveillance screens above it, two computers, and a printer.

"Isn't the footage stored on the hard drive?" Adrián asked.

"The robbers wiped the hard drive." Ms. Finch's mouth twitched, and she looked like she might burst into tears.

"How did these robbers know where the security equipment is kept and how to wipe the drive?" Stevenson asked.

"Exactly what I was wondering," Adrián said. Staying one step ahead of Stevenson was proving more difficult than he thought it would be.

"Let's see what you've got," Stevenson said. "Maybe there's something the thieves missed." He sat down at the desk and started typing on one of the keyboards. "Password?"

"I'll type it in." Ms. Finch reached around Stevenson and typed in the password.

Por favor. She's suddenly concerned about security. Talk about too little too late. "We're going to need access to all your computers." Adrián stood behind Stevenson, watching the computer screen.

The thieves were tech savvy. They'd erased the footage from the robbery, but not from any time before the robbery.

Stevenson played the footage from the day before.

"*Mira.*" Adrián pointed at the screen. "Look." Just after eleven at night, a security guard buzzed a man in through the back door. "Who is that?"

Ms. Finch leaned closer to the screen. "That's just one of our trustees."

"Oh." Adrián tried not to sound too disappointed. "We need to interview the security guard, the one on duty last night."

"Patience," Stevenson said. "Patience." When he stood up, he almost knocked Ms. Finch over. "Pardon me." He took her elbow. "Are you sure you're okay?"

"Yes." She forced a smile. "I only hope the FBI can recover the paintings."

"We will." Stevenson patted her shoulder.

"How many paintings were taken?" Adrián asked.

"It seems only two. Rembrandt's *Christ in the Storm on the Sea of Galilee* and Bouguereau's *Innocence.*" She inhaled loudly. "But they left such a mess, it's difficult to tell for sure."

"That's an odd pair." Adrián tipped his hat back and scratched his forehead.

"Both religious works," the director said. "Obviously, the Rembrandt is by far the most valuable and the Bouguereau is very popular."

"Yes, well..." Stevenson stepped over to the printer. "There must be a backup of this printout on the computer someplace." He looked at Adrián. "You stay here and recover what you can from the computer. I want to see where the thieves tied up the guard."

"Of course," Ms. Finch said.

"And we'll need the guard's contact information," Adrián added.

"Of course," she repeated.

"Do you mind if I come with you to see the basement and *then* get the stuff off the computer?" Adrián asked. He needed all the clues he could get if he was going to solve this case, impress the boss, and get the job. *Keep the target in view.*

Stevenson glanced at Ms. Finch and then gave Adrián the side-eye. "Stay here until you've finished."

"But—"

"That's an order." The tone in Stevenson's voice meant business.

Por Favor. I'm not a child. Adrián nodded. He didn't like being under someone else's thumb. "Yes, sir."

"I'll be back," Stevenson said. "Don't go anywhere." He put his hand on the small of Ms. Finch's back and followed her out.

Adrián tapped at the keyboard. What was to stop him from investigating the basement when Stevenson wasn't looking?

For the next half hour, Adrián went through the security logs. The CCTV recordings didn't show anything else suspicious. But he found a backup of the security printout. He unwrapped a *Chupa Chups* and scanned the printout record from last night. The minimalist security system worked on heat sensors. All he could tell from the printouts was whether anyone had entered a gallery or not. Not much to go on.

Ay! What is this? The thieves had been in the building for over an hour! Why would they stay so long and destroy so many paintings just to take two? What robbers take their time and hang around for an hour?

That can't be right. Must be a glitch.

Adrián looked around the room. There had to be an automatic alarm that notifies the police, or at least a panic button.

Why didn't the guard press the panic button? *There is something fishy about this security guard. I have to interview him ASAP.*

He needed to inspect the basement where the guard was held. *Was he in on it? Was he really tied up?* Why did those local cops let him go home? He huffed. *Idiota.*

To hell with Stevenson, I'm going to the basement. Adrián pushed back from the desk. The chair tipped over as he stood up. He righted it, straightened his fedora, and headed back to the elevator.

Shifting from foot to foot, he waited for what seemed like an eternity until the elevator arrived. *Finally.* He punched the button for the basement. With a jolt, the ancient elevator started its descent, complaining all the way.

This place is falling apart. Probably all sorts of safety violations. No wonder they got robbed. He shook his head. *If this is the state of security in America, it's a wonder they have any art left.*

The elevator doors opened as slowly as two tectonic plates moving away from each other. Adrián wedged his body through the opening doors before they'd finished parting. He stepped out into the hallway.

Dios mio! No way.

From the back it sure looked like her. Slim frame, long, wavy, blonde hair, cute little *colito.*

He took the *Chupa Chups* out of his mouth. "Jessica? Is that you?"

"Adrián?" She whipped around to face him. "What are you doing here?"

He smiled. His heart was racing. There she was. Standing right in front of him. The inimitable Jessica James with her eyes as blue as Cala Mondragó lagoon.

Chapter 7

When Jessica left Italy, she never thought she'd see Adrián Garcia again. She knew he was interning at FBI headquarters in Washington. She knew it was a possibility they would run into each other someday. But what were the chances they'd be on the same case in Boston?

"Great to see you." She gave him a hug. Although they hadn't left Amelia on the best terms after the grappa incident, she was glad to see him.

"You too, *linda.*" His face cracked into a huge smile.

"Big case, huh?" She raised her eyebrows.

"The biggest. Those paintings must be worth over one hundred million dollars." His hands were flying as he talked.

"Forget about the money." She smirked. "Those paintings are masterpieces. The Rembrandt is the only sea-scape he ever painted."

"I doubt the museum wants to forget about the money." He was grinning from ear-to-ear.

"What's so funny?"

He tilted his head. "I'm just happy to see you."

She nodded. "Me too."

"Want one?" He held out a lollipop.

She smiled. Adrián and his suckers.

"What have you found out?" she asked as she took the candy.

"Not much more than the local police came up with." He glanced around as if looking for someone.

She followed his gaze. He was staring into the furnace room where Marshal Colt was chatting with another FBI agent and the museum director.

"How about you?" he asked, turning his attention back to her.

"Remember in our class on organized crime and art theft, we learned how the mafia uses art to get their guys out of prison?" She lowered her voice. "I think this could be the Boston mafia."

"Organized crime?" He waved his lollipop in the air. "Did you find any evidence to that effect?"

"The security guard told us that the thieves used zip ties to bind his wrists and feet and put a hood over his head." She leaned closer. "Then the thief announced, 'My good man, this is a robbery'." She bit the jagged edge of her fingernail.

"You interviewed the guard already?" Adrián's face soured like he was sucking on a lime.

She nodded. "Doesn't that sound like something a mafioso would say?" She chuckled. "I mean who else says that? And the hoods. Classic mafia."

"Did the guard say why he opened the door in the middle of the night to let the robbers in?" Adrián asked with a smirk.

"The thief was dressed like a cop and the guard thought he was for real." She shook her head. "Then again, the guard is a twenty-something pot-head."

Talking to that guard had reminded her of conversations she'd had with some of her stoner friends. Jack came to mind. Jackass may do dumb stuff, but he was still one of the smartest people she knew. Unlike that dummkopf security guard.

Crapulence. Jack had left her three messages yesterday.

Weird messages. Like something was up. *I really need to call him back.*

"We should work together on this case," Adrián said. "After hours." He ran his hand through his thick hair. "Two heads are better than one." He smiled and popped his sucker back into his mouth.

Last time she collaborated with Adrián, he'd left her holding the bag… the barf bag. He'd taken credit for their work. He'd gotten the internship. And she was relegated to a mere alternate. Then again, it wasn't his fault she couldn't hold her grappa. Give her good ole Jack Daniels any day.

"Okay." She shrugged. "Why not?"

"If we solve this case, we will both get jobs with the FBI for sure." His hands moved as if he were directing a symphony. "Maybe even in the same place… you and me, together."

"A rising tide floats all boats."

"Boats?" He scrunched up his nose. "Did the thieves use a boat?"

"Just a figure of speech."

"Garcia, did you finish with the computer already?" A booming voice made Jessica whirl around. It was the FBI guy. Adrián introduced him as Detective Stevenson. Something about him reminded her of an aging actor from the '70s. Maybe it was the hair, and there was lots of it—on his head, on his upper lip… and the chest-hair exploding out of his V-neck shirt. *All he's missing is the bellbottoms and the super wide lapels.*

"Almost finished," Adrián said, pulling the sucker out of his mouth. "I came to see if you needed help."

Stevenson glanced back at the museum director. "I'm fine."

The museum director, Ms. Finch, had the slouched posture and puffy eyes of a defeated woman. On a better day, with her buzz cut and red horn-rimmed glasses, she would surely be considered hip and cool. Then again, losing some of the museum's most valuable pieces would knock anyone for a loop. *Poor woman.* She was bearing up, all things considered.

When Marshal Colt sauntered into the foyer, all heads turned. Jessica thought of the line from a novel. *The marshal was the kind of woman that would make a bishop kick in a stained-glass window.* What she wasn't was a woman whom men could kick around. She was hot, but she was also tough as ten-month-old jerky. *These dudes better not mess with her, or they'll be the ones getting kicked right in the teeth.*

"Let's get back to headquarters." Marshal Colt tucked a lock of dark hair behind her ear. "Then you can go through the report from the local police and write up our own." Her face brightened. The marshal seemed to be enjoying giving Jessica orders.

Jessica punched the button for the elevator.

"Hey, how about dinner?" Adrián asked, his eyes full of hope.

"I'm kinda busy writing reports." She glanced over at Marshal Colt, whose body language screamed "get away from" to Stevenson.

"But you've got to eat," Adrián said. "I could come by with take-out. Where will you be?"

"You've got my number," she said. "Call me later."

"Sure thing." He smiled and tipped his hat. "We can compare notes."

The elevator door opened. "Yeah," she said as she stepped inside.

"We make a good team," he said into the closing doors.

He was right. Until the grappa, they had made a good team. In Italy, they'd solved the last case together. It wasn't his fault she didn't turn in her report on time.

━━━

LEXI REVVED THE ENGINE. Why did D.C. have to send that

stalker, Stevenson, with his grabby hands and slick-backed hair? Last time they worked together on a case, she'd had to knee him in the nuts after he pinned her against a wall and tried to reach up her skirt. Dirty SOB. She'd reported him, for all the good it did. Since then, he'd kept his paws off her.

Just thinking about Stevenson made her blood boil.

"Hand me a pop from the backseat." Lexi pulled out onto Fenway. Fenway Park greenway reminded her of where she grew up. One thing you could say about Tennessee. It was green.

The cowgirl was nice enough to flip the tab on her can of Diet Dew. "Thanks." She took a sip. *Ahhhh.*

"How can you drink that stuff warm?" Jessica asked. "It's bad enough cold."

"After that shitshow back there, I need my Dew." She guzzled half the can.

"I think this might be one of the biggest art heists in history." The cowgirl smiled. "Probably organized crime."

"The agency is pulling out all the stops." Lexi downed the rest of the Dew. "Sending agents up from national headquarters." She shook her head. "As if we can't handle it."

"It's not standard operating procedure?"

"No." Lexi wasn't used to having a sidekick.

"What's next?" The cowgirl's voice was full of excitement. Wait until she realized that most of the job was shuffling papers.

"You write up a report on the crime scene." Lexi gunned it as she entered the freeway. "Then coordinate with the local police."

"And what will you do?" The cowgirl asked.

"My job."

They rode the rest of the way in silence. The cowgirl had enough sense to keep her trap shut. Lexi didn't want anybody telling her how to do her job. She'd had enough of that in the army.

When she got back to the office, Lexi went straight for the computer. She settled into her desk, snagged a Snickers from her desk drawer, and googled the latest mafia arrests. The cowgirl just might be onto something with her mafia theory.

Organized crime was rampant in Boston—the Winter Hill Gang, the McLaughlin Gang, Irish mobsters, the Patriarca Family, the DeNunzio Brothers, Italian mobsters, and renegades like Spucky Spagnolo, Ponytail Parillo, and Bobby the Cigar. The list went on and on.

Out of the corner of her eye, she saw the cowgirl standing across the room, staring at her. "Why aren't you working?"

"I don't have a desk." The cowgirl shrugged.

Good Lord. She shook her head. *Not a lot of gumption. Without it, she wouldn't get far in the FBI.* "There's a whole table and two plastic chairs. What more do you need?" She pointed to the long table that stretched the length of the far wall. She was lucky to have an office with a nice big desk and an extended metal table—not the prettiest, but plenty functional.

"A secure computer." The cowgirl raised her eyebrows.

"Oh." Lexi jerked her thumb over her shoulder toward the door. "Go ask HR. And ask them to get you your own office while you're at it." She hoped to hell the FBI didn't expect her to share *her* office with Nick's ex-girlfriend. It was awkward enough working with her.

Her cheeks burned. Dammit. Why did she have to think about Nick? She closed her eyes. His soft hair. His soft lips. His... *Stop it, Lex.* Her eyes flew open. *Stop daydreaming about Nick Schilling. Who knows where he is now.* With WitSec, he could be anywhere. *And who knows when he'll be back… if ever.* So just forget about him.

"What do you think about the case?" the cowgirl asked.

"Huh?" Lexi cleared her throat.

"Could it be mob related?"

"Could be." She didn't look up from her keyboard.

"Any kingpins go to prison lately?" The cowgirl went to

the window and sat on the sill. "Someone big enough to need a hefty ransom like the Albertina Carpenter haul?"

"Ransom?"

"In my art crimes class, we learned about lots of cases where mafia bigshots used precious art to buy their way out of prison."

Lexi was beginning to see what Nick had obviously seen in this skinny mess of a woman. She clearly did not comb her hair, but at least she had a good head on her shoulders. "Let me do some research." Maybe the cowgirl was onto something. A mob boss with an army of foot soldiers could easily organize a robbery from inside.

Who would think of something like that? Edward "Eggs" Benedict came to mind. He was well known for stealing a Rembrandt in broad daylight from the Museum of Fine Arts. These days, Eggs worked alone. Still, it was the sort of ballsy stunt he'd try. "We should interview Eggs Benedict."

The cowgirl laughed. "What about French Toast?"

"Edward Eggs Benedict is a known art thief."

"How will we find him?"

"Easy." Lexi continued searching the computer data base. "He's in federal prison in Norfolk. If he didn't plan the Albertina Carpenter hit, he'll know who did."

The cowgirl came up behind her and looked over her shoulder at the screen. Lexi twisted around to face her. "Shouldn't you be heading to HR?"

"Yup," the cowgirl said. "On my way." She did an about-face.

Lexi nodded but didn't look up. *Thank goodness*. She had her office to herself again. She wasn't used to sharing. Her office... Nick... or anything else.

For the next half hour, Lexi searched the data base for organized crime figures who could have been involved in this type of heist.

"Any luck finding a crime boss recently interred?"

Lexi's hand flew to her chest. "You scared the bejeezus out of me."

"Sorry." The cowgirl was standing in the doorway. "What have you found?"

"Give me a minute. It's only been half an hour." *Geez. What does she expect?* "Shouldn't be too hard to find." A high-profile kingpin recently locked up. "What happened with HR?"

"I'm afraid you're stuck with me." The cowgirl slouched into a chair at a table. "HR said we're roommates."

Could this day get any worse? Lexi grabbed another Snickers bar out of her desk drawer.

The cowgirl stood there looking at her with big blue puppy dog eyes. *What the hell.* She held out the candy bar.

▭

JESSICA SLID into the marshal's chair. It was still warm from the marshal's perfect derrière. The cursor was flashing on the screen, daring her to touch the marshal's keyboard. Though the marshal had asked her to go over the security printout from the robbery and write up a summary, she felt like she was trespassing.

Behind the open file, was the smiling face of a baby. *Must be her and Nick's daughter.* Jessica closed the file to get a better look at the baby. She was a pretty little thing. But with parents like Nick Schilling and Marshal Ava Gardner, she was bound to be pretty… and smart… perfect, actually.

The marshal didn't seem like the maternal sort. But you never could tell. *I wonder what it would be like to have a baby? Must be horrible.*

In sixth grade, she'd passed out during the sex-ed film of a woman giving birth. She shuddered just thinking of the bloody spectacle. Growing up witnessing her own mother's depression—and feeling responsible for it—she'd never wanted to have children.

Anyway, she could barely take care of herself, let alone another human being for cripe's sake.

A cat. Maybe I should get a cat as practice. Having someone else dependent on me would take me out of my own head. I wonder if my new apartment accepts pets. No, she'd better not look at cat videos on the marshal's computer.

Distracted by thoughts of kittens, Jessica scrolled through the computer back-up record of the security printout. Screen after screen of screaming caps and exclamation points telling the guards someone had entered the Blue Room, the Green Room, or the Impressionist Gallery. Seventy-two minutes of second-by-second alerts as the thieves moved through the museum.

Seventy-two minutes. That was a long time for a robbery. Usually, thieves got in and out as fast as they could… *unless they know the cops aren't coming.*

Did the thieves have someone on the inside?

Twenty minutes later, the marshal returned with a laptop.

Crapulence. Her hands froze over the keyboard. If she stopped now, she'd have to start over on that laptop. "Want your computer back?"

The marshal peered over her shoulder. "No. Keep at it." She slid a laptop out of its case and installed herself at a table in the corner of the office. "I'll search for kingpins recently incarcerated."

"Sounds like a plan." Jessica went back to scrolling.

They worked in silence for another half an hour.

"Bingo." The marshal swiveled around in her chair. "Angelo Tick Tock Tommaso was locked up last month for racketeering."

"Is he a crime boss?"

"You've never heard of Tick Tock Tommaso?" The marshal chuckled. "He's the head of the Boston Italian mob."

"Could some of his henchmen have pulled off the heist hoping to use the art to bargain his way out?"

"Let's go ask him."

"Okay." Jessica stood up. She was happy to leave the printouts for a while. Page-after-page of ALERT-INVESTIGATE IMMEDIATELY got her nothing but blurred vision. All she'd learned was the thieves took their time cleaning out the Blue Room.

"Not now. Tomorrow." The marshal went to a small refrigerator and pulled out a Diet Mountain Dew. "Want one?"

Jessica shook her head. She did want caffeine. But a Starbuck's Caramel Macchiato was more her speed. She thought of Nick. He used to call her "Dolce" because when they first met, she'd spilled her sweet coffee all down the front of her little black dress. He'd said she smelled like dessert. *I wonder if he'd said that to Marshal Hottie, too?*

She went back to the printouts. ALERT-INVESTIGATE IMMEDIATELY over and over, line after line. Her mind wandered to Nick… and cats… and Adrián.

Would he call her? Would she go out with him? Work. It was just work. One thing was for sure. No more grappa.

Wait! She scrolled back to the previous screen. *That's odd.* She double-checked the list of stolen paintings and their locations in the museum.

What the heck. The stolen Bouguereau was in the French Gallery and not in the Blue Room. According to the security logs, the thieves never set foot in the French Gallery. But if they didn't take the Bouguereau, who did?

Her phone buzzed. *Adrián. Wait until he hears about this!*

Chapter 8

Later that night, Jessica met Adrián at a fancy bar in the basement of a posh hotel on the Charles River. He'd suggested the place. "The hippest place in Boston." It was dark and smelled like burnt cedar incense.

The bar was decorated with tiny white lights. Old-fashioned bar stools lined the long wooden bar. With lava lamps and Formica tables, the place had a vintage wannabe sort of vibe.

Jessica snacked on smoked almonds from a thick ceramic bowl shaped like a boot. Installed in a cozy corner booth, they were already on their second round.

"How did you find this bar?" she asked.

"It's a lounge, not a bar," Adrián corrected her. "Used to be a jailhouse."

Now, with its pale blue lights, psychedelic wallpaper, and velvet bar stools, it was more jailhouse rock than jail.

"How appropriate." Next round, she'd order a Cosmopolitan. Her usual Jack-n-Coke seemed too bar and not enough lounge.

"What did you learn about the robbery?" Adrián skewered a maraschino cherry with a bamboo cocktail spear. He was drinking a Rob Roy cocktail. Something her Aunt Mary used to drink at the Bulldog bar on Main Street. Jessica never could develop a taste for scotch… or bitters.

"Have you heard of Eggs Benedict?" She finished her Jack-n-Coke and waved to the waitress.

"The breakfast food with muffins and ham?"

"The art thief." She leaned closer to him. "He's in prison, but Marshal Colt thinks he could have orchestrated the heist from his cell."

"Interesting." Adrián sipped his cocktail.

The waitress took her order. She waited until the waitress was out of ear shot. "How about Tick Tock Tommaso? Heard of him?"

"The gangster?" His eyes widened. "He's a big time mafioso. From Sicily."

"He was busted last month for racketeering." She popped a smoked almond into her mouth. "Could be his men hit the museum to use the paintings to negotiate his release."

"Clever." He had dimples when he smiled. Must have been the dim lighting… he was looking like a young Antonio Banderas.

You already have a boyfriend, Jess, and you don't need another, especially not while working the case that will decide the course of the rest of your life. Jessica inhaled deeply and let out the breath. *Crapulence. I need to call Jack.* "What about you? What did you find out?"

Adrián raised his eyebrows. "I think that guard is in on it. The one who opened the door." His hands were dancing as he spoke. "I mean, who does that? Just open the door in the middle of the night?"

"He was contrite when we interviewed him—"

Adrián interrupted. "Did you expect him to confess?"

She tightened her lips. Sometimes Adrián was kind of mean. "If you'd let me finish… I saw something really strange on the security printout."

"I'm listening," he said, his intense brown eyes boring a hole in her face.

Unnerving. She sipped her cocktail only to discover it was gone. When she glanced over, Adrián was still staring at her. "Okay, so when I was scrolling through the heat-map print-outs, I noticed something weird—"

"I'm listening."

Dang. He's impatient. "The thief took the Rembrandt from the Blue Room—"

"Not Bouguereau's Innocence," Adrián interrupted. "That was from the French Room."

"As I was saying…" She gave him the side-eye. "On the security printout, there is no record of the thief setting foot in the French Gallery." She looked him in the face. "So, who took *Innocence?*"

"The security guard," Adrián said. "Has to be." He grinned. "I knew it." He pulled a *Chupa Chups* from his pocket and unwrapped it.

"He must have taken it down and handed it to the thief." She blew at her bangs. "How else could they have taken it?"

"Good question." Adrián waved for the bartender. "Let's go ask him."

"What?"

"Let's go interview the guard." Adrián took a few bills from his wallet and threw them on the table. "Frank Mutton, 616 Church Street, Apartment 10."

"Good memory." She blinked at him. "But it's Motton, not Mutton."

"Did you see his sideburns? And that hair?" Adrián chuckled. "Let's go have a chat with Mr. Frank Lambchop." He adjusted his fedora and stood to go.

"Shouldn't we wait for Marshal Colt or your guy, Detective Stevenson?"

"Why? We're as good as they are."

"I doubt that. Anyway, they're our supervisors." She twisted a lock of hair around her finger.

"If you don't have the guts, I'll go by myself." He turned on his heels. "We'll see who solves the case."

"Wait." She went after him. "Wait for me." Why did she always end up following these rule-breaking bad boys? What choice did she have? She wanted to solve the case… No. She *needed* to solve the case. Her future depended on it. "I'll go with you."

"Good girl." He popped the sucker into his mouth. "You can drive."

▭

FRANK LAMBCHOP MOTTON lived in a fourth-floor walkup in Dorchester. Once the home to Irish and Caribbean immigrants, Dorchester had been taken over by students. Close to the University of Massachusetts, and not far from Boston University, the neighborhood was full of low-cost rentals in disrepair.

Jessica had stood on this same stoop earlier that afternoon with Marshal Colt. Now she was practically hyperventilating while waiting to be buzzed up. *This really is a bad idea. What will the marshal do when she finds out? I'll lose my internship. Breathe. Just breathe. What the marshal doesn't know won't hurt her.*

Adrián pressed the buzzer again. No answer.

Loud rock music was blaring out of the brick apartment building. Was there a rooftop concert going on?

Adrián pressed the buzzer a third time. Nothing.

She stepped in front of him and held her finger down on the buzzer. The music was so loud she couldn't tell if anyone responded over the intercom. But suddenly the door buzzed.

Adrián opened the door, and she slipped in after him. Since she'd been here before, he let her lead the way. Either that or he was afraid Lambchop might pull a gun on them.

Yup. The blaring music was coming from Frank's apartment. Either they were having band practice or putting on a concert. It was a wonder the neighbors hadn't called the cops. She didn't recognize the song. Perhaps it was an original. They were actually pretty good. Swinging rock with a sweet melody and a badass beat.

Adrián pounded on the door for a minute solid. Finally, the music stopped. He pounded again.

A stick of a man with more tattoos than skin answered the door. "Dude," he said. "We're practicing for a gig. Did our psycho neighbors call the cops on us again?"

"We're not here about the music," Adrián said. He flashed his temporary FBI badge. "We're here to speak to Frank Motton."

"Franko." The tattooed stick of a man yelled back into the apartment. "Visitors." He left the door open but disappeared behind it.

Adrián stepped inside after him.

"Going rogue is bad enough." Jessica grabbed his arm and pulled him back into the hallway. "Let's not mess this up."

Frank Motton poked his furry face around the door. "You lookin' for me?"

"FBI," Adrián said. "We want to ask you some questions about the Albertina robbery." He pushed past Frank and went into the apartment.

"You again." Frank groaned. "I already told you. I don't know anything."

With wavy hair down to his waist and a full-on beard, Frank Motton looked like a Wookie. A Wookie wearing a stained heavy-metal T-shirt and frayed jeans. "They tied me up down there and put a hood over my head, for God's sake. It was terrifying, man."

"Let's get right to the point," Adrián turned abruptly. Frank almost ran into him. "Why did you go into the French Gallery last night?"

"What?" Frank's furry brows furrowed. "I was making my rounds like I always do."

"Why did you open the side door?"

"What?" Frank's lashes fluttered over his glassy eyes.

"You heard me." Adrián took a step closer to him. "Why did you open the side door?"

"I didn't, man." Frank took a step backwards.

"Security logs show that the door was opened at twelve-ten, just nineteen minutes before the robbery." Adrián's hands did a menacing dance.

"I don't know, man." Frank wiped his forehead with the back of his forearm.

"Did you take the Bouguereau off the wall and hand it out the door to someone?" Adrián's voice was strong and deep.

"What?" Frank's eyes got wide. "No way."

"Then why did you open that door?" Adrián sauntered into the living room like he owned the place.

Jessica was seeing another side of Adrián. A scary side.

"I didn't have anything to do with the robbery." Frank flushed, rushing to beat Adrián into the living room. "You've got to believe me."

"You're the only person who set foot in the French Gallery last night," Jessica said, trailing behind them. "*Innocence* was stolen from the French Gallery."

"Explain that." Adrián stood arms akimbo, his hands still for a change.

"I can't. Look, I didn't do anything."

Whoa. Is he crying?

"Or maybe you decided to help yourself to a painting?" Adrián towered over poor Frank.

"Look man, I told you." Frank's voice cracked. "I didn't do it."

"Then why did you open the side door?" Adrián's tone was demanding.

"I swear, man." Frank pushed a strand of hair out of his face. "I didn't do it."

"Either you're lying and you're working with the thieves, or you're the worst security guard in the world." Adrián huffed.

"Yeah. I know." Frank hung his head.

"Negligence at best," Jessica said. "Felony at worst." She got a whiff of eucalyptus and camphor and glanced around the filthy apartment.

"Yeah, man. I know." Frank was in tears. "I suck."

"We're going to have to search your apartment," Adrián said, pushing past Frank.

Jessica dashed around him and stood in front of him. "We can't do that," she whispered. "We don't have a warrant."

"We can't give him time to hide it." Adrián glared at her. "Whatever it takes, I'm getting those paintings back."

"If we break the law, then we're as bad as the robbers." Jessica pulled at his elbow. "Let's go."

"Go ahead," Frank said in a loud voice. "Search the place." His voice got even louder. "Have at it. I ain't got nothin' to hide."

He must be warning someone to hide the drugs. The whole lot of them looked stoned and the place reeked of weed… weed and that weird, minty smell.

Adrián tore through every drawer, closet, and cupboard in the apartment. Jessica watched, in awe of his determination. She grimaced as he threw Frank's underwear out of a dresser drawer.

"Was that really called for?" She stood in front of Adrián and looked him in the eyes. "I don't think you're going to find the missing paintings in Frank's underwear drawer. Let's go."

Adrián insisted on going through the rest of the apartment.

A bong under the kitchen sink. A box of condoms in the nightstand. A roach in the ashtray. But no paintings. The place was clean. Well, not exactly clean, but nothing hot, as in stolen.

"I told you," Jessica said when they came up empty-handed. "Now, let's saddle up and get outta here."

"Honey, I'm home." A singsong voice came from the doorway. "Where's the welcome wagon?"

Holy crap. She smelled him before she saw him. Eucalyptus and camphor. "What are you doing here?" Jessica's pulse quickened. The Gutenberg Bible nutcase and his goth girlfriend.

Goth-Girl waved at Frank and rubbed her baby bump.

With a cowlick standing straight up in the middle of his head, Dean Braugh stood there, grinning from ear to ear. "I live here, darlin."

Chapter 9

Adrián was sharing a suite with Stevenson at the Residence Inn not far from the Albertina Carpenter Museum. The suite had two bedrooms on either side of a common living area and a small kitchenette. The carpet was the color of dirt, which made it impossible to know whether it was clean. And the sectional sofa was an unappealing beige faux leather.

Papers, files, and photographs were spread out on the coffee table in the living area and all over the bar that separated the living area from the kitchenette. With every passing day, they gathered more information, and more reports piled up in every corner. Soon, the entire space would be plastered in paper.

Despite his late night with Jessica at Lambchop's apartment, Adrián had gotten up before dawn. By the time Stevenson finally got up at seven, Adrián had already drunk the entire Mr. Coffee pot of the swill Americans called dark roast.

Stevenson wandered into the living room wearing his plaid flannel pajamas. "You're up early." He yawned. His hair was sticking straight up, no doubt from all the grease he used on it.

He looked like a graying Beaker from the Muppets. Even his eyes were starting to bug out like Beaker's.

And you're up late. Adrián frowned. "I'm working on the case."

"Early bird gets the worm, eh?" Stevenson padded into the kitchen in his fuzzy slippers. He opened the refrigerator, removed a carton of milk, and then poured Cheerios into the last clean bowl in the place.

Birds. Worms. Tides. Boats. *Why can't Americans just speak plain English?*

"What have you found?" Stevenson asked, standing at the bar, his mouth full of Cheerios.

What a slob. Adrián looked away. He hated to watch Stevenson eat. And he hated to share intel with anyone. But Stevenson was his boss. And it was Stevenson he had to impress if he wanted to get a permanent job with the FBI. He closed Frank Motton's file and sat it atop the stack of folders on the coffee table.

"The security guard denies having anything to do with the heist. But he opened a side door to the French Gallery just minutes before the robbery. And he was the only one to step foot in there."

"Okay." Cereal bowl in hand, Stevenson padded into the living room.

"Remember the Bouguereau was taken from the French Gallery." Adrián ran his hand through his hair. "So Motton must have taken it."

As much as that hippy security guard denied taking part in the robbery, Adrián knew he was in on it… and he was determined to prove it.

Obviously, the guard wasn't stupid enough to hide anything at his own apartment. Adrián had to get *el loco* to crack. He'd tail him night and day if necessary. Frank Motton would screw up. And when he did, Adrián would be there.

"What else you got?" Stevenson dropped into an overstuffed chair and put his slippered feet up on the edge of the coffee table.

Isn't that enough? Motton is guilty. Adrián flipped through the file looking for more.

"Let's make a list of possible suspects." Stevenson slurped milk from his bowl.

Why did they need more suspects when they had the perpetrator already? Adrián sorted through the file folders until he found the one on Black Cat Security. He did wonder about the security firm. "Is it just a coincidence that the museum gets a new security system, and a new director, and then gets robbed?"

"They didn't have *any* security before they installed that system." Stevenson scoffed. "At least the heat sensors and the entrance videos give us a fighting chance. Imagine if we didn't have any surveillance at all."

"I guess." Adrián shook his head. He wasn't convinced.

"I'll go talk to the museum director again today," Stevenson said, a strange gleam in his eyes. "She might be able to tell us something about the security firm."

"Do you think she could be in on it?"

"Ms. Finch?" Stevenson sat up straight and then put his cereal bowl on the floor next to the chair. "She's the victim here, not the perpetrator."

Adrián glanced around the room. *Qué marrón. What a mess.* "If you say so." Adrián went back to the file. Black Cat Security. They installed the system just over a month ago. *Pretty suspicious. A few weeks after they install the system, the place is robbed.* "I'll check out this Black Cat Security."

"Good idea." Stevenson stood up. "I'll shower and get dressed and then we can make a game plan for the day. Why don't you make some more coffee?"

Who does he think I am? His servant? Adrián begrudgingly got up and went to the kitchen. He rinsed the coffee pot, put a new filter in the machine, scooped double the recommended coffee into the filter, and then filled it with water. *I suppose he expects me to do his dishes, too.*

If Adrián had to stay in this pigsty, he would have to break down and clean before the place became infested with God-knows-what American parasites.

Ring. Ring. Adrián looked around for the source. The hotel phone was on the desk in the corner of the living room. Adrián answered it.

"Stevenson, why aren't you answering your cell phone?" A gruff voice barked from the other end.

"Stevenson is in the shower," Adrián said.

"It's nearly lunchtime," the man said. "Why isn't he working?"

"We are working."

"Who is this?" the man demanded.

"Garcia, Adrián Garcia, the intern. Who is this?"

"Vereen, Gerald Vereen, head of the FBI."

Mierda.

"I got a tip off that the Albertina Carpenter heist might be a Dr. No."

What in the hell is a Dr. No? "Uhuh."

"Big time collector, Rockefeller Vanderbilt. He arrived at his townhouse in Louisburg Square last week. Tell Stevenson to get down there and interview him before he skips town in his private jet."

"Yes, sir."

The line went dead.

Caramba. Adrián's heart was racing. He'd just spoken to the director of the FBI.

But what did he mean? *Rockefeller Vanderbilt. Louisburg Square. Dr. No.*

Adrián grabbed his laptop and searched Google.

Wow. Rockefeller Vanderbilt was an oil baron and one of the richest men in the country…. And he had one of the most important private collections of Dutch art in the world. *The*

Rembrandt. Of course. Vanderbilt would probably give anything to get his hands on it.

Louisburg Square was a neighborhood in Beacon Hill and one of the most exclusive areas in the United States, with townhouses worth over fifteen million dollars. *No me digas. No way.*

Dr. No. *The first James Bond movie with Sean Connery?* What did that have to do with Vanderbilt or the robbery?

"Who was that on the phone?" Stevenson asked. He was wearing a robe and rubbing his head with the towel.

"Gerald Vereen."

"The director?" Stevenson dropped the towel on the floor. "What did he want?"

"Wants us to interview Mr. Rockefeller Vanderbilt."

"Who?"

"One of the richest men in Boston. He collects Dutch art. The director thinks he might be a Dr. No." *Whatever that is.*

"Dr. No." Stevenson picked up the towel. "Interesting. Looks like we have another suspect. I'd better call Vereen back."

What? Doesn't he trust me? Adrián scowled.

Stevenson disappeared into his bedroom. He reappeared a couple of minutes later, fully dressed and talking on his cell phone. "Got it. Meet Colt at Louisburg Square at noon." He grimaced and then glanced over at Adrián. "Got it."

"Marshal Colt?" Adrián asked. Jessica would be there too. This could be fun. No way he would give her a head-start.

"Apparently, Rocky Vanderbilt has been trying to buy another Rembrandt for years." Stevenson buttoned his suit jacket.

"And Dr. No?" Adrián asked.

"Dr. No from James Bond." Stevenson chuckled. "Rich villain who had a stolen Goya on display in his lair."

"A movie villain. What does that have to do with our case?"

"Just go with it." Stevenson gathered up his wallet and keys from the counter. "Look. Colt and I have some history," he said. "She's one of those gals, you look at her wrong and she cries sexual harassment." He smiled. "Know what I mean?"

No means no. Dr. or not. Adrián nodded. Stevenson was not only a slob but also a creeper.

"Why don't you meet Marshal Colt at Louisburg Square and I'll take Ms. Finch to lunch." He winked. "To get more information out of her about the security system."

Instead of interviewing a prime suspect, he wants to go on a date? And this guy is an FBI agent. Adrián turned up his lip.

"Deal?" Stevenson knotted his tie.

Anything to get away from Stevenson. "Sure." *Now I can get to Vanderbilt before the luminous Jessica does.* "Glad to help."

———

LOUISBURG SQUARE WAS A WELL-GROOMED neighborhood of three-story, redbrick townhouses with bay windows and flower boxes. From the outside, it didn't look that much different from other posh neighborhoods in Boston.

Adrián adjusted his tie, and then rang the doorbell.

"Just a minute." A man's voice came from inside.

Adrián shifted from foot to foot.

A petite man wearing a pink polo shirt answered the door. With his short, sandy hair and pressed slacks, he looked more like a tennis pro than a butler. "You must be the G-man," he said. "Vereen warned me you were coming."

So much for the element of surprise. "Yes, I'm Adrián Garcia." *Why is the director of the FBI tipping off a suspect? Is this how they do things in this country? It's all about money.*

"Come in, Mr. Garcia." The man gestured him inside. "My staff has the morning off. So, I'm afraid we're on our own."

"Mr. Vanderbilt?"

"Yes. Sorry." The man extended his hand. "Call me Rocky."

He looks familiar. His grip was hard as if to compensate for his small stature, and his unflinching eye contact made it clear that no one was going to get the best of Rocky Vanderbilt.

Vanderbilt led Adrián through the marble foyer to the first room on the right. There were two walls of built-in bookshelves stocked with neatly arranged hardbacks and one shelf of ancient leather-bound books. *Must be the library.*

A third wall boasted a magnificent stone fireplace above which hung an imposing portrait of a solid woman with cascading blonde hair. She was dressed in a regal cape and crown, looking up from a large book. Adrián recognized it as Rembrandt's *Minerva in her study*, one of the Dutch master's finest.

"Nice Rembrandt," Adrián said, taking a seat on a high-backed burgundy chair. *Ajá.* Vanderbilt was the trustee on the CCTV video—the one who visited the museum the other night.

"Isn't it, though?" Vanderbilt sat behind a desk near the only window, an oversized bay window that looked out on the square. "You probably already know I have the largest *private* collection of Rembrandt paintings in the world."

"I know that you've been trying to acquire more." Adrián paused for effect. "Through any means necessary?"

"I'm always looking to expand my collection," Vanderbilt said with a smirk. "Provided it's within my means."

"Do your means include theft?" Adrián asked.

"Everything I do is perfectly legal." Vanderbilt shifted some papers on the desk. "Perhaps you would like to talk to my lawyers?"

"Did you have anything to do with the theft of the Rembrandt from the Albertina Museum?" Unblinking, Adrián stared down the tycoon.

"Absolutely not," Vanderbilt said. "Anyway, do you think I'd tell you if I did?" His eyes danced when he smiled.

"Absolutely not."

Chime. Chime. Chime. The doorbell rang.

"Excuse me." Vanderbilt stood up. "Someone's at the door. One of your colleagues perhaps?" His fancy sneakers squeaked on the floor as he walked to the foyer. "Don't you always travel in pairs?" At the threshold, he turned back. "Or is it packs?" He disappeared.

As he fumbled to get the listening device out of his pocket, Adrián's heart was pounding. He jumped up, dashed across the room, and attached the quarter-sized eavesdropper under Vanderbilt's desk. *Any means necessary.*

As he hurried back to his seat, he heard the familiar voice. *Aja. The inexorable Jessica.* She wasn't far behind him. At least, he'd gotten there first. Not that it helped him get any information out of the sly tycoon.

When the door to the library opened, Adrián leaned back in his chair and tried to look relaxed.

"Ladies," Vanderbilt said as he ushered Jessica and Marshal Colt into the room. "Mr. Garcia, I'm afraid our interview is over. I have business to discuss with these two charming women."

"But—" Adrián stood up. He wished he'd planted more bugs.

"Good to meet you, Mr. Garcia," Jessica said, coming toward him, her hand outstretched.

What is she playing at? Puzzled, he played along and extended his hand. The jolt of electricity when his palm held hers surprised him, and his face twitched.

Jessica winked. "May I present Mrs. Roth?" She gestured toward Marshal Colt, who had a gurgling baby slung across her body.

He didn't let go of her hand. Instead, he squeezed it as

hard as he could. She tightened her lips and pulled out of his grip.

Not fair. She wasn't playing fair.

"I'm Dr. Tyson," she said, glaring at him. "I represent Mrs. Roth's artistic interests."

"Ladies," Vanderbilt said cheerfully. He led them to the sitting area. "Mr. Garcia," he said not so cheerfully. "I'm afraid you'll have to show yourself out."

Chapter 10

Great. The baby just puked on her navy blazer.

Lexi wondered why she was going along with the cowgirl's hairbrained charade. Oh yeah. Because the stupid babysitter called in sick again. Mrs. Faheem wasn't home. And she had a pacifier pinned to her lapel.

If she hadn't had baby Sammy strapped to her chest, she would have intervened by now and set the record straight.

No, she wasn't an art investor. No, the cowgirl was not her representative. She was a federal marshal and Blondie was an intern with an overactive imagination.

Where did Jessica come up with this shit?

Lexi had to hand it to her. Whatever else she was, the cowgirl was a good actress. If it hadn't been for Jessica's quick thinking, Rockefeller Vanderbilt might have slammed the door in their faces.

"Mrs. Roth is interested in adding a Rembrandt to her Dutch collection." The cowgirl walked over to the fireplace. "Minerva. The virgin goddess of war… and of peace. Those Greeks and their contradictions." She stood smiling under the painting as if she were modeling it instead of admiring it. "Priceless."

Lexi stared up at the ugly thing. The woman in the painting looked like a pudgy man with the expression of someone who'd just relieved himself of excess air.

"Everything has a price," Mr. Vanderbilt said. "Even Adrián Garcia."

"The FBI man?" Jessica asked. "Do you collect those too?"

"You could say I've owned a few over the years." Mr. Vanderbilt grinned.

Lexi felt like socking him in the face. How many FBI agents had he bought off? If Mr. Vanderbilt thought *her* loyalty was for sale, he had another thing coming. "Do you have a Rembrandt for sale or not?"

The cowgirl gave her the stink eye. "What Mrs. Roth means is, do you know of any Rembrandts that we might be able to purchase?" She sat down on the couch next to Mr. Vanderbilt. "It's a surprise gift for her husband. Something intimate, not for the whole world to see, if you know what I mean."

Baby Sammy was squirming and kicking. *Come on, kid. Chill out.* Lexi paced around the library, bouncing her up and down in the Baby Bjorn. It was impossible to be tough when interviewing a suspect with a kid strapped to your boobs. Still, the cowgirl was taking the act a bit too far.

"Cute baby," Mr. Vanderbilt said. He didn't sound like he meant it. "My staff is out until this afternoon, or I'd offer you ladies some coffee." He chuckled. "I'm on my own this morning."

Did Vereen know the staff would be out this morning when he set up the interview? Probably. *Clever. Very clever.*

Interviewing the staff could prove more useful than talking to Mr. Vanderbilt. It wasn't like he would admit it if he had stolen the Rembrandt. Maybe the staff had seen something suspicious in the last couple days.

Lexi would have to track down the staff… without baby Sammy and without Jessica James.

"About the Rembrandt," the cowgirl said, leaning closer to the suspect. "Any ideas where we might find one to purchase?"

"Depends," Mr. Vanderbilt said.

Lexi stopped in her tracks and perked up her ears. "On what?"

"Can you pay cash?" he asked. "And what kind of provenance would you expect?"

"It's a birthday gift," the cowgirl said. "Not an investment."

"I see." Mr. Vanderbilt stood up, walked over to Lexi, and patted the baby on her furry, little head.

Sammy's face turned the color of a ripe tomato, and she started screaming.

"Sweet kid," Mr. Vanderbilt said.

Now Lexi was sure he didn't mean it.

"I might know of a painting that's just come on the market," Mr. Vanderbilt said. "I might be able to put you in touch with a guy who can tell you more about it." The baby's screaming must have persuaded him to finally get down to business.

"Which painting?" The cowgirl asked.

Mr. Vanderbilt sat down next to her. "Something very special." His voice was nearly inaudible.

"The Rembrandt taken from the Albertina Museum?" Lexi asked. Things were getting interesting.

"I don't know anything about that." Mr. Vanderbilt said. "I've only heard there could be a very unique Rembrandt on the market."

"From whom?" Lexi asked.

Mr. Vanderbilt scowled. "Are you sure you're not from the FBI?"

"Do we look like we're from the FBI?" the cowgirl asked.

Mr. Vanderbilt glanced over at Lexi bouncing the baby and shook his head. "Not really."

"Excuse Mrs. Roth's impatience," Jessica said, sweetly. "The baby is teething, you see. And the nanny called in sick. It's been one of those days."

As if on cue, Sammy spit up again.

Mr. Vanderbilt nodded. "I see that." He wrinkled his nose. "Why don't you talk to my lawyer?" He got up, went to his desk, and grabbed a business card from a holder. "He might be able to help you." He handed the card to Lexi.

She stared down at it. *What in Sam Hill?*

Rocky Vanderbilt's lawyer was the infamous mafia lawyer, Santo Romano. Santo Romano had defended some of the biggest organized crime bosses in the country. He was famous for getting some big fish off the hook. Lexi remembered seeing him in action when she worked with WitSec.

Maybe Vereen is right, and Rocky Vanderbilt is our Dr. No.

"WHAT'S THE RUSH?" Jessica white-knuckled the handhold. Why was Marshal Colt always in such a hurry?

The baby was strapped into a car seat in the back, and every time the marshal accelerated, the kid chirped like a squirrel.

"The faster I go, the quieter Sammy gets." The marshal glanced over at Jessica. "She loves it."

Yeah right. "Either that or she's terrified." What would it be like to have the marshal as a mom? And a dad off someplace in WitSec? *Poor kid.*

Jessica knew something about a missing dad. After her dad died in a trucking accident, twelve-year-old Jesse had to grow up quickly and take care of herself and her gin-swilling mother. At least the marshal was only addicted to Mountain Dew.

"Nice work back there," the marshal said.

"Thanks." Jessica smiled. "Obviously, Rocky doesn't like the FBI, so I figured we'd better improvise."

"Maybe you could warn me next time?"

"It was all kind of spontaneous." Jessica let go of the handheld and gripped the passenger seat. "Maybe we could develop some sort of code."

"Code?"

"Yeah. Like, if I say, 'Sammy's diaper needs changing', then you're Mrs. Roth." Jessica giggled. "And if you say, 'fetch me a baby-wipe', then I'm Dr. Tyson, your art expert."

"That assumes I bring Sammy along when we interview suspects." Lexi stomped on the accelerator. "Not sure the boss would approve."

"What he doesn't know…"

Lexi smiled. "Hand me a pop, would you?"

Jessica reached into the back seat and snagged a can of warm Diet Mountain Dew. "Aren't you worried about becoming addicted?"

"It's just pop." Lexi scoffed. "It's not like it's cocaine."

"That color." Jessica grimaced. "It's just not natural."

"Neither is the color of your hair, but I'm not busting your butt."

Point taken. Jessica had gotten a few highlights to celebrate getting the internship. "Do you think Vanderbilt is our perp?"

"Could be." The marshal swerved into the parking lot behind headquarters. "Let's make up a list of suspects and go over everything we've got so far."

Yeah. You're jacked up on Mountain Dew. What about me? I haven't had my second cup of coffee yet. "Mind if I run across the street to Starbucks first?"

"Aren't you worried about getting addicted?"

"Okay. Okay." Jessica unclipped her seatbelt. "To each their own poison."

"Make it snappy." The marshal went around to the back

to fetch Sammy. "I don't want the baby to start yowling again."

"Don't blame me if your baby cries."

"But she likes you." The marshal fastened little Sammy into the Baby Bjorn.

"I'm your intern," Jessica said. "Not your babysitter."

"Using the baby as a prop was your idea, sister." The marshal gave her a salute. "Get your coffee and then get your butt upstairs. We have a thief to catch."

"Yes, sir." Jessica stood at attention and returned the salute. Then she took off at a gallop toward her caramel macchiato Frappuccino.

MARKER IN HAND, Lexi stood at the whiteboard. "Suspects. Rocky Vanderbilt, our Dr. No."

"And his lawyer." The cowgirl was sitting at the desk cradling Sammy in her lap. "Sounds like one or both knows where to find the missing Rembrandt."

"Either that or he was blowing smoke up our butts." Lexi wrote "Rockefeller Vanderbilt" at the top of the board. "Who else?"

"The stoner security guard." Jessica rocked the baby back and forth. "He is the only person who went into the French gallery. And he opened the side door, supposedly to have a smoke. Even if he wasn't the mastermind, he might be an accomplice."

Lexi wrote "Frank Motton, security guard," and said, "and his roommate, the Harvard bible thief?"

"Yeah, Dean Braugh. He's a real kook. And his girlfriend is a piece of work too."

"Okay. Dean Braugh." Lexi wrote down his name.

"What about that crime boss?" The cowgirl laughed. "Mr. Egg McMuffin."

"He's the art thief, not the crime boss." Lexi wrote "Eggs Benedict" on the white board. "The mafioso is Tick Tock Tommaso." She wrote his name on the board too. "That's four so far. Anyone else?"

"The museum director, Ms. Finch?" Jessica bounced the baby in her lap.

Was that a Snicker's wrapper sticking out of the cowgirl's jacket pocket? Has she been in my stash? "You think she could be involved?" Lexi squinted at the wrapper. "Any evidence?"

"My gut tells me she's innocent." Jessica tickled the baby. "She was genuinely broken up about it. Wasn't she, baby Sammy?"

Why does everyone start talking babytalk around babies? "Does your gut have a lot of experience with criminals?" Lexi asked.

"As a matter of fact—"

"Okay, okay." Lexi laid the marker on the tray of the white board. "Let's review our suspects."

"Our Dr. No rich art collector, Rockefeller Vanderbilt, more than hinted that he knows the location of the missing Rembrandt. So, he's suspect number one." The cowgirl carried the sleeping baby over to Lexi and held her up like a peace offering.

"Frank the security guard was behaving suspiciously on the night of the robbery." Lexi took the baby. "Did he say anything that makes you think he's in on it?"

"Not really." The cowgirl shrugged.

"What's your gut tell you about him?" Lexi smirked.

"Not a thief. Pothead, yes. Art thief, no."

"Speaking of art thieves, we should interview Eggs. If anyone knows who could have pulled off a heist like this, it's Eggs." Lexi strapped Sammy into the sling and then gathered up her diaper bag. "I'll arrange it for tomorrow."

"Don't forget about Dean Braugh."

"Right. The bible thief."

"It can't just be a coincidence that he's the security guard's roommate." The cowgirl followed Lexi around the office. "Maybe Adrián and I should tail him."

Lexi stopped in her tracks. "Adrián, the Spanish intern assigned to stalker Stevenson?" She narrowed her eyes. "Stevenson is a dirtbag. I'd just as soon we keep our dealings with him to a minimum… and strictly business. Got it?"

The cowgirl stood there blinking.

"What?" Lexi slung the diaper bag over one shoulder and her purse over the other. Baby Sammy was snuggled between them. "Let's knock off early."

"Adrián is a good guy," Jessica said.

"Is that what your tummy tells you?"

"We can trust him." Jessica slouched into her ratty cowboy jacket.

"If you say so." Lexi left the cowgirl sputtering in the doorway.

If her gut tells her to trust Adrián Garcia, she needs to see a gastroenterologist.

Chapter 11

Adrián slid down in the back seat of the Uber. He watched as Vanderbilt left his townhouse in a black limo.

"I'll be back in a few minutes," Adrián said to the Uber driver. He got out and ducked behind the car door.

When Vanderbilt's limo was out of sight, he went to the door.

I still can't believe that sneaky Jessica. Pretending to be an art dealer. He'd heard everything. Thankfully, the little bug under the desk picked up the entire conversation. He wasn't going to let the transcendent Jessica James get the better of him.

He pressed the doorbell.

A woman wearing jeans and a starched white blouse answered the door. "I'm sorry," she said with a strong accent. "Mr. Vanderbilt just left."

Adrián flashed his temporary FBI ID card. "I'm here to talk to you."

The woman put her hand to her chest. *"Dios Mìo."* Her body froze, but her eyes looked like she wanted to run.

"It's okay," he said in Spanish, drawing out the words, trying to emulate her Mexican drawl. "I just want to ask a few questions about Mr. Vanderbilt. You're not in any trouble."

"*Ay.*" Her face relaxed. "Okay."

"Can I come in?" he asked, in his brightest tone.

She led him through the townhouse to the kitchen, which was in the very back with windows overlooking a well-manicured courtyard. The kitchen's gingham curtains and shiny stainless-steel appliances gave it a cheery feel. Obviously, the woman was more comfortable here than in the foyer. She sat at a small table and gestured for him to do the same.

"My name is Adrián," he said. "What's yours?"

"Maria." The woman looked down at her hands. "I don't know anything." Either she was incredibly loyal to her employer, or she was afraid of something… or both.

Adrián pulled a *Chupa Chups* from his jacket pocket. "Would you like a lollipop?"

She shook her head.

He shrugged. Hoping to put her at ease, he unwrapped the lolly and popped it into his mouth. He pulled out another and held it out to her. "Sure you don't want one? Best lollipop in the world."

She smiled weakly and took the candy. "For my son." She sat it on the table next to her.

"How many children do you have?"

"Three." She smiled for real. "Two boys and a baby girl."

Adrián held out two more lollipops. "One for each."

"*Gracias.*"

It was working. Little by little, the muscles in her jaw relaxed.

"I'm interested in Mr. Vanderbilt's art collection."

"I don't know nothing about that."

"Did you by chance see him bring in any new paintings this last week?"

"I don't know. Mr. Vanderbilt is always moving paintings around."

"Which paintings did he move yesterday?"

"Yesterday?"

"Or today?"

"I don't know. He might have moved some."

Adrián gritted his teeth. He was losing his patience. He took a deep breath. "Did you see what any of them looked like? Did they have people in them? Or animals? Or boats on the sea?"

"Boats on the sea." Her eyes lit up. "Yes. Mr. Vanderbilt had a picture of a boat. He took it out to be restored, I think."

"When?"

"Maybe half hour ago." She shrugged. "I don't know."

Mierda. I should have followed him. Too late now. "Do you know where he went? To get the painting restored?"

She shook her head. "Sorry."

"Did you see any of the other pictures Mr. Vanderbilt moved or bought recently?"

She thought for a minute. "Just that one with the boat." She smiled.

"Can you show me where he stored it or had it hanging before he took it out to be restored?" His pulse quickened. *Could it be?* Had he found the Rembrandt? *The Storm on the Sea of Galilee,* Rembrandt's only seascape.

"I guess so." She gathered up the *Chupa Chups* and put them into her purse, which was sitting on the kitchen counter. "Mr. Vanderbilt had it in the closet of his office. I saw it when I was cleaning in there early this morning."

Why would he put a painting in a closet? Unless he's hiding it?

Adrián followed the housekeeper up the stairs, down the hallway, and into the office. The dark burgundy curtains and heavy, oak furniture reminded him of his father's study at home in Madrid.

As a boy, Adrián loved to sneak into his father's study and play with the colorful ink and fine fountain pens adorning the desktop. Whenever his father caught him, Adrián would try to hide under the big wooden desk. Once, as he flew under the desk, he tipped over the red ink bottle.

The next week, he was sent to Catholic boarding school in Italy.

"In here," Maria said, opening the closet door. She stood there blinking at the empty space. "It was here this morning when I cleaned."

Adrián moved closer and peeked inside the closet. "May I?" He pointed at the floor.

Maria was wringing her hands. "I don't know. Mr. Vanderbilt might not like it…"

Before she could object, Adrián was on his hands and knees examining the carpet. "Is this where you saw the painting?" He looked up at Maria. "Leaning against this filing case?"

She nodded.

He pulled a pair of tweezers from his pocket, along with a tiny plastic evidence bag, and then plucked some fibers from the carpet. Perhaps wood splinters from the picture frame or paint flakes had made their way onto the carpet. Everything left a trace. The Art Crime Forensics department should be able to tell him if they were from late nineteenth century France.

"I think we should go now." Maria's voice trembled. "Mr. Vanderbilt will be home soon."

Adrián stood up… but not before attaching another listening device to the filing cabinet. "*Gracias*, Maria." He smiled down at her. "You've been very helpful."

"*Por favor*, go now," she pleaded.

"Of course." He followed her back down the stairs, through the foyer, to the front door. "May your children enjoy the lollipops in good health."

She nodded nervously and then shut the door in his face.

━━

WHEN ADRIÁN GOT BACK to the hotel suite, Stevenson was

already there lounging around with his feet on the coffee table, watching daytime television. An empty pizza box lay open on the floor next to a crumpled Coke can. *How is it possible this guy is the Division Director?* Adrián shook his head. *Unbelievable.*

"Enjoying your vacation?" Adrián asked, dropping the car keys on the counter.

"Actually," Stevenson sat up and clicked the remote to turn off the TV. "I got some very interesting intel from Eliza." He chuckled.

"Eliza?"

"Ms. Finch, the museum director."

Adrián took a seat on the couch across from his boss. "I'm all ears."

"Remember she told us she started two months ago?" He raised his eyebrows. "Well, the former director left under a cloud… a rather dark cloud."

"Okay." He couldn't stand looking at the mess. He jumped up, gathered the pizza box and empty can, and took them to the trash. "The dark cloud?"

Stevenson got up and followed Adrián into the kitchenette. He opened the refrigerator and took out another can of Coke. "The former director was run out on a rail after he used museum funds to fly his girlfriend around the world with him." He snapped the tab on the can and then took a sip. "Apparently, he wasn't too happy about getting fired."

"You think he's a suspect?" Adrián asked. He pulled a garbage bag out from under the sink, flipped it open, and proceeded to tidy the common area of the suite. Stevenson had left candy bar wrappers, take-out boxes, and soda cans all over. There were messy days and people who were a mess every day. Stevenson was an everyday sort of mess.

"There's more." Stevenson grinned. "Just before he was fired, he was told to upgrade security after a credible threat. He hired Black Cat Security, but he was out on his ear before they finished installing the system." Stevenson headed back to the living area and planted himself in a beige faux leather chair.

"Interesting." Adrián stuffed a Chinese food container into the garbage bag. "This former director might have arranged the robbery as severance pay." He scooped up a pile of pistachio shells from the bar and dropped them into the trash. "And he might have convinced the security company to help him."

"Exactly."

"We need to interview this former director." Adrián tied the trash bag shut and put it in the hallway outside the hotel room door.

"Ah," Stevenson said. "There's the rub. The dude has flown the coop. No one knows where he is."

"Okay, that's suspicious."

"Indeed." Stevenson downed the last of his Coke and crushed the can between his palms. "But I made us an appointment with the head of Black Cat Security." He glanced over at Adrián and then dropped the can onto the floor next to his chair.

Pendejo. Does he think I'm his maid? Adrián ignored him and tried not to look at the crumpled can.

"How'd you get on with Rocky Vanderbilt?"

"Didn't get a lot out of him." Adrián didn't tell him that he'd planted bugs in Vanderbilt's townhouse, or that Jessica had gotten the name of Vanderbilt's lawyer. "But I did talk to his maid." Maria evened the score. Jessica one. Adrián one.

"And what did she have to say?" Stevenson absentmindedly flipped through a file folder.

The least he could do is pay attention. "She saw the Rembrandt."

That got his attention. Stevenson dropped the folder back onto the table. "The stolen Rembrandt?" He stared at Adrián with his mouth hanging open.

"Maria saw Vanderbilt put it in his closet. But when we

looked for it, it was gone." Adrián pulled the tiny baggie from his pocket. "I collected carpet fibers from where it was sitting."

"We need to get that to forensics." Stevenson got up off his butt and strolled over to the kitchen to take a look at the fibers. "I'll send it off." He held out his hand.

Adrián flinched. Should he give the evidence to Stevenson and let him take all the credit? What choice did he have? Stevenson was his boss. He handed over the baggie. "Can you give me a copy of the requisition?"

"Don't you trust me to do my job?"

No. Actually I don't. "What is it you Americans say, I just like to dot my I's and cross my T's." He shrugged. "Let me know as soon as the results are back, okay."

"I'll put in the request right now." Stevenson shoved some papers off the counter to reveal his laptop underneath.

Adrián squeezed his eyes shut. *What a slob. I've got to solve this case soon. I can't take much more of this guy.*

Stevenson tapped on the keys. A minute later, the portable printer on the coffee table buzzed to life. "There's your copy."

Adrián lifted it out of the printer tray, folded it into a square and put it in his pants pocket.

"I'll drop this off at HQ first thing in the morning." Stevenson stuffed the evidence bag into the pocket of his jacket. "Now, let's go interview Black Cat Security." He picked up Adrián's car keys off the counter. "You drive." He tossed the keys at Adrián. They bounced off his chest and onto the floor.

Qué Cabrón. Adrián snatched the keys off the floor.

Stevenson was standing in the doorway. "Get a move on."

Adrián strode across the suite to the entrance. He was just about to shut the door when he saw it out of the corner of his eye.

That crumpled Coke can next to Stevenson's chair. Adrián tried to ignore it, but he couldn't.

Ay. Tonto del culo.

He ran over, picked up the can, threw it in the trash, and then slammed the door shut on his way out.

◻

A ROUND-FACED MAN was waiting for them in front of a renovated warehouse at Charleston waterfront. The warehouse had been converted into condos, except for the basement, one corner of which housed Black Cat Security.

The guy was wearing an ugly, green cardigan sweater and khaki slacks. He extended his hand to Stevenson and introduced himself. "David Black. I'm the owner." He pushed his glasses back on his nose and led them into the building and down concrete stairs into the basement. "In here."

The room was only half finished. Pipes and wires ran across the ceiling. One of the walls was concrete blocks. And it smelled dank and salty from the harbor air.

The guy sat down behind a desk—the only furniture in the large room. He pushed his glasses back up his nose again as he opened a laptop sitting on a scratched-up metal desk. "I'll show you around the system we installed at the museum."

Adrián looked over his shoulder as the guy explained the bare-bones security system. Motion and heat sensors in every room and CCTV cameras at every exit. That was it. No automatic locking mechanisms. No door alarms. Nothing to alert local police of a breech except for one panic button at the guard's desk. A panic button that wasn't used.

"Why such a paltry system?" Adrián asked, pushing his hat back on his head.

The owner pushed his glasses up his nose yet again. "It's all the museum could afford."

That gibed with what the museum director, Ms. Finch had told them. The museum was underfunded and understaffed. No wonder they were robbed.

"The former museum director had the system installed," Adrián said. "What was his name?" He looked at Stevenson.

"Jim Johnston," Stevenson said. He stood with his legs wide apart and his hands stuffed into his pants pockets.

"That's correct." The owner wrapped his torso in the cardigan as if a stiff wind had just blown through the room. "We worked with Mr. Johnston."

Were they in this together? *David Black is nervous, like he's hiding something. And the former museum director, Jim Johnston, is missing in action.*

"Do you know how we can get in contact with Mr. Johnston?" Stevenson asked.

"You could try Janie," the owner said, glancing up from his desk.

"His girlfriend?" Adrián asked.

"No." The owner blushed. "His wife."

Interesting. Mr. Black is on a first-name basis with his client's wife. "Do you know how we can contact Janie?" Adrián asked.

"She's probably at home." The owner troubled a button on his sweater. "In Medford."

"Do you happen to have her address or phone number?" Adrián asked.

"Ah… well… I might." The owner fumbled with papers on his desk, as if the wife's contact info might be somewhere in the stack. "Actually." He stopped searching. "I think I remember her cell number." He laughed nervously and then recited the phone number.

"Can I borrow a pen?" Stevenson asked.

The owner handed him a pen, and Stevenson wrote the number on his palm.

Sigh. Adrián shook his head. *How does this guy keep his job?*

"What can you tell us about Jim Johnston?" Adrián asked.

"Wasn't home much. Always traveling." The owner picked up a pencil from his desk. "Seemed nice enough. I don't know." He tapped the pencil on the edge of the desk. The sound echoed through the cavernous room. "I didn't really know him."

"But you know his wife." Adrián towered above him.

"I've met her." The owner bit down on the end of the pencil.

"Were you sleeping with her?" Adrián asked.

"Garcia, careful," Stevenson said.

"I'm married," the owner said.

Adrián glanced over at Stevenson. "I'll take that as a yes."

Chapter 12

His tongue hanging out, Camo obediently sat by the door watching as Lexi tore around the apartment looking for her wallet.

She was going to be late for dog training. *Where is it? Dammit.* She sighed. If the army doctor hadn't insisted, she never would have gotten a dog. *Camo is my ticket back into the FBI. What choice do I have?* The special training came with the dog.

Aha. The diaper bag. My wallet is in the diaper bag. She still wasn't used to carrying a diaper bag as a purse.

She found the diaper bag on her bed. She'd left it there when she changed Sammy before dropping her off with Mrs. Faheem.

Lexi rummaged in the bag. Pampers. Vaseline. Handcuffs. Taser. Gun. Baby Powder Spray. Sammy's teething ring. *Where in the hell is my wallet?* She tipped the bag upside down and dumped the contents on the bed.

Dragging his leash behind him, Camo came to her side and nudged her elbow. He must have sensed that she was agitated. He was trained to comfort her during a PTSD flash-back. His job was to bring her back to the present. The nightmares too. He woke her up if she was screaming in the night. His wet nose on her cheek. Even when she frantically batted his nose away, he forgave her. If she could only forgive herself.

Survivor's guilt. That's what the therapist called it. She felt guilty because she was the only person to survive the Taliban attack on the convoy. Her boyfriend at the time had died in front of her eyes, and her injuries had claimed the life of their unborn child. A little girl.

Sammy. Thank the Lord for Sammy.

There it was. Her wallet. It had gotten folded inside a diaper. At least, it was a clean one and not a dirty one. She grabbed it and stuffed it into the back pocket of her slacks. "Come on Camo."

The dog picked up his leash in his teeth and handed it to her. *Wow.* Sometimes this dog totally blew her mind.

JESSICA PACED BACK and forth on the scuffed-up, wood floor of her studio apartment. She'd had to find something cheap to rent and didn't have much time to look.

The one room apartment sat atop a history professor's house in Allston. Its battered appliances, smudged walls, and door—black with palm prints, bore witness to dozens of university students who'd lived there before her.

Although her place was crappy, the neighborhood was cool. The avenues were lined with cafés, bookstores, shops, and divey student hangouts. Just her speed. It seemed apt that the Boston suburb was named after the romantic painter, Washington Allston, a Harvard graduate.

Her stuff was still in boxes, and to keep up her pacing, she had to zigzag around them. It was just a year-long internship, so she packed light. Then again, even if this had been the last move she'd ever make, she didn't have much. A box of her grandmother's vintage dresses. A few boxes of books, of course. And a small box of letters and presents from ex-boyfriends. Nick… and Michael before him.

All Jack ever gave her was unwanted advice and some tome of Rilke's poems. Why wasn't he answering his phone? *As mom says, absence makes the heart grow fonder… for somebody else.* Supposedly, they were still a couple. But she hadn't seen him for over two months, and she hadn't talked to him since she got back from Italy. Maybe he'd found someone else. Maybe that's what he wanted to tell her. Maybe that's why his messages were always so cryptic.

Since Jack wasn't home, she called Adrián. Yeah. The marshal told her not to. But being alone was not her forte. In fact, nothing scared her more. Maybe that's why she'd stuck with so many bad boyfriends. She'd rather be with Mr. Wrong than by herself.

Adrián invited her to have a drink with him in a bar near his hotel.

After half an hour on the 57 bus, she was in front of the Residence Inn. Adrián was waiting for her in the lobby. He looked dapper in his dark fedora, wool jacket, and jeans. *Who wears a wool jacket in June?*

He took her across the street to a bowling alley called Lucky Strike.

Holy Crap. She hadn't seen this much neon since her trip to Las Vegas. The Lucky Strike bowling alley had a video arcade with a wall of flashing lights, a sports bar with giant televisions, a billiard room, and, of course, a bowling alley. She followed Adrián into the bar.

The music was so loud she could feel it vibrating in her gut. *It's gonna be hard to talk about secret FBI intel in this place. We're going to have to yell.* "Maybe we should go someplace else," she shouted.

Adrián took her hand and led her through the crowded bar. Once they got past the giant screens, he pulled her into a cubicle and slid a door shut. *Wow. A tiny private room.*

It reminded her of the private dining rooms in her favorite sushi place back in Chicago. She used to go there with Lolita, aka The Poker Tsarina. Her best friend from Northwestern University. She hadn't seen Lolita since before she went to Italy. She wondered when she'd see the feisty Russian again. *Always interesting times with Lolita.*

Adrián turned off the television and sat down in the booth tucked into the corner. "This is for private parties," he said, taking off his jacket, and revealing a black T-shirt and jeans. And he was wearing sneakers.

He's more casual than usual. America must be wearing off on him. "How'd you get this room?" she asked.

"I've gotten to know the owner." He flashed his FBI badge. "And this works like magic."

"Is the owner a pretty woman?"

"How well you know me." Adrián smiled.

Actually, she hardly knew him at all. She'd spent a few weeks in class with him in Italy. They'd hit it off. They made a good investigative team. That's it. "Did you get any new info on the Albertina heist?"

"Not much." Adrián shrugged. "How about you?"

"Let's get some drinks, and then I'll tell you." She thought of the marshal's warning. Just because Stevenson was a sleazeball didn't make Adrián one too.

"What can I get you?" Adrián asked.

"Not grappa, that's for sure."

He laughed.

"Jack-n-Coke." A safe choice… well, most of the time anyway.

"Coming right up." He slid the door open and left the private room.

She watched through the open door as he strode across the room to the bar. He did have a nice way of filling out a pair of jeans. *Dang.* Couldn't she just be friends with a cute guy?

Obviously, the answer was a hard no. *Hormones. It's just hormones.*

When Adrián returned with the drinks, she felt her face get hot. Good thing he couldn't read her mind. He sat a tall glass in front of her. "The bartender made it a double. On the house."

"Don't tell me… another pretty woman?"

"No." He grinned. "I've become a regular, so I get special treatment." He sat across from her in the booth and then lifted his glass. "To teamwork."

"Teamwork," she repeated, clinking her glass against his, which was no easy feat since he was drinking a martini out of what looked like a glass funnel. "What have you learned about the case?" She took a drink and grimaced. *Whoa. Strong. Jack with a splash of Coke.*

"You first," he said, sipping his martini. "What did you get out of Vanderbilt?"

"He was very sly." She got up and slid into his side of the booth, and then lowered her voice. "I think he knows something he's not telling. Either that or he's lying."

"Why do you say that?" He twirled the plastic toothpick that was impaling two green olives.

"He just wouldn't deny anything outright." She wondered if she should tell him about the lawyer. Maybe not… or at least not until they interviewed this Santo Romano. "Okay. Your turn. Whatcha got?"

He ran his hand through his hair. If they were playing poker, Jessica would say that was his tell. She didn't know him well, but she'd seen him do it enough times to know he did it when he was nervous. *Does he consider this a date? Or is it something else?* He had been hitting on her in Italy.

"We interviewed the owner of the company that installed the security system at the Albertina." He took a sip of his martini. "He was lying too."

"Is everyone a liar?" As Jack would say, it was a rhetorical question. *Of course, everyone lies. It's human nature.* Jack. She felt a twinge of guilt. She still hadn't returned his calls.

"I don't think his lie has anything to do with the robbery," he said. "But you never know."

"What was he lying about then?"

"He was having an affair with the former museum director's wife." Adrián slid an olive off the toothpick and popped it into his mouth.

She squinted at him. "Could that have something to do with the robbery?"

"I don't know." He finished his drink. "Want another?"

"Okay. But, this time ask your friend to put some Coke in it." She drained her glass and handed it to him.

"The waitress will take the empties." He sat it back down on the table and then motioned for her to let him out of the booth. "Don't go anywhere."

She stared at the last lonely olive in his glass, trying not to look at his butt. *Butt versus olive. Butt versus olive. Butt.*

She took a peek.

Adrián returned with two more drinks. She tasted hers. Thank goodness it had more Coke in it. She slid further into the booth to let Adrián sit down.

"Did you get to talk to any of Vanderbilt's staff?" Adrián asked. He pulled a lollipop out of the pocket of his jacket. "Want one?"

Absentmindedly, she took it. "No. Did you?"

He unwrapped a lollipop and gazed down at her with his dark eyes. The irises where just a shade lighter than the pupil. "Yeah. But she didn't know anything." He ran his hand through his hair again. "It was a total waste of time." He stuck the sucker in his mouth.

Chapter 13

The next morning, fighting a hangover, Jessica went into the office early. She wanted to get a head start on the case and review Edward "Eggs" Benedict's file. *Ack.* Just reading the name *Eggs Benedict* made her stomach flip. Adrián was a bad influence. At least, she hadn't blacked out like she did in Italy.

Sipping a double mocha Frappuccino, Jessica slid the chair up to the table and opened the laptop assigned to her. She tapped in the security codes and read about one of the greatest art thieves of all time.

Edward "Eggs" Benedict was sixty-three years old. He grew up in Sturbridge, Massachusetts where his dad was a policeman. *Wow. Talk about rebelling against your parents.*

Eggs robbed his first museum when he was eighteen and got caught. But two weeks later, he escaped from the Vermont jail and disappeared until last year when he robbed another Boston Museum in broad daylight. He was suspected of committing dozens of art thefts and three bank robberies. *Accomplished guy.* He often worked with some mysterious part-ner, who always dressed in black and hid his face... some guy called Cobra, who was supposedly meticulous in removing paintings from their frames. Eggs and Cobra's most famous heist involved three small Degas sketches that had never been recovered.

Jasmine and strawberries. Jessica could smell her before she entered the room. Was it perfume or just fruity dryer sheets? Sometimes, Jessica's super sense of smell was a menace. Like a canary in a coal mine, she could smell things no one else could. Heck. She could probably track an animal just with her sense of smell.

"You're here early," the marshal said, dropping her purse on a chair. In her tight navy blazer and matching skirt, she looked like Ava Gardner playing Margaret Thatcher.

"Where's the baby?"

"She's with Mrs. Faheem again. Stupid babysitter has gone AWOL." The marshal was breathless like she'd run up the stairs. Maybe she had. She was in tiptop shape, unlike Jessica.

Jessica's only exercise was walking to Starbucks to ask for more whipped cream on her Frappuccino.

"Ready to drive inland to interview Eggs?" the marshal asked.

He would have to be called Eggs. Her stomach roiled. "Sure thing, boss." She slapped the laptop shut and jumped up from her chair. Dizzy, she grabbed the edge of the table. *Arggh. No more quick movements today.*

"Are you okay?"

Jessica didn't dare tell her she'd been out with Adrián last night. She nodded. "Yeah. Fine." And she didn't want to tell her boss that she was hungover either. As far as she could tell, the only poison the marshal drank was Diet Mountain Dew.

After an exciting half hour of the marshal weaving in and out of traffic, blaring her siren, and flooring her Charger, they pulled into the parking lot at Norfolk Federal Prison. By some miracle, Jessica managed not to toss her cookies. Even on a good day, riding shotgun with the marshal was like riding a bucking bronco.

Aside from the twenty-foot wire fence around the perimeter, the federal prison's red-brick building could have passed for her undergraduate college dorm. Inside was a different story. Security cameras, metal gates, automatic locks, armed guards. It was intimidating, to say the least. Even Jessica's FBI badge didn't ward off a pat-down and a trip through the metal detector.

Too many locked doors to count, three hallways, and a corridor later, they arrived at a small visitor's room.

"Have at it," the guard said. "I'll be right outside if you need me."

"Is he dangerous?" Jessica asked. She'd never been in a prison before.

Well. That wasn't quite true. She'd visited Jack in prison a few times. She cringed thinking about the time he broke into the medical lab to free the animals at her behest and then served two years in prison for his trouble.

"Everyone in here is dangerous, Ma'am." The guard sniffed and patted his gun.

Including you. Jessica stayed close to the marshal as they entered the tiny windowless room.

"Visitors," the guard said to Eggs.

Eggs looked up from the book he was reading. Jessica tried to get a look at its spine. *The Wealth of Nations* by Adam Smith. Odd reading for an inmate. *I bet his interpretation of the invisible hand is a wee bit different than most free market economists'.*

Eggs Benedict looked younger than the mugshot in his file. He had kind eyes and a receding hairline. His fair complexion was freckled from the sun. He looked like a fun grandpa and not a criminal.

"Welcome, ladies," he said smiling. "Have a seat." He gestured across the table to a couple of chairs.

Should she sit down? Jessica waited for the marshal to make the first move. She didn't want to mess this up.

"We've come to ask you about the Albertina Carpenter

Museum heist," the marshal said. She tugged at the bottom of her blazer.

"A pretty big haul." Eggs laid his book on the table. "Impressive."

"It has your fingerprints all over it."

Is the marshal just trying to goad him? From what Jessica had seen, Eggs and his partner were meticulous, and the Albertina heist was a mess.

"Now, now, marshal." Eggs crossed his legs and leaned back in his chair. "As you well know, I was locked in this cell when it happened. Do you think I'm a magician?" He chuckled.

"I wouldn't put it past you," the marshal said. "It's the kind of brazen stunt you love."

"True." His face tightened in concentration, and he nodded. "True."

"Did you have something to do with the Albertina heist?" the marshal asked again.

"I wish I did." He slapped his knee. "I'd be a very wealthy man… and the greatest art thief of all time." He thought a minute. "Oh wait. I *am* the greatest art thief of all time."

"Looks like you have competition," Jessica said. Maybe she could use his arrogance to trap him. "Whoever pulled this off is the new world champion."

"You don't want someone else taking credit for your masterwork, do you?" The marshal got in on the goading.

"I see what you're doing," he said with a smirk. "I wish I could oblige you lovely ladies. But truly, I didn't do it."

"Do you know who did?" Jessica asked.

He shook his head.

"Who might do something like this?" the marshal asked, her finger hovering over her iPad. "You know everyone in the business. Come on Eggs throw us a bone."

"You want a bone?" His sly smile made Jessica's skin

crawl. His forehead creased, and he screwed up his face. "I might have an idea."

"Who?" The marshal tapped her iPad ready to take down the name.

"I hesitate to say." He sighed.

"Spit it out," the marshal said, dropping into the chair across from Eggs.

"You know, you remind me of my ex-wife." Eggs grinned. "I like that."

"Quit stalling and give us a name." The marshal used her official no-nonsense voice.

"When she got frustrated with me…" Eggs winked. "She'd blush all the way to her cleavage too."

"You're really getting on my nerves—"

"That's what she always said." Eggs interrupted. "Before she kicked me out of the house, and I escaped to our cabin in Wallis Cove. She eventually took that too—"

"What do you need, Mr. Benedict?" Jessica interrupted. "Cigarettes? Chocolate? We can get it for you if you help us out." She hoped she wasn't overstepping.

"Mr. Benedict is my dad. Call me Eggs."

"You're going to be scrambled eggs if you don't give us that name." The marshal could be scary when she put her mind to it.

"I tell you what I want…"

"Name it," Jessica said, her heart racing.

"Get me out of here, and I'll tell you who hit the Albertina."

"If you know, you're going to tell us now." The marshal pounded her fist on the table.

"Get me out, and *then* I'll tell you." He crossed his arms over his chest.

"How about you tell us, and then we'll get you out." The marshal stared him down.

"Like I said…" Eggs grinned. "You remind me of my ex,

and I wouldn't trust her as far as I could throw her." He chuckled. "Judging by the last time I tried, that's not very far."

"Are you a wife beater, Mr. Benedict?" Jessica felt like kicking the grin off his pasty face.

"You've got it backwards. My wife was the beater—"

"An egg-beater?" Jessica smirked.

"Good one." Eggs howled. "I like you too."

"Okay," the marshal said. "Here's what we'll do. We'll ask for a deal to shorten your sentence in exchange for the name of the person who committed the robbery."

"Can you get me protection too?" Eggs raised his eyebrows.

"What do you mean?" the marshal asked.

"If I give up Cobra, I'm a dead man." He slapped his palms on the table.

The guard opened the door and peeked inside. "Everything okay in here?"

"Fine," the marshal said.

"Cobra. Your partner?" Jessica asked.

"Former partner." Eggs got a faraway look in his eyes. "Those were the days."

"You sleep on it, and we'll come back tomorrow." The marshal snapped the case of her iPad shut. "And you'd better not be dicking us around." She glared at him.

Eggs smiled. "The last thing I'd want to do after months in this hellhole is dick you lovely ladies." He winked again. "I'm looking forward to you coming… back."

Jessica's stomach flipped. She couldn't wait to get away from Eggs and out of that prison.

—

"NOW WHERE, BOSS?" Jessica gripped the dashboard of the Charger as it lurched onto the freeway.

"Let's run through our leads." The marshal floored it and

cruised past a semi-truck. "I need to ask the chief about a deal for Scrambled Eggs."

"Do you think our perp could be Egg Benedict's former partner Cobra?"

"A mess like the one at the Albertina…" The marshal took a sip of warm Dew. "Doesn't fit his M.O.—Cobra was known for his meticulous robberies."

"I saw that in the file." Jessica bit a fingernail. "He had respect for the art, unlike our thief." It had to be organized crime. *Who else would make such a gawd-awful mess?* "What about Tick Tock?" Tick Tock Tommaso was the incarcerated crime boss looking for a big-time bargaining chip. What could be bigger than the art heist of the century?

"He should be easy to find since he's in jail." The marshal slammed on the brakes to avoid back-ending a Toyota. "We should talk to him. But we still need to find his henchmen… the ones who might have carried out the robbery. Both Eggs and Tick Tock are in prison. So, if either one of them did it, they had to have guys on the outside."

"Mafia guys." Jessica furrowed her brows. "I might know someone who can help us find them."

The marshal glanced over at her. "Hand me a pop."

Jessica reached around the seat and snagged the last can of warm Mountain Dew. She popped the top and passed it to the marshal. "My friend Lolita. She knows all the big-time mobsters."

"Your friend Lolita." The marshal sighed and shook her head. "Don't tell me. A sorority sister from school."

"Do I look like a sorority girl?" Jessica took pride in *not* looking like a sorority girl.

"You're blonde."

"Well, if it makes you feel any better, Lolita isn't."

"Okay. Tell me more about this Lolita." The Charger swerved to miss a piece of a tire shed by a truck.

Where to start? Lolita, her best friend. Lolita, the honors business student. Lolita, the Poker Tsarina hosting high-stakes games all over the country. Lolita, the undercover agent working with the Chicago police. Lolita, the head of the Russian mafia. Lolita, the bravest and most loyal person I know.

"Lolita Durchenko is heir to the Russian crime family dynasty known as Bratva."

"Durchenko?" The marshal thought a second. "Part of the Yudkovich clan?"

"Anton Yudkovich was her grandfather." *And the head of the international Russian syndicate out of Moscow.*

"Lordie. This gal's a friend of yours?"

"My best friend." Jessica put her hand over her heart. When she did, she felt the *Chupa Chups* Adrián gave her. It was in her shirt pocket.

"You sure know how to pick 'em."

Jessica pulled out the lollipop, unwrapped it, and popped it into her mouth.

The marshal's eyes got wide. "Where'd you get that?"

"What?"

"That sucker."

Crapulence. She was busted.

"I told you to keep it professional with Stevenson's team, including your buddy, Adrián Garcia… and now you're exchanging lollipops?"

Jessica fingered the fringe on her jacket. *What's the big deal about talking to Adrián… or Stevenson for that matter? Aren't we on the same team?* She wanted to ask *why not,* but instead she said, "I'm sorry."

"Well, what did you tell him?" The marshal's dark eyes flashed daggers in her direction.

"Nothing." Jessica felt her face get hot. "I swear." Her mind was racing. What had she told him? She couldn't remember. She really should watch the drinking.

"Did he tell you anything?"

"Yes." Jessica perked up. "He talked to Vanderbilt's maid. She didn't know anything. It was a total waste of time."

"Great." The marshal yanked the steering wheel. The Charger made a hard right turn.

"Where are we going?" Jessica grabbed the dashboard.

"To talk to that maid."

LEXI PARKED the Charger across from Vanderbilt's townhouse. "You stay in the car."

"Shouldn't I go with you?" The cowgirl's voice broke.

What a whiner. This intern was turning out to be more trouble than she was worth. Having her around was like having another kid to babysit. "No. Stay put until I get back."

Lexi slammed the car door, marched across the street, and rang the doorbell. She tugged at the bottom of her blazer, and then pressed the buzzer again.

A slender woman with brown skin answered the door. "Can I help you?" she said with an accent.

"Federal Marshal Lexington Colt." Lexi flashed her badge. "I'd like to ask you a few questions about your employer."

The woman's dark eyes filled with terror. "*Lo siento, pero, no hablo inglés.*"

"You just spoke English."

"*Lo siento,*" the woman repeated. "I'm sorry."

"Has your employer purchased any new paintings recently?"

"*Lo siento.*"

"Have you seen any of these?" Lexi pulled out of her pocket a printout with pictures of the stolen paintings.

The woman gazed down at it. Wringing her hands, she shook her head.

"Let me guess." Lexi sighed. "*Lo siento.*"

Red-faced, the woman shrugged.

Something about this woman didn't sit right. The maid was hiding something. Either that or Adrián was right. A total waste of time.

Lexi punched up Stevenson's number on speed dial. She hated working with the S.O.B., but she needed to know what he and Adrián had gotten out of the maid. *Dammit.* No answer.

Wait. Adrián speaks Spanish. Lexi folded the printout and jammed it back into her jacket pocket. *Someone is withholding information. Is it the maid or Adrián Garcia? That's the million-dollar question…*

Chapter 14

While Stevenson was holed up in his bedroom, Adrián rushed around the suite picking up trash and throwing it away. *What a pig.* How could anyone live like this? Grumbling, Adrián straightened a stack of file folders. I didn't sign up to be this *pendejo's* maid.

Stevenson emerged from his room. He tugged at the waist of his pants to pull them up over his muffin top. "You're back. What did you find out?" He plopped into a chair in the sitting area of the living room.

Adrián tied the trash bag shut and deposited it in the hallway. This routine was getting old. Stevenson made messes, and Adrián cleaned them up.

Adrián dashed back to the living room. "Here's what I've got." He slid a notepad out from under a pile of papers on the coffee table. He took his Montblanc pen from his jacket pocket and wrote the number *one* with a circle around it on the top of the pad. "Rocky Vanderbilt had one of the stolen paintings in his closet."

"Did the forensics report come back already?" Stevenson chewed on a granola bar.

"No." Adrián stared at the wrapper, which was crumped

up on the coffee table. *Why can't he pick up after himself? Ignore it. OCD. Maybe my mother is right.* He shook his head to clear his thoughts. "But I'm sure of it. Vanderbilt is our Dr. No."

"Don't get cocky." Stevenson smirked. "Until we have hard evidence, everything is on the table."

Everything's on the table, indeed. Stevenson's garbage. Adrián ignored him. He wrote the number *two* and circled it. "Vanderbilt's lawyer knows something." He put a question mark next to "Vanderbilt's lawyer." *What is his name? Who is this mystery lawyer? And what does he know?*

Adrián had heard Rocky Vanderbilt tell Jessica to talk to his lawyer about buying the Rembrandt. Was this lawyer fencing paintings for his rich client?

"And who is Vanderbilt's lawyer?" Stevenson went to the refrigerator and grabbed a Budweiser.

"I don't know, but I plan to find out." Adrián rifled through the file folders on the table. In the middle of a stack, he found it. Edward Benedict's FBI file. It was a good two inches thick. "I've scheduled an interview with Edward Benedict."

Stevenson spit out a mouthful of beer. "What? When? Why?"

"I got a tip." Adrián wrote the number three and circled it. "Edward Eggs Benedict is in prison—"

"Tell me something I don't know," Stevenson said, slamming the beer can down on the counter. "I put him there."

"Then you know about his penchant for bravado and art." Adrián put an exclamation point next to the art thief's name.

"That old coot couldn't orchestrate his way out of a paper bag, let alone plan a major art heist from his prison cell." Stevenson brought his beer and joined Adrián in the sitting room.

The hotel suite had gotten progressively more crowded with Stevenson's fast-food wrappers, tabloid magazines, and brochures from all the sightseeing he was doing. Like a living, breathing, organism, the junk in the living area kept expanding and contracting. Stevenson threw stuff down, and Adrián picked it up. *Let it go. Let it go.*

Adrián stared at the legal pad to avoid watching Stevenson guzzle beer. "Well, that's not what I heard." He put another exclamation point next to Eggs Benedict.

"Where'd you hear it? From him?" Stevenson moved a pile of folders off the coffee table with his foot and then reclined in his chair, feet up on the table. "The egotistical, old fool."

Adrián wanted to knock his feet off the table and tell him to pick up his stuff. He'd never known such a messy person in his life. The disorder was driving him mad. That's why he did most of his work at the bowling alley. Both places smelled of stale beer. But at least the bowling alley was tidy.

"Okay then." Adrián put his pen down and gave Stevenson the side-eye. "What have you got besides another date with the museum director?"

Stevenson jerked his feet off the table and sat upright. "I warned you. Don't get cocky."

"What have you learned from the lovely Ms. Finch?" Adrián gave him a fake smile.

"For your information, a friend of a friend of hers might know where the former museum director is hiding out." Stevenson's lips twisted into a smug grin.

"So now he's hiding out?" Adrián shook his head. "A friend of a friend…"

"Look, buddy. Quit bustin' my chops." Stevenson swigged the rest of his beer and then crushed the can between his hands. "Remember who's the boss here."

"*El burro sabe mas que tu.* A donkey knows more than you." Adrián said under his breath. *Why do I have to put up with this pendejo? Why can't I just work solo? Oh, right. Because that ass is the boss.* He heard his father's voice in his head, *ten minutes of patience, ten years of success.*

"What'd you say?" Stevenson stood up and puffed out his chest.

"Nothing." Adrián took a deep breath. If he wanted to succeed, get a permanent job with the FBI, and get out from under his father's thumb for good, he *had* to be patient. *Not one of my virtues.*

"Where is he?" Stevenson asked in a mocking voice to his hand. He turned his head and spoke to his other hand. "I thought you'd never ask." He turned back again. "I'm dying to know."

Stevenson's mocking tone made Adrián cringe. He already had one arsehole father. He didn't need another.

When Adrián went to Italy to pursue art crimes, it had made his father livid. Before he left for America, his father told him to get his *maltido* act together and come back to the family business or he'd disinherit him.

Yeah, right. Disinherit me from those stupid grocery stores. What do I care?

Stevenson stopped his silly charade, stepped right in front of Adrián's chair, and stood glaring down at him. "He's in the Bahamas."

"Jim Johnston is in the Bahamas?" Adrián picked up his pen, wrote the number *four*, circled it, and then scribbled "Jim Johnston, former museum director, Bahamas."

"You'll be happy to learn that I'm going after him while you stay here, collaborate with Miss Fussybutt Lexington Colt, and follow up the rest of our leads." Stevenson rubbed his hands together. "In fact, I'd better go pack. Eliza and I are leaving on the red-eye tonight."

"Eliza Finch?"

"I've got her on the hook." Stevenson made an obscene gesture with his fingers. "I'm not going to lose her now."

Disgusting. At least I'll be rid of him for a while. *Gracias a Dios.*

After Stevenson disappeared into his bedroom, Adrián

called an Uber to take him out to Norfolk prison. He was going to interview Edward Benedict. He couldn't bring himself to call the gangster "Eggs."

THE UBER DRIVER GOT LOST, and it took over an hour to reach the prison.

"Wait here," Adrián said. "I'll be back in twenty minutes."

"But—"

"Don't worry." Adrián hopped out of the back seat before the driver could object. "I'll pay you for waiting." The driver would either be there when he finished, or he wouldn't. If he wanted to get paid, he'd better be there.

The prison was surrounded by a ten-foot, concrete wall topped with barbed-wire. Through the window, he saw two armed guards standing in a guard station that looked like a treehouse perched on the corner of the wall. He shuddered.

Dios mío. It must be awful to be locked up in a place like this.

A guard patted him down and then led him through the maze that was the prison to a visiting room. Adrián avoided making eye-contact with anyone, especially the armed guards.

Edward Benedict was waiting in the tiny room, reading a book.

"I've been expecting you," Benedict said. "They told me you'd come." He glanced up from his book. "The other two were better looking."

Other two? He must mean Jessica and Marshal Colt. *Mierda. They beat me to it.* "I'm Adrián Garcia from the FBI. I'm here to ask you—"

"About the Albertina heist." Benedict interrupted him. "I know."

"What do you know?"

"Nothing you don't. I heard about it on TV." He went back to his book. "Virtue is more to be feared than vice," he read from the book. "Because its excesses are not subject to the regulation of conscience." He looked up. "What do you think of that?"

Adrián didn't even understand what it meant. It sounded like something Jessica would say. *Don't let him goad you.* "You don't know anything about the heist?"

"Nope." He went back to reading.

"Do you know who might have pulled a job like this?"

"Nope."

"If you had to put money on it, who would you bet did it?"

Benedict looked up. "How much money?"

"Your life's savings." Adrián held his gaze in a game of chicken to see who would look away first.

"My life's not worth much." Benedict chuckled.

"Your daughter Heather's life then." Adrián had memorized every detail in his file, especially the personal ones. According to the file, Mr. Benedict had one daughter with with a childhood sweetheart.

Benedict dropped his book on the table with a loud thud. "What does Heather have to do with this?"

"Hypothetically. If you had to say who pulled off the heist, and Heather's life was on the line, who would you bet on?"

"I don't bet." Benedict glared at him from across the table. "If you cross that line, your life will be worthless."

"Is that a threat?" Adrián's palms were sweating.

"Fight fire with fire." Benedict opened his book. "Interview over."

Adrián leaned forward. "What if I told you I could get you out of this place?" he whispered.

Benedict closed his book. "I'm listening."

"Tell me who pulled the Albertina heist, and you're a free

man." Adrián kept his voice deep and steady. He touched his St. Christopher's medal.

Benedict squinted at him. "Do you have the authority to get me out?"

Adrián pulled a folded paper from his pants pocket. *Ay.* The forensics report on the fibers. Wrong paper. He stuffed the report into his jacket and patted his pockets until he felt paper crinkle.

Smiling to himself, he pulled a second folded sheet from his pocket and passed it across the table. Amazing how easy it was to lift a logo and put it on letterhead.

Benedict eyed him suspiciously and picked up the letter. He read it and looked up in surprise. "The governor will give me a full pardon?"

Adrián ran his hand through his hair. He nodded and then held out his hand and wiggled his fingers.

"Cobra." Benedict put his head in his hands. "The governor better get me out of here now, or I'm a dead man."

"Who is Cobra?"

"I told you what you wanted to know. Now go do your job and leave me alone." Benedict laid back on the bed and put his arm over his eyes. "Guard," he yelled and then turned back to Adrián and whispered, "If you don't get me out of here in the next twenty-four hours, I'm dead."

Wow. This guy is so dramatic. Adrián smiled. He'd put on a pretty good act himself.

Adrián left the visiting room and made his way back through the maze to the entrance. *Gracias a Dios.* The Uber driver had waited.

On the drive back to Boston, Adrián called Jessica. *Come on. Answer.* The phone went to voicemail. *Mierda. Where is she?*

I must get to Cobra before she does. But who is Cobra? Does Jessica know?

He tried her again. This time, he left a message. He had to tempt her with some bit of information. But what? What could he tell her that wouldn't give her an advantage? Something harmless. Something she already knew.

"Hey Jessica. It's Adrián. I found something. Meet me at Lucky Strike at nine tonight so we can share intel."

Where is she? Maybe she'd already found Cobra… or Vanderbilt's lawyer.

Ay di mí. If I don't watch it, Jessica is going to solve this case before I do. Then she'll get the job, and I'll have to go back to Madrid and work for my father as a cashier at one of his stupid grocery stores.

Adrián rubbed his temples. To think, his father threatened to disinherit him from a chain of supermarkets. He shook his head. *Who cares what my old man thinks?*

He patted his pockets looking for an aspirin. He found two, popped them in his mouth, and swallowed.

Chapter 15

Lexi got up from her desk and went over to the table where the cowgirl was eating her lunch. "How can you eat that stuff?" Munching on the last of her fries, Lexi peered down at the unappetizing gray chunks mixed with brown granules and green pods.

The cowgirl was shoving the stuff into her mouth like it was grandma's homemade apple pie. "One woman's poison…" She reached up and flicked a piece of French fry off Lexi's lapel.

"Are you ready?" Lexi asked. "Or are you going to eat some Styrofoam for dessert?"

The cowgirl knocked back the last of her carrot juice. "Yup. Ready."

"You've got an orange mustache." Lexi handed her a napkin.

"Thanks." She scrubbed her upper lip. "Better?"

Lexi nodded, crumbled the Wendy's bag, and tossed it into the trash can.

"Good shot," the cowgirl said, nibbling on some revolting trifecta of quinoa, tempeh, and edamame from some health food store in Brookline. She'd insisted they stop there on the way back from Norfolk.

"Let's pay Tick Tock a little visit." Lexi slung her purse over her shoulder. "And ask him if that stolen art is his get out of jail free card.""

"Does he know we're coming?"

"The warden knows. I don't know if they told Tick Tock." Lexi rummaged through her purse. "Hopefully not." She withdrew her car keys and held them up. "The element of surprise."

An hour later—just past the Moose Sanctuary and Cedar Swamp—they arrived at Massachusetts Correctional Institute Maximum Security Prison, a short, squat and blaringly white building in the middle of nowhere.

Inside, all the furniture was bolted to the concrete floor. The rows of cells stacked on top of each other three stories high looked like a dog pound. The place smelled of bleach, obviously used to camouflage the scent of urine.

Lexi watched on CCTV from a glass cage atop a panopticon as a guard clamped Tick Tock into leg irons and handcuffs, and then led him out of his cell and up the corridor. She had asked the guard to give her a visual on the creep before she questioned him. It always helped to size-up your opponent in advance.

The guard led them back through the bleach-soaked prison to a small windowless visiting room. Tick Tock sat on one side of a table, and they sat on the other.

Angelo Tick Tock Tommaso's silver hair fell to the collar of his orange jumpsuit. He made the chair he was sitting on look like it belonged in a dollhouse. Even through the prison-issue one-piece number, you could tell he'd been working out. Probably not much else to do in the joint. His face was lean and tanned. For an old geezer, he wasn't bad looking.

"Hey, Angelo," Lexi said.

"Marshal Colt. Lost any witnesses lately?" He grinned.

She cringed. Tick Tock's son-in-law, Jimmy Giordano, had been in Wit-Sec in West Yellowstone under her protection. He was the first witness she lost. Unfortunately, he wasn't the last, which was why she was now working in the "shoplifting" division of the FBI. "Guess that was your lucky break."

"Not so lucky," he said. "I'm still in this joint." Jimmy was going to testify against Tick Tock. Luckily, Jimmy's assassination persuaded Tick Tock's daughter to turn on him.

"Yeah. That's why we're here." Lexi cleared her throat.

"Who's she?" Tick Tock lifted his cuffed hands in the general direction of the cowgirl, who was as quiet as a possum playing dead. "Your daughter?"

"No." Lexi scowled at him. *What the—do I look old enough to be her mother?* "This is my intern, Jessica." *Come on, Lex. Don't let the crook get to you.*

"Nice to meet you," the cowgirl said, making a complete ass of herself. *Who says that to a gangster inmate at the federal pen?*

"This isn't a social call," Lexi said, scooting her chair closer to the table. "Did you hire your thugs to hit the Albertina Carpenter Museum and steal a couple of pricey paintings so they could make a deal to get you out?" Despite her racing heart, Lexi stared down the kingpin. "Well?"

"You overestimate my power." Tick Tock laughed. "From in here, I can't even get a pack of smokes, let alone pull off an art heist like that one." He looked at Jessica. "Darlin', do you have a cigarette for a harmless old man?"

Lexi let out a guffaw. *Harmless old man, my patootie.*

"We can get you a pack of cigarettes in exchange for information." Jessica played with the fringe of her jacket... *a bad habit, one of many.*

Tick Tock furrowed his bushy brows. "First you think I stole millions of dollars' worth of art to get out of this joint. And now you think you can just offer me a measly pack of cigarettes." He shook his head. "Typical government men...

Excuse me, I mean government broads." He stretched the word broads.

Jerk. Lexi exhaled. "Look. If you do know something about the Albertina heist, *and* we recover the loot, we *might* be able to shorten your sentence."

"You want to get out of here, don't you?" the cowgirl said, stating the obvious.

"I'm not going to say anything else without my lawyer present." Tick Tock folded his arms over his chest and sat back in his chair.

"Give us something in good faith, and we'll talk to the DA about shortening your sentence." Lexi held her breath. It was his right to demand his lawyer. In fact, if they were going to make a deal, he was just being prudent.

"Call my lawyer."

"Who is your lawyer?" Jessica asked. "We will call him… or her."

"Santo Romano." Tick Tock leaned into the table. "Tell him I want to see him. Tell him to get down here on the double."

"Santo Romano," Lexi repeated. *Good Lord.*

"That name is familiar." Jessica turned to her with a question on her face.

"That's right. Best lawyer on the East Coast." Tick Tock smiled. "If anyone can make a deal, it's Santo."

"Santo Romano is Rocky Vanderbilt's lawyer," Lexi whispered into Jessica's ear. "He might know the whereabouts of the stolen paintings."

"How about an appetizer?" Jessica asked. "Just a tidbit to show us you're serious."

"You've got quite an appetite for a little girl." The gangster puckered his lips.

"Did your men rob the Albertina?" Jessica asked. "And if not, who did?"

"How about Edward Benedict and his partner? They're

the art thieves, not me." Tick Tock threw up his hands. "I'm just a lowly racketeer."

A lowly racketeer, my behind. Try the biggest crime boss in Boston. "Benedict is in prison." The marshal leaned across the table. "Did your men rob the Albertina to cut a deal to get you out?"

"Lawyer." Tick Tock folded his arms across his chest.

"I think we'll pay Mr. Santo Romano a visit." Lexi got up, went to the door, and knocked. The guard opened it. "We're done here."

"Lawyer," Tick Tock repeated.

"Come on, Tommaso," the guard said. "Let's get you back to your cell before the other inmates think you're getting special treatment and decide to beat the crap out of you."

Tick Tock hooted with laughter. "Those ladies wouldn't dare." As the guard escorted him out of the room, he turned back and smiled. "Nice chatting with you, ladies. Get me Romano, and then maybe we can dance."

Once Tick Tock was out of the room, the cowgirl let out an audible exhale. "Wow, that guy's a piece of work."

"Tell me about it." Lexi shook her head. "That whole family is bad news." She stood up and brushed invisible crumbs off her skirt.

"Next stop, Santo Romano?" the cowgirl asked.

"Damn straight."

<hr>

"SHOULDN'T we pick up baby Sammy?" Jessica white-knuckled the handle on the passenger door of the Charger as the marshal skidded around a corner.

The marshal gave her the side-eye. "You're missing *my* baby?"

Jessica loosened her grip. "We're going to pay Santo Romano a visit."

"Right…" The marshal's Tennessee drawl was coming out.

"And he's Rockefeller Vanderbilt's lawyer." Jessica wiped her sweaty palms on her jeans. Riding with the marshal was hair-raising.

"Yes?" The marshal furrowed her brows.

"When we interviewed Vanderbilt, we had Sammy along, and I was an art dealer, and you were my client."

"Hand me a pop," Lexi said, wiggling her fingers in Jessica's direction.

Jessica felt around in the back seat, then cranked her head around. "You're out. No more pop."

Lexi's lip quivered.

Geez. She's totally addicted to that fluorescent-green swill.

"I'd better stop and get some gas."

"Fess up. You mean some Diet Mountain Dew."

"Whatever." The marshal swerved into the nearest gas station. "You pump. I'll be right back."

Jessica got out and went around to the gas pump. *Where is the gas cap on this beast?* As soon as the pump clicked to life, she pumped the gas.

Yup. I knew it.

The marshal came back with two six packs of Diet Mountain Dew.

"That stuff will kill you," Jessica said.

"Gotta die of something." The marshal put the sodas—save one—in the backseat and hopped back into the driver's seat. "Ready to go talk to the most popular lawyer in town?"

Jessica had barely shut the passenger door when the marshal squealed out of the gas station. *Crapulence.* She grabbed the seat cushion and sunk her stubby fingernails into it. *No wonder the marshal drives like a maniac. She's always totally jacked up on Dew.* "As I was saying." She swayed back and forth with the movement of the car. "Vanderbilt may have told his lawyer to expect an art dealer and a rich beatch with a baby."

"Who you calling rich?" The marshal laughed.

So, she does have a sense of humor after all. Good thing, or Jessica would be out on her ear.

"Sammy does seem to disarm even the jerkiest jerk." The marshal squinted. "But my daughter is not a prop in our criminal investigation."

"Of course not." Jessica paused for effect. "She's part of the team!"

"I don't know." One hand on the wheel, the marshal sipped her soda.

"You want to beat Stevenson, don't you?" Jessica raised her eyebrows.

The marshal made a quick right onto a side-street.

"Where are we going?" Jessica asked.

"To get the baby." The marshal guzzled the rest of her Dew. "I have to let Camo out anyway."

"Camo?"

"My dog."

Wow. Jessica didn't figure the marshal was the type to have a baby, let alone a dog.

Twenty minutes later, the Charger pulled up in front of a three-story brownstone in Roxbury.

"You want to get out while I find a parking spot?" the marshal asked. "It might take a while."

"I'll ride along." *What was she going to do? Just stand out on the curb?* Jessica didn't want to risk the marshal taking off and leaving her standing there.

After circling around the apartment building like a vulture for a half-hour, the marshal lucked into a spot four blocks away.

"Nice neighborhood." Jessica enjoyed urban walking. People-watching and window-shopping in a big city were two of her favorite pastimes.

"If you say so." The marshal picked up her pace.

Gawking at various ethnic restaurants and boutiques,

Jessica could hardly keep up. They passed a group of women speaking an Asian language, Vietnamese maybe. Others they passed spoke some sort of Creole.

"A Taste of Haiti." Jessica pointed at a divey café. "Have you eaten there?"

"No."

"Want to try it?" Jessica stopped in front of the café.

"No." The marshal kept walking.

"Why not?" Jessica took off after her.

"One woman's poison…" The marshal turned the corner and marched up the sidewalk to her apartment building.

Jessica struggled to keep up.

Inside, the three-floor walk-up was clean but like a boxer who'd seen better days, it showed the scars of past defeats. As they climbed the stairs, Jessica's cowboy boots clacked on the wooden steps. She walked the rest of the way on her tiptoes. When they reached the third floor, the bitter smell of garlic and stewed tomatoes intensified.

The marshal knocked on the door of apartment 3B.

A middle-aged woman with amber eyes and straight, black hair pulled into a bun answered the door. Like the building, it was obvious she'd once been a stunning beauty, who was now showing the scars of her past.

"Miss Lexi," she said with a warm smile. "Samantha is sleeping." She opened the door wide, and the scent of spices as warm as her smile wafted into the hallway. Cinnamon. Cardamom.

Jessica's mouth watered.

"Won't you and your friend come in while I go get the baby?" The woman left the door open but disappeared into the back of the apartment.

"What is she cooking?" Jessica asked. "It smells delicious." She peeked into the apartment, which was decorated with colorful fabrics and oversized pillows. Jessica could imagine herself tucked into the cozy space enjoying a nice, curried dal.

"Mrs. Faheem's apartment always smells like this," the marshal said with a shrug. "I guess she likes to cook."

Mrs. Faheem delivered the baby, who was no longer asleep. "There, there little button," she said. "Go to your mama." She passed the squirming baby to the marshal, who held the baby tight to her chest as if she was afraid of dropping a priceless package.

Jessica followed the marshal across the hall.

"Can you hold her a minute?" The marshal handed her baby Sammy while she fished her keys out of her purse. She unlocked the apartment door. "Come on in."

The marshal's apartment was the opposite of Mrs. Faheem's. Whereas Mrs. Faheem's place was warm and inviting, the marshal's place was cold and sterile. The place barely looked lived-in. She hadn't even unpacked her moving boxes.

"You must be Camo." Jessica knelt to cuddle the golden retriever. "Who's a good boy?" She scratched his ears. "Yes. I've heard so much about you."

Camo wagged his tail and licked her face.

"What are you, the dog whisperer?" asked Lexi.

"I'm an animal person. I grew up on a ranch." Jessica gave Camo a headbutt. "Can I give him a dog bone?"

"You carry dog bones with you?"

"Don't you have any?" Jessica asked.

"No." The marshal had Sammy on one hip and the diaper bag on the other. "Can you take the dog out for me?"

"Sure." Jessica found Camo's leash hanging on the hook by the door. She fastened it to his collar. "Camo, wanna go out?"

Camo wagged his tail and turned his lips up into what she swore was a smile.

"Good boy." Jessica smiled down at him. "Come on, buddy."

Outside, the spring breeze was fresh and cool. The spindly

trees growing out of the sidewalk had sprouted buds and were attracting bees.

Camo waited and let Jessica take the lead. *Wow. What a good dog.* She clicked her tongue and off they went.

She took him to a park the size of a saddle horn. Not even a quarter of a square block, it was so small it would have been laughed out of Montana. Camo sniffed around a hedge and left his calling card. Then they ventured onto the grass so he could do his business. She turned her head and watched the cars go by to give him some privacy.

Wait. Is that Adrián? She strained to see the car parked at the stoplight. The guy in the backseat sure looked like Adrián. *What's he doing here?* The car sped through the intersection.

Her phone buzzed, and she pulled it out of her pocket. Speak of the devil.

———————————————

Chapter 16

———————————————

Gracias a Dios. Finally. She answered.

"Hey Jessica. What are you doing?" Adrián asked, knowing full well what she was doing. She was walking a dog in that park across from the marshal's apartment in Roxbury. He'd tracked her down.

"Weird. I just saw a guy that looked just like you, and now you're calling me." She sounded surprised.

"I've been calling you for the last hour." He tried not to let the desperation seep into his voice.

"Why? What's up?"

He heard barking.

"I have some new intel." He shifted the phone from one ear to the other.

"Really? What?"

"Meet me at Lucky Strike at nine tonight, and I'll tell you." He held his breath.

"Okay. If we're done by then."

The Uber circled back around the block and past the park again. Adrián watched as the irrepressible Jessica James threw a stick for the dog.

"Why? What are you doing?" *Are they working on the case night and day?* His stomach grumbled and he glanced at his Rolex. He'd missed lunch.

"I'll tell you tonight." The dog was panting in the background. *Did she have her phone on speaker?* "I've got to go." She hung up.

Adrián hated to think of the Uber fare. Norfolk. Then Roxbury. Now back to his hotel in West Fens… during rush hour. Wait until Stevenson sees the bill. Good thing he's off in the Bahamas with Ms. Finch.

Adrián shook his head. *Really? A vacation with a suspect? Completely unprofessional.*

He stared out the window at the bumper-to-bumper cars in the next lane. Since he was stuck in traffic, he might as well make the best of it. He tapped his phone awake and made some notes.

His money was still on the security guard, Frank Lambchop Motton, who was probably working for Rockefeller Vanderbilt. With a man inside, and his resources, it wouldn't be hard for Vanderbilt to pull off the Albertina heist, especially given their lax security.

Evidence. I need evidence. How could he prove his theory? More importantly, how could he recover the stolen paintings? If he could solve the case and retrieve the art, then he'd be assured a plum job as an art detective… and not just any art detective, an *FBI* agent. *That will show my father.*

"You know what?" he said to the driver. "Let's go to Louisburg Square instead."

"You want me to change direction?" The driver cranked his head around to look at Adrián. "In this traffic?"

"Don't worry. You'll get paid." Adrián really should have learned how to drive a car. But his father had a chauffeur, and growing up in the city, he hadn't needed to drive a car. His scooter had always been enough. *How in Hades am I going to stakeout Vanderbilt's townhouse in an Uber?*

Forty minutes later, Adrián was staking out Vanderbilt's

townhouse, slouched down in the backseat of the Uber, sucking on a *Chupa Chups*. He still had a couple of hours to kill before it was time to meet Jessica at the Lucky Strike.

He watched Vanderbilt's door. Maybe he would get lucky, and Muttonhead or Vanderbilt would screw up, and he'd catch them in the act of transferring the paintings.

His stomach growled again. He'd missed lunch, and now he was going to miss dinner too. *Gracias a Dios* for *Chupa Chups*.

A black limo pulled up across the street. The door to the townhouse opened. Adrián scooted closer to the window and peered out. Vanderbilt exited the building and got into a limo.

"Follow that limo." Adrián rewrapped the half-eaten sucker and stuck it back in his pocket. "Don't lose them."

"Dude," the driver said. "Do you think this is the movies?"

"I'll give you a big tip." He reached in his wallet, pulled out a twenty-dollar bill, and waved it at the driver.

"I don't know." The driver cranked his head around again. "But this is weird."

"FBI." Adrián pulled his identification badge from his pocket. "I'm commandeering this vehicle."

"Like heck you are."

Adrián pulled a hundred-dollar bill from his wallet and flashed it at the driver. "Will this do?"

"Plus, another tip for the trip to the prison too."

"Okay. Okay." Adrián watched the limo disappear onto the horizon. "Just catch up to them. Hurry."

The driver threw the car into gear, pulled out into the street, and stomped on the accelerator.

"Faster."

They followed the limo through the streets of Boston to the waterfront. Adrián was on the edge of the seat, grasping the headrest of the passenger seat in front of him. "Don't let him see you."

"Faster. Slower. Make up your mind."

"There." Adrián pointed. "They stopped." *Finally*. His heart was racing faster than the Uber. "Stop the car."

The Uber driver slammed on the brakes, and Adrián's head whiplashed into the back of the seat in front of him. "*Ojo!* Watch it." He rubbed his forehead. "I haven't paid you yet."

The limo driver got out and went around to the backseat and opened the door for Vanderbilt. The wealthy art collector got out and strode up the street.

Adrián gave the tycoon a healthy head start, and then took off after him. "Wait for me," he said on his way out of the Uber.

"You haven't paid me yet," the driver said. "I'm not going anywhere."

Ducking under awnings and into alleyways, Adrián trailed the tycoon to a swanky rehabbed warehouse. It had been converted into a multiuse building with cafés and boutiques on the first floor and offices on the upper floors.

Vanderbilt entered the building, and, holding his breath, Adrián trailed after him. The tycoon looked both directions before entering an office suite on the third floor. He disappeared inside.

Careful not to be seen, Adrián tiptoed to the door. *Santo Romano, Attorney at Law* was etched into the glass on the door.

Gotcha. Vanderbilt's lawyer. It had to be. Talk about lucky strikes. Adrián glanced at his watch. Seven o'clock already. He had one hour to get back across town to the Lucky Strike. He texted Jessica and told her he was stuck in traffic.

After loitering in the hallway for another fifteen minutes, Adrián knocked on the door. No answer. He knocked again. Nothing.

He tried the doorknob. The door was unlocked. He opened the door and peeked inside. No one. The office was empty. Where had they gone? There had to be a back door.

Sí. There was another door at the back of the room. A second exit. Adrián rushed across the room.

"Can I help you?" a deep voice said from the doorway.

Meirda. A husky security guard glared at him.

"*Lo siento,*" he said. "I'm lost."

The guard scowled at him. "I'll show you out." He had his hand on his sidearm.

"*Gracias.*" Adrián followed the guard. He wasn't about to argue with a big dude with a gun.

After they stepped out into the corridor, the guard pulled a giant keyring from his belt and locked the door behind him.

Tomorrow, I'll come back for Santo Romano.

The Uber driver was leaning against the car, smoking a cigarette. When he saw Adrián, he dropped it and crushed it under his shoe. "About freaking time."

Adrián had the Uber driver drop him off at the Lucky Strike bar. He cringed as he handed him two hundred dollars as a tip. *Ay.* He could have put a down payment on a scooter with just one day's Uber fare. Stevenson was going to explode when he saw the bill.

Every time Adrián entered the Lucky Strike, he thought of that scene in *The Big Lebowski* when Jesus licked the bowling ball. He smiled. *What a great movie.* The sound of bowling balls striking pins cheered him up. Until the Lucky Strike, he'd never set foot in a bowling alley. Now, he never wanted to leave. The sounds, the lights, the shoes… he loved it.

He only saw the back of her head, but he knew it was her. The irreplicable Jessica James was waiting in a booth across from the bowling alley. Her long, wavy hair reflected the ambient light. As he approached, her slim silhouette came into view. The fringe on the sleeve of her leather jacket swayed as she took a sip of her drink.

She looked too young to be drinking whiskey. He liked that about her.

"You came." He bent down and kissed her cheek.

"You thought I'd stand you up?" She scooted over and made room for him.

He slid in next to her. "I'm just glad you didn't."

"So, what's this big intel you've got?" Her eyes sparkled in the glow from the fake electric candle in the middle of the table.

"I just came from Vanderbilt's lawyer's office." He waved the waitress over and ordered a draft IPA beer.

"You found Santo Romano?" Her mouth dropped open. "At his office in —?"

"*Sí.* In that converted warehouse on Pearl Street." Maybe his tone was a little too triumphant. But it wasn't like he was telling her anything she didn't already know.

"Pearl Street… downtown?"

Is she playing dumb? She'd found out about the lawyer two days ago. Surely, she and the marshal had interviewed him by now. Santo Romano was the key to the case. "Haven't you been there already?"

"No. We went to his house, but he wasn't there." She took a drink. "And his office didn't show up in any of our searches."

"Really?" *Vaya.* He'd given her important intel, after all. "You haven't been to his office?"

"Where is it exactly?" She tapped her phone. "I want to write it down."

Mierda. Now he'd have to tell her. *What the hell. It will make the game more exciting.* He rattled off the address. *No big deal. She hasn't even interviewed him yet. I'll just have to get to him first.*

He would have asked her for the lawyer's home address, but he didn't want to admit he didn't have it.

"What did Santo Romano have to say for himself?"

He also didn't want to admit he hadn't even seen the guy, let alone talked to him. "Not much. Denied everything."

"Come on," she said. "It can't be a coincidence that

Romano is the lawyer for both Rocky Vanderbilt and Angelo Tommaso."

"Who the hell is Angelo Tommaso?" he blurted out.

The waitress delivered his beer. He grabbed it and took a drink.

"I told you about him. The big-time crime boss Tick Tock Tommaso. He's locked up in federal prison for racketeering."

"Ay, Tick Tock Tommaso." *How could I forget that? I'm an idiot.* "Right. I knew that."

"Well, what did Romano say about Tick Tock?" She twirled the twizzle stick in her cocktail.

"Nothing. He claimed client confidentiality and wouldn't say anything." Adrián sipped the IPA. Jessica was always so trusting and nice. He hated to lie to her. Then again, Romano would probably claim client confidentiality. *What is the chance of getting anything out of a slick lawyer like him?* Then again, the ingenuous Jessica James had her devious ways.

"Maybe we will have better luck." She drained her drink.

"What makes you think so?" he asked.

"We have a secret weapon." Jessica smiled.

"What do you mean?"

"Baby Sammy." She winked at him.

"*Si, claro.*" He pulled a *Chupa Chups* from his pocket. "I'll show you my secret weapon."

"Are you like James Bond?" She laughed. "Is your lollipop going to explode?"

"You'd better watch it." He aimed the *Chupa Chups* at her. "Or I'll use it on you."

▭

THE NEXT MORNING, Adrián got up early and paced around the hotel suite waiting for the dealership to open. It was ridiculous trying to stake out and tail suspects in an Uber.

One more Uber and that's it. The Uber to the dealership.

Adrián was waiting at the entrance when the salesman showed up to open the showroom. A shiny red 946 Vespa called out to him from a platform in the center of the show-room. It was just like the scooter he'd rented in Italy.

"I'll take that one." He pointed at the beauty from across the room.

"Don't you want to test-drive it?" the salesman asked.

"No." Adrián handed the salesman his credit card. "But can you hurry and get it ready? I want it now."

"Yes, sir."

Adrián paced the showroom waiting for the salesman to finish all the *maltido* paperwork. "*Deprisa*," he repeated under his breath. *Quickly*.

He glanced at his Rolex. It was nearly eleven. Jessica and Marshal Colt were probably interviewing Santo Romano by now. He pounded his fist into his palm. "Can you hurry?" he yelled at the salesman, who was still tapping away at the computer.

"Only a few more minutes and you'll be good to go." The salesman flashed a practiced smile.

Adrián ran his hand through his hair. *Come on, man. Hurry up.*

Finally. Thirty minutes later, the salesman handed him the key to his new Vespa. *Yes*. He couldn't wait to hop on it and zip through Boston. Nothing quite like riding a scooter through metropolitan traffic.

"This matching helmet is our gift to you," the salesman said, smiling his insipid smile.

Adrián grabbed the helmet. "Thanks."

"I'll take you to your new ride."

The salesman led him across the lot to a new red Vespa 946. "This gorgeous lady only has twenty-four miles on it."

"Great." Adrián threw his leg over the saddle and turned the key. The Vespa purred like a kitten. His heart soared. He was in love. He kicked up the stand, revved the engine, and took off. In his rearview mirror, he saw the salesman standing there gaping.

He hadn't been this happy since his first day at riding school when he was eight. His father insisted he learn to ride and hunt. He could care less about hunting. But riding horses had been his childhood passion.

This little Vespa was the Andalusian of scooters. While cars and buses sat idling in the lunchtime rush hour, he weaved in and out of traffic and back and forth in between lanes, flying across town.

He parked the Vespa across from the rehabbed warehouse on Pearl Street. His heart was pounding as he climbed the stairs to the third floor. He could have taken the elevator. But as his hundred-and two-year-old grandfather always said when asked how he'd lived so long, "Read poetry every day, and always take the stairs."

Adrián did not have an aptitude for poetry, but at least he could climb stairs.

He stood in front of the etched glass door listening to voices coming from inside. He couldn't make out what they were saying. Gingerly, he turned the doorknob. It was unlocked. *Why shouldn't it be? It's an attorney's office.*

"Can I help you?" a bespeckled woman asked from behind a desk. "Do you have an appointment?"

"No, ma'am." Adrián crossed the room. "I'm with the FBI, and I'm hoping to talk with Mr. Romano."

"I'm sorry," the woman said, pushing her glasses further up her nose. "Mr. Romano is booked solid all day."

"It's imperative I speak with him." Adrián towered over the desk.

"Would you like to make an appointment?" She looked over the top of her glasses at her computer screen.

"Just a few minutes of his time." Adrián picked up a stapler off the desk. "That's all I need."

The woman scowled, reached across the desk, and

grabbed the stapler out of his hands. "I'm sorry, but you'll have to make an appointment."

Laughter was coming from the other room. Women's laughter. A baby let out a yowl.

Ay. Mierda. They beat me to it.

Chapter 17

Jessica had pulled her hair back into a tight ponytail and worn one of her great-grandmother's vintage dresses—the black one, the only one Jessica hadn't torn while climbing over a fence or falling down an embankment. How in the world had her great-grandmother kept them in such perfect condition? And how had Jessica ruined them so fast?

Now she just had to psyche herself into the part of a fancy art dealer. She took a deep breath and forced a warm smile.

Santo Romano's office was heavy, dark, and dripping with masculinity. It stank of stale cigars and ill-gotten gains.

So, this is what a big-time mafia lawyer looks like. Santo Romano was well-dressed in an expensive tailored suit; and he was wearing a blocky, gold ring on a pinky finger and a thick wedding band on a ring finger. His hair was so short and perfectly shaped, she guessed he visited the barber every week.

"I hope you're not here to tell me the brat is mine." Santo Romano winked, and his lips turned up into a snide smile.

Jessica forced a laugh. "We're here to discuss art, not paternity."

"That's a relief." Romano pretended to wipe his brow.

"My client is looking for a Rembrandt as a gift for her

husband." Jessica gestured toward the marshal, who was bouncing the baby up and down, trying to quiet her. "He's a collector. You may have heard of him? Philip Roth."

Romano squinted at her and then glanced over at the marshal. "Why do you think I can help you?"

"Mr. Rockefeller Vanderbilt sent us your way." Jessica adjusted the blazer she'd borrowed from the marshal. It was too big in all the wrong places.

"Rocky sent you?" Romano opened his palms wide. "Why didn't you say so?"

"Can you help us procure a Rembrandt?" Jessica asked. "Preferably something rare and special."

"Aren't all Rembrandts rare and special?" Romano asked.

"Something unique," Jessica said. She couldn't come right out and say they were looking for the only Rembrandt seascape, the one stolen from the Albertina.

"Do I look like an art dealer?" Romano looked up at her from his desk. He hadn't invited them to sit down.

"Mr. Vanderbilt—"

"He's a client and a friend."

"He said you might know where we could find a Rembrandt." Jessica shifted from one foot to the other. "Something that just came on the market."

Romano continued to play this evasive game for the next fifteen minutes.

"Can you help us or not?" the marshal asked, impatiently. "The baby needs her nap."

"That depends," Romano said.

"On what?" the marshal asked.

"How much you can pay."

"That depends," Jessica said.

"On what?" Romano asked.

"On the painting. What can you get?"

"Well, I don't know much about art." He fiddled with the trunk of the elephant-shaped paperweight.

Here we go again. This guy was as slippery as a brown trout in Hell Roaring Creek. Jessica blew at her bangs. Her feet were killing her. The marshal had dressed her up to look like a businesswoman, navy blazer, matching skirt, and low-heeled pumps that pinched her toes. *If this is dressing for success, then I'm destined for failure.*

"I can't tell my Monet from my Manet." Romano chuckled.

Why can't he give us a straight answer? "We don't want to take up any more of your time," Jessica said. "But if you come across a Rembrandt for sale, please let me know." She pulled a pen out of her pocket. "Can I give you my number?"

He slid a pad of sticky notes across the desk. "Sure."

"I assure you." Jessica wrote her cell phone number on the tiny pad. "My client is very interested in any Rembrandts that might be for sale."

"Rembrandts," he repeated. "You know, I think I heard something the other day..." He launched into a long story about a friend of a friend's nephew.

Baby Sammy was fussing again. The marshal unclipped the pacifier from her lapel and stuck it in the baby's tiny mouth. Sammy twisted her head back and forth and batted the pacifier away. It flew a couple feet before landing on the floor. Sammy started bawling at the top of her lungs.

"Take her," the marshal said, handing the baby over to Jessica.

Jessica held the dense little bundle tight to her chest and softly sang *Home on the Range.* When she got to the antelope playing, Sammy's kicking and flailing stopped. The more she sang, the more the baby relaxed.

The marshal, on the other hand, was far from relaxed. "Look Romano. Let's cut the crap." She opened the diaper bag and pulled out her badge. "FBI. We have reason to believe your client knows the whereabouts of the Rembrandt stolen from the Albertina Carpenter Museum." She snapped her badge in its case and stuffed it back into the diaper bag. "Tell us what you know about it."

"Cobra is my client." Romano stood up. "And I never breach a client's confidence." He came around the desk, stomped across the office, opened the door, and made a sweeping gesture. "Good day ladies."

"Does Cobra have the stolen painting or know its whereabouts?" the marshal asked.

Jessica bounced the baby as she watched. *I thought she said the Albertina heist wasn't Cobra's M.O. That's why she hadn't put him on the list of suspects. Either the marshal is keeping things from me, or she's as cool as a mountain stream.*

"I'm not answering any more of your questions." Romano gestured for them to leave. "You've wasted enough of my time with your little charade. Did you rent that brat?"

The marshal looked like she might spit in his face. Instead, she grabbed Sammy out of Jessica's arms and stormed through the office door. Jessica followed on her heels.

"Don't come back." He slammed the door after them.

"See you in court, asshole," the marshal shouted, as she turned and flipped the bird at the closed door.

"That was illuminating," Jessica said.

"Yes, very." The marshal shifted Sammy to her other hip.

"Where is this Cobra?"

"Cobra. Also known as Snake-Eyes. Eggs Benedict's sometimes partner. Elusive as the Tennessee Saw-whet owl." The marshal pressed the fob to unlock her car. "Who knows where he is now. He dropped off the radar twenty years ago."

"Why would he come out of retirement?" Maybe he had a thing for Rembrandts and Bouguereaus.

"Your guess is as good as mine." The marshal revved the engine. "Buckle up."

"For all the good it will do, the way you drive." Jessica fastened her seatbelt and grabbed the handhold for good measure.

On the way back to the office, the marshal insisted they stop at McDonald's for lunch. Jessica countered with Whole Foods. They split the difference, and settled on Taco Bell, which to Jessica's mind wasn't much of a compromise. But at least she could get a bean burrito.

By the time they reached FBI headquarters, they'd downed two burritos and one giant soda each. Jessica belched as loud as a sailor after shore leave. The marshal gave her the side-eye, and they both laughed.

As soon as they got upstairs to the office, they both hit their computers. The marshal held baby Sammy on her lap and typed with one hand. Jessica sat across the room at the table, tapping away on the laptop.

Her mind was whirling with questions.

Where was this Snake-Eyes? Did he steal the paintings? If so, who was he working for? Tick Tock Tommaso? Rocky Vanderbilt? Edward Eggs Benedict? And where did Frank the security guard and his roommate Dean Braugh fit in? Were they part of the heist too?

Jessica didn't have the security clearance to get very far with the FBI data base. And her google searches didn't yield anything but newspaper articles about crimes this mysterious Snake-Eyes had committed. *Whoa.* You name it, Cobra had done it. Including murder. But he'd never served time because the FBI could never find him, let alone prove anything.

It was as if Cobra was a tornado leaving destruction in his path, but too fast for anyone to catch… or even get a good look at. The file was full of different sketches of a short stocky figure dressed all in black with a balaclava over his face.

"I'm not getting anywhere with my search for Snake-Eyes," Jessica said, looking up from her laptop. "How about you?"

"Just what's on Eggs Benedict's rap sheet." The marshal laid the sleeping baby in its car seat. "It's as long as *War and Peace*… and it's mostly war."

"So is Tolstoy." Jessica closed her laptop and stretched. "Maybe we should parallel-process."

"Parallel-process?"

"Yeah. I'll go back and reinterview Frank Motton and Dean Braugh, while you look for Cobra." She stood up and did a full sun salutation.

"What in the hell are you doing?"

"Yoga." Jessica did another downward dog.

"Quit flashing your butt at me and go." The marshal waved her away.

"To interview Motton and Braugh?" Jessica asked. Was the marshal really sending her out on another assignment? Alone?

"Good idea." The marshal went back to her computer. "I'll track down Snake-Eyes."

"Want me to call my friend?" She couldn't believe she'd just suggested calling Lolita again. True. Lolita Durechenko knew the world of mobsters. And she was tough as a two-by-four. But she was also a wild card. With Lolita, you never knew what might happen.

The marshal looked up from her computer and narrowed her eyes.

"My friend Lolita Durechenko." Jessica stretched her arms behind her back. "I told you about her. Bratva. Russian mafia."

"We're not desperate enough to call in your chums from school." The marshal clicked her tongue.

"Not yet anyway."

"Bad enough I have to report to Stevenson," the marshal said under her breath.

"I thought you were avoiding him." Jessica picked up her backpack off the chair.

"I wish." The marshal shook her head. "I send the obligatory report via email."

"I thought you hated him."

"I do." The marshal looked up from her computer. "It's called the chain of command. Speaking of… aren't you supposed to be on your way to talk to Motton again?" She got up from her desk, went to the fridge, and pulled out a pop. "Be sure to check in afterwards."

"Yup."

"It's three-thirty now," the marshal said. "Call me by five with a progress report."

"Yes, sir." Jessica gave a crisp salute.

"And don't call me sir."

Jessica shrugged. "Yes, Federal Marshal Colt."

The marshal nodded and then waved her away again. The desk phone rang, and the marshal answered it. She looked at Jessica and held up one finger.

Jessica stopped in her tracks in the doorway and waited. "What's going on?" she mouthed.

The color drained from the marshal's face. She hung up and then just sat staring at the computer screen.

"What is it?" Jessica asked. Something was wrong.

The marshal sighed. "Eggs Benedict is dead."

"What?" Jessica stood there blinking. "We just saw him."

"Yeah, and someone wanted to make sure we didn't see him again." The marshal put her face in her hands. "Dammit."

"I don't get it." Jessica went back to her table and dropped into the chair. "We talk to him and then he dies?"

"He was killed. Murdered in the prison yard." The marshal shook her head. "Obviously, our perp got word that Eggs was about to spill the beans." The marshal pounded her fist on the desk. "Dammit."

"How is that even possible?"

"The guard." The marshal closed her eyes. "And other prisoners." She grimaced. "Whoever did this must be very powerful."

"What do we do now?"

The marshal sighed again. "You go interview Frank Motton as planned. I'll go back to the prison and get the details on Mr. Benedict's murder."

"Could it be Snake-Eyes?"

"It could be anyone." The marshal waved her away. "He tried to warn us."

"I guess we should have listened." Jessica shrugged.

"You think?" The marshal's face was blotchy. She didn't look well.

"We're going to catch whoever did this." Jessica went to the marshal and put her hand on her shoulder. "Together."

▭

JESSICA TURNED the ignition in the rental car, synced her phone with the car speaker, and called Lolita. An art heist was one thing. A dead robber with mob connections was quite another. Only the mafia could have orchestrated a murder in prison in a matter of hours. Time to bring in an expert on organized crime.

"My Montana friend." Lolita's voice was as refreshing as a summer rain during fire season. "Drank any bad grappa lately?"

"Very funny." Jessica started the car and pulled out of the parking lot. "I'm in Boston, working for the art crimes division of the FBI."

"Impressive," Lolita stretched the *r* into a purring sound. With her shiny black hair, sage green eyes, and agile karate moves, Lolita did remind her of a cat.

"I'm driving, so I can't talk long." Jessica tried to look at the GPS and merge into traffic at the same time. She didn't know her way around Boston yet. Given her sense of direction, she could get lost in puny Whitefish, Montana for cripes sake. "Have you heard of a gangster by the name of Cobra, also known as Snake-Eyes?"

"Snake-Eyes," Lolita repeated.

"Cobra." She heard Vanya's voice in the background. Vanya was Lolita's second cousin and a bit of a gangster himself. He'd been in and out of Bratva like a gopher in a Montana field. "He's a myth."

"Vanya knows him?" Jessica asked. "Does he know where to find him?"

Lolita said something in Russian, presumably to her wiry cousin. "He says Snake-Eyes doesn't exit."

"He is a suspect in the biggest art heist in history." Jessica blew at her bangs.

Lolita whistled. Then more muffled conversation in Russian. "In Boston?"

"The Albertina Gardener Museum." Jessica swerved to miss a man who was talking on his cell phone instead of paying attention.

Vanya was talking in the background again. "Cobra is a fairytale. Like Santa Claus, only bad."

"You mean Santa doesn't exist?" Jessica chuckled.

"I know some rich Harvard boys itching for a well-run high stakes poker game," Lolita said in her sultry Poker Tsarina voice.

No. Not poker. Not again. Lolita was famous for hosting high-stakes poker games for the rich and famous. Unfortunately, not all the rich and famous were honest. In fact, some were downright crooks."

"What are you suggesting?" Jessica asked, although she knew full well what her resourceful friend was up to. "I hope you're not planning to come mess up my shot at a real job."

"More like save your job." Lolita laughed. "We'll call you when we get there."

"You're coming to Boston?" Jessica nearly rammed the car in front of her.

"See you soon, *milaya*." Lolita made kissing noises and then hung up.

Whenever Lolita used Russian endearments, Jessica knew to expect trouble. The marshal wasn't going to be happy about a couple of Chicago Russians interfering in their investigation. Jessica should have kept her big mouth shut. Then again, if anyone could root out a mobster, it was Lolita and Vanya.

Trouble never travels alone. Lolita was one thing… her half-cocked cousin Vanya was quite another. Last time Vanya met Marshal Lexington Colt, he'd coldcocked her with his gun and left her for dead in a frozen parking lot. *The marshal won't be happy to see him again.*

Jessica didn't have time to think about Lolita and her crazy cousin Vanya. Anyway, Lolita was right. She'd saved Jessica's butt more times than she could count on all her fingers and toes.

Jessica shoved a cassette tape of Gregorian chants into her ancient tape player—one of the few things on the car that still worked.

She had to get in the right mindset to interview Frank the security guard and his bible-stealing roommate. Their rundown apartment was only a block away.

She put on the brakes and slowed to a cruise. Snagging a parking spot in Boston was even harder than snagging a paddlefish.

There she was. Standing on this dilapidated porch yet again. At least it was quiet. The last time, the music had been so loud and Adrián had been so pushy. She was lucky she didn't lose her internship.

Frank Motton buzzed her in. She climbed the creaky, wooden stairs to the fourth floor. The building reeked of stale beer and onions.

She grabbed the banister and immediately regretted it. The splintered wood was coated in a film from decades of student parties and test anxiety. She wiped her palm on her jeans.

Frank was waiting for her at the top of the stairs. "No more good cop, bad cop?"

She squinted at him. *Good cop, bad cop?*

"Your friend, Agent Garcia, he's not with you this time?" Frank took a rubber band off his wrist, pulled his long, wavy hair into a ponytail, and wrapped the band around it. "That guy is scary, man."

"Just me," she said. *Crapulence. Maybe I shouldn't have told him I'm alone. Dude looks harmless enough, but you never know.*

As she stepped into the apartment, she got a whiff of marijuana smoke mixed with sandalwood incense. A long, half-burned, stick of incense stuck out of the dirt of a potted plant.

Under attack, her sinuses swelled, and she had to blow her nose. She pulled a Kleenex from her jacket pocket. With her allergies, she always carried tissues.

"Look, man. I told you everything I know," Frank whined. He flopped into a ratty upholstered chair.

Does he have a cat? The shredded fabric reminded her of her mom's living room. "I just want to ask a few more questions, and then I'll be out of your hair." Given the equally ratty state of his hair, Jessica regretted that turn of phrase.

"What's your relationship with Dean Braugh?" she asked.

"Dean is my roommate," Frank said with a questioning look. "Why are you asking about him?"

"Where is he?" she asked. "Is he here?"

"He and Gloria went to his mom's place in Middleton." Frank picked at his thumbnail.

Middleton. She wrote it down. "Gloria?" *Oh, right. The goth girlfriend.*

Frank blushed. "Dean's girlfriend."

"When will he—they—be back?" She held her phone ready to type.

"I think he's coming back tonight." He grabbed a bronze Ganesh off the cluttered coffee table and dropped the statue back and forth from hand-to-hand. "Not sure about Gloria."

Tonight. She'd have to come back again later. "How long have you known him?"

Frank scrunched up his face in concentration. "Um. Like maybe four years?" He put the statue back and picked up a small rubber ball. He squeezed it in his palm.

"Where did you meet?" She tapped her phone awake to take more notes.

"Um. College." He kept squeezing the ball.

"Where did you go to college?"

"Actually, I dropped out to play music." He dropped the ball on the floor and picked at the hole in the knee of his jeans.

"Before you dropped out, where were you?"

"Boston Community College." An unruly lock of hair escaped his ponytail.

Fair enough. Given her own humble background growing up in a trailer park, and being a first-generation college student herself, she could appreciate the courage it took to make that leap of faith.

"Did you know Dean tried to steal the Guttenberg Bible from Harvard's library?" She stared into his furry face waiting for the answer.

"Wow." Frank's eyes lit up. "That's crazy, man." With both hands he pushed the hair out of his face.

"So, you didn't know about it?" She shifted from foot to foot.

He shook his head. "You can sit down, if you want." Frank pointed to a sunken, stained couch across from him.

She hated to think of everything that had gone down on that couch. She shook her head. "You didn't know your roommate broke into the Harvard library?"

"Nah." He freed his hair and fiddled with the rubber

band. "Dean and Gloria keep to themselves." He glanced around the room like he was looking for something.

She followed his gaze. The dude was as nervous as a stallion on gelding day. "Didn't you know he spent last week in jail?"

"No ma'am." At the mention of jail, a shadow fell over Frank's face.

It was a long shot, but she had to ask. "Could Dean be involved with the Albertina robbery?"

Frank glanced around again like he expected a SWAT team to bust in. "No. How could he if he was in jail last week?" His knee was bouncing up and down. *The dude seems totally strung out.*

"Let's switch gears." Jessica tapped her phone. "On the night of the robbery, you opened that side door. We know you did, so don't deny it."

Frank screwed up his mouth.

"The security tapes show that you opened it." She tapped her foot.

Frank stared down at his hands. "Look, man. I went outside to smoke a cigarette. Just for, like, a minute."

"You left your post to smoke?" Jessica asked. "And you opened the side door? Pretty irresponsible behavior." *I'm a fine one to talk about irresponsible behavior.* She thought of the time she and Jack broke into her dissertation advisor's office to smoke something more than tobacco. *Good old Jackass.*

"Actually, I do it every night." Frank's hands were shaking as he wiped them on his jeans. "I always stop on my rounds for a quick smoke."

Is he telling the truth? "Did you see anyone or anything unusual the night of the robbery?"

"No ma'am." Frank tilted his head. "Wait a sec."

"Go on," she encouraged.

"There was a car parked in the alley." He stretched the rubber band until it snapped.

His incessant movement was making her nervous. "What kind of car?" she asked.

"I don't know." He shrugged. "It was dark." He pulled a pack of Marlboro Lights from his shirt pocket. "Do you mind?"

She shook her head.

"Want one?" He held out the pack.

She held up her hand. "A big or a small car?" *Now we're getting somewhere.*

"Big." His knee was bouncing a mile a minute as he lit up his ciggy.

"Do you remember anything else?" She set her phone to record, and took notes too, just in case.

"There was a stocky guy in the car smoking." He pointed to an overflowing ashtray on the coffee table. "He was wearing a black beanie."

"A black beanie." She typed it into her phone.

"I thought it was weird coz it was warm out." He shrugged and blew out a cloud of smoke.

She stifled a cough. "You couldn't tell what kind of car it was, but you could tell there was a guy inside smoking and wearing a beanie?" She squinted down at him.

"I saw the glow of his cigarette." He looked up at her with glassy eyes. "I guess it could have been a woman… all I saw was the glow."

"Anything else you remember?"

He shook his head and picked at his holey jeans again.

"What can you tell me about the French Gallery?"

"What do you mean?" He played with the skull-shaped ring on his pinky finger.

"You were the only one to go in there that night, and a painting is missing from that room." She paused. "How do you explain that?"

"I can't. I told you I don't know… why don't you believe me?" He pleaded. "Maybe the security system messed up.

Maybe the robber went in there too. I don't know." He put his head in his hands.

"Okay. Calm down." She didn't want him to start crying again. "If you think of anything or remember anything else, please contact me right away."

He lifted his head and nodded.

"You've been very helpful, and I appreciate it." She smiled down at him. *You catch more flies with honey than with vinegar, as mom always said.*

"Thanks," he said weakly.

"If you're innocent, you have nothing to worry about." Of course, she'd read enough existentialism and watched enough film noir to know that wasn't true.

"I am innocent!" His voice was shaky. He stubbed out the cigarette. "I'm not guilty, man."

She thought of Kafka's story *The Trial*. The main character said, "I'm not guilty, there's been a mistake," and the priest responded, "That's exactly what a guilty man would say."

Chapter 18

Adrián had just parked his Vespa across the street from Frank's apartment building when he saw Jessica slip through the front door. *Mierda. She beat me again.* He lowered the shield on his helmet so she wouldn't recognize him. Seventeen minutes later, he watched her come out again.

What information did she get out of Frank Lambchop Muttonhead?

He waited a few more minutes before he kicked the kickstand, threw his leg over the scooter, removed his helmet, and hung it on the handlebar. He crossed the street to Frank's building and pressed the buzzer for 4A. No answer. Holding his finger on the buzzer, he determined to solve this case before the incomparable Jessica James. Still no answer.

Muttonhead had to be in there. Otherwise, what was Jessica doing inside for seventeen minutes? He pressed the buzzer again. He slammed his whole hand into all the buzzers at once. Maybe someone would buzz him in.

Buzz. It worked. He slid inside and took the stairs, two at a time. He was going to question Muttonhead if he had to break the door down to do it.

All his buzzing had attracted attention. A lady on the second floor poked her head out and stared at him as he zipped past. Another woman carrying a garbage bag passed him on the stairs. She clung to the wall like he might bite. When he reached the third floor, another girl flew past him like she thought Adrián was contagious. *The tenants in this building aren't very friendly.*

When he reached the fourth-floor landing, he heard groaning coming from Frank's apartment. He knocked on the door. "FBI, open up."

"Glory be." The man's voice was strained.

Was he praying?

The man groaned again.

Adrián knocked again. "Open the door."

Nothing. The groaning had stopped. The man inside was quiet.

"Open the door, or I'll kick it in." Adrián had never kicked in a door in his life. *But that guy sounds hurt, and this door looks rickety.* He slammed his shoulder against the door. He did it again, this time putting all his weight into it. He took a few steps back, got up some momentum, and went at it again. The door burst open. The momentum sent Adrián flying into the apartment.

Mierda. That hurt. He skidded to a stop in the foyer. "Anybody home?"

No one answered. He'd heard someone. He was sure of it.

Something wasn't right. Adrián wished he had a weapon. He took a few more steps into the apartment. "Hello?" No answer.

He rounded the corner into the living room.

Dios mío. Feet stuck out from behind the couch. Someone was lying on the floor behind the beat-up sofa. His heart racing, he moved in to investigate.

Frank Motton lay staring over at the wall with dead eyes, his mouth twisted into a hideous oval. He had a syringe sticking out of the crook of his arm. And he had a huge bleeding gash across his forehead.

Adrián's hands were trembling. He'd never seen a dead body before. He felt like he was going to be sick. He bent down for a closer look.

Santo cielo. He must have overdosed and then fell and hit his head on the edge of the coffee table. Adrián put on gloves and examined the corner of the table. His hands shook even more as he touched the corner. *If only I'd come in sooner. I might have been able to save him.*

A red blossom grew around Frank's head. The gash was still bleeding. Tears welled in Adrián's eyes. He covered his mouth and looked away. Soon the bleeding would stop. *The dead don't bleed.*

Adrián forced himself to look. On the floor near Frank's head was a bunch of junk that must have fallen off the table when he fell. A red rubber ball. A weird elephant statue. A heavy glass ashtray. Cigarette butts. Lots of cigarette butts.

He turned Frank over on his back to get a better look at his face.

Adrián's head was spinning. The taste of bile filled his mouth. He touched his St. Christopher's Medal. *Dios mío.* Now he was praying.

I should call the police. He pulled his phone from his pants pocket and made the call.

"Hello."

He stood there frozen with the phone to his ear.

"Adrián?" It sounded like an accusation.

He couldn't speak.

"Adrián, is everything okay?" Jessica asked, her voice full of worry.

His eyes stung.

"Adrián, what's going on?" Her voice was strained.

"He's dead." He could barely get the words out.

"Who's dead?"

"Frank, Frank Motton." His hands were shaking so bad he nearly dropped his phone.

"How is that possible?" she asked. "I just saw him a few minutes ago."

"He overdosed." Adrián stood staring down at the dead body. As the pool of blood grew, so did his nausea.

"Stay there," she said. "I'm only ten minutes away."

———

HOW COULD Frank Motton be dead? *I just saw him a few minutes ago. Did he shoot-up right after I left?* What was Adrián doing there? *I hope he isn't breaking the rules again, especially if a guy is dead.* So many questions swirled in her mind.

Jessica did a U-turn and headed back to Frank's apartment.

When she arrived at the apartment, she found the door wide open. Adrián was nowhere to be seen. "Adrián?" No answer.

She tiptoed into the living room, where she'd been interviewing Frank. "Oh my God." She clasped her hand over her mouth.

The same glassy eyes that had averted her gaze earlier, now stared up at the ceiling. She'd seen dead bodies before—too many in her twenty-five years on the planet. But those sightless eyes were always as uncanny and unsettling as the first time. She never got used to seeing death… and she hoped she never did. Death was part of life, that was a fact, but that didn't make it pretty.

Adrián appeared from the back of the apartment. His face was wet, and he wiped his mouth with the back of his hand. "Sorry," he said in a small voice. "I was sick."

"I know what you mean." Jessica crossed the room to Adrián and put her arm around him. "It's awful." She held him close.

"You're trembling," he whispered and wrapped his arms around her.

"So are you." She moved into his embrace.

They stood there clinging to each other for another minute.

"Did you call 911?" she asked, pulling out of the hug.

"Not yet." His face was pale. "I meant to, but…" His voice trailed off.

She pulled her phone out of her pocket and called the marshal.

"Frank Motton is dead."

Silence.

"I interviewed him, left his place, and a few minutes later Adrián called. He found Frank dead."

"Adrián Garcia? Stevenson's boy wonder?"

"He found Frank dead of an apparent overdose."

"Don't touch anything," the marshal said. "I'm on my way."

Without touching anything, Jessica knelt next to Frank's head and surveyed the items forming a halo on the blood-stained carpet. The contents of the overflowing ashtray had now spilled. The Ganesh statue Frank was tossing from hand-to-hand when she interviewed him. The rubber ball Frank had been squeezing less than half an hour ago.

Something looked off about the halo of blood around his head. Had he been moved? She came around to the other side of the body and bent down to examine the needle sticking out of Frank's arm. "That's odd."

Adrián stood over her, looking away from the body. "What?"

"The needle is stuck in his right arm."

"So?"

"Frank was right-handed." She remembered him squeezing the ball in his right hand. And every time he'd taken something off the coffee table, it had always been with his right hand. "I'm sure of it."

"So?" He took a few steps backwards, away from the body.

"If you were going to shoot-up, wouldn't you use your dominant hand to inject your nondominant arm?" Like in charades, she acted out injecting herself with an invisible syringe.

She stood up, walked around the coffee table again, and looked at Frank's bleeding head from a different angle. "I don't think he hit his head when he fell."

"What do you mean?" From across the room, Adrián stared over at the body and then looked away again. "He has that gash, and he's bleeding."

Even in profile, she could see the color drain from Adrián's face. "Are you okay?" she asked. "Do you need some water?"

"The sight of blood." He nearly choked on the word *blood*.

"Gosh. Have you considered a different career path?" If he couldn't stand the sight of blood, maybe the FBI wasn't the right choice. Not that she liked the sight of blood... but come on.

"I thought in the Art Crime Division all the blood I'd see would be in the paintings of Caravaggio or Artemisia Gentileschi." He sucked in air. "Not spreading out over a dirty carpet."

"Wouldn't that be nice." She went to his side. "I would love to see an Artemisia Gentileschi."

"Of course, you would." He bent over and put his hands on his knees.

"Why do you say that?" She rubbed his back.

"All those women cutting off men's heads." He groaned.

"Symbolic castration as revenge for sexual assault." She tilted her head. "Seems fair to me."

Adrián ran both hands through his hair and stood up again. He looked like he might pass out.

"Why don't you go sit in the kitchen and wait for the

marshal?" She patted his arm. "I'll join you in a minute." She wanted a closer look at the stuff around Frank's head.

"Okay." Breathing heavily, he left the room.

Thank goodness. She couldn't take care of Adrián and examine the scene before the marshal arrived.

Jessica went back to the corpse. She knelt next to the blood stain on the carpet and leaned over trying not to touch anything… or get blood on her pants. Underneath the stale smell of cigarettes, a strong pungent odor hit her nose. *Pickles.* Why did she smell pickles? Pickles and mint. Pickled mint? *Weird.*

What a sickening mess. I don't blame Adrián for refusing to look.

The ashtray and butts, the red ball, the statue, all were floating on a lake of blood. She leaned closer. *Yikes.* She started to fall. She grabbed the edge of the coffee table to keep from toppling into the mess.

There was something different about the statue. It wasn't just sitting on the bloodstain. Ganesh's trunk had blood on it and a strand of Frank's hair.

What if Frank didn't fall and hit his head? What if someone hit him on the head and that's why he fell? The ashtray and cigarette butts must have flown off the table when Frank struggled with his attacker.

Maybe Frank was hit on the head with the statue, and then injected with the heroin… or pickle juice.

Holy crapulence. Jessica's hand flew to her mouth. *That makes Ganesh the murder weapon.*

Frank didn't overdose. He was murdered.

Chapter 19

Maybe the cowgirl was right, and Frank had been murdered. Lexi cracked open a Mountain Dew and slumped down in her chair. It had been a long night, and she was running on fumes. The trip across town to examine the murder scene had about done her in.

After taking Camo out and putting Sammy to bed, the first thing she did when she got home was take a shower. She always took a shower after examining a murder scene—as if she could wash away the blood and death.

How had a simple art heist turned into murder? The bodies were stacking up. First, Eggs Benedict, and now Frank Motton. This wasn't about catching a thief. It was about catching a killer.

Could it be a mob job? The mafia could easily have arranged for a hit in prison. And they could easily have made Frank's death look like an accidental overdose. Those mafia thugs had skills.

Lexi tightened the belt on her terrycloth robe and leaned her elbows on the table. Was she ever going to adjust to her new life? *A new baby, a new dog, a new job.*

The box containing her dishes still sat unpacked in the

corner of the kitchen. She hadn't cooked a single meal on the gas stove. The only food in the refrigerator was string cheese and Mountain Dew. And the only thing in the cupboard was Camo's dog food.

She put her head in her hands. No. Boston didn't feel like home. Since she got back from Afghanistan, no place did. Not even her hometown, Gleason "Tater Town" Tennessee… not that she'd given it much of a chance. She'd been back exactly once in the last five years.

She glanced at her phone. *Good Lord. It's midnight already.* She finished the can of pop and tossed it in the trash. After checking on Sammy, she stripped off her robe and crawled into her cold, lonely queen bed.

These days, she slept with one eye and ear open, on high alert. The baby's crib was right next to her bed, so she could sense whenever Sammy moved. *What if Sammy stops breathing?* She shivered and reached for the pill bottle on the nightstand.

▭

"LORD, HELP ME," Lexi screamed, thrashing, and kicking. She was stuck. It was no use. She was going to die along with the rest of them.

What the— She woke up in a sweat with Camo licking her face. *Dammit.* Her recurring nightmare. *It's the same every time.*

Her pillowcase was wet. *Tears? Sweat? Drool?* She rolled over and stared at the crib. Sammy's little face looked so peaceful. *Does the baby dream? I hope her dreams are better than mine.*

Lexi closed her eyes and drifted back to sleep.

She was with her platoon in the desert. There was a loud noise… like an explosion. She hid behind a tanker truck.

She dug her fingernails into her palms so hard it woke her up again. Camo nudged her arm.

"When I come out everyone is dead… but not just

dead…" She sucked in air. "Eviscerated. Like they were turned inside out."

Camo barked and nudged her again. She glanced at the clock on the nightstand and sighed. *Three in the morning.* Since her tour in Afghanistan, she'd learned to live on little sleep. Then when Sammy came along, the level of sleep deprivation skyrocketed.

Still, feeding and comforting the baby took her mind off that horrible dream. Lexi got up and threw on her bathrobe. She peeked over the crib. Little Sammy was fast asleep. So peaceful. *I hope the world is kinder to her.*

Camo licked her hand. He'd done his job. He'd woken her from the nightmare. He'd comforted her. *How could he sense her anxiety? The smell of terror?* However he did it, she was impressed.

She went into the kitchen, took the box of milk bones down off the refrigerator, scooped out one, and handed it to him. "Good boy."

If only the dog could stop the nightmares from coming. If only he could sense them before they started.

PTSD was a tricky bastard. It would sneak up on you when you least expected it. That was why her therapist had told her to take the dog with her everywhere. She was supposed to take Camo to work with her. *What am I? Blind?*

"You have a mental illness," her doctor had said. "It's nothing to be ashamed of." Then he'd prescribed a big bottle of yellow horse pills and a therapy dog.

Lexi padded into the bathroom and fetched the pills from the medicine cabinet. She popped two in her mouth and bit down. The bitter taste was her punishment. She deserved it. It made her feel better.

She went back to the kitchen, opened the fridge, and pulled out a can of Diet Mountain Dew. *Breakfast of champions.* The sound of the pop-top was always reassuring. She flopped into a chair at the breakfast table and sipped the Dew.

Camo sat next to her. She stroked his head.

She'd messed up again. Two people had been killed on her watch. And she hadn't even seen it coming. She'd been transferred to Art Crimes Division because WitSec witnesses had been killed on her watch. And last night, the only witness to the Albertina heist was murdered… on her watch.

What's next for me? Meter maid?

Her army track record sucked. Her FBI track record sucked. She sucked.

She sat there in a stupor sipping her Dew and stroking the dog.

A high-pitched wail snapped her out of her stupor. The baby was crying, and Lexi felt like joining her. Maybe Sammy was having nightmares too. Was PTSD carried through breast milk?

Lexi padded back into the bedroom and lifted Sammy out of the crib. "There, there, little mite." She kissed the baby's fuzzy head, and then laid back on the bed with Sammy nestled on her chest. The baby's rhythmic breathing was more calming than those bitter pills. Lexi closed her eyes. *Just as long as I don't go back to the desert… not again.*

She realized she'd dozed off when her phone woke her up. Trying not to disturb the baby, Lexi reached for her phone and slid it off the night table.

Good Lord. It's only four-thirty. What's happened now?

"Colt here," she whispered into the phone so as not to wake Sammy.

It was the cowgirl.

"This better be good to wake me up at four in the morning." Lexi carefully shifted the baby onto the bed.

"I know who killed Frank Motton."

"Who?" Lexi sat up. "Never mind. Meet me at headquarters in an hour."

She fed and changed the baby and left her cooing in her crib. Then she fed the dog. As she cracked open another

Mountain Dew, her hand trembled. She stood in front of the refrigerator and guzzled the pop.

Camo left his food bowl half-full and came to her side. He looked up at her with anxious eyes.

"Don't look at me like that." She crushed the empty can and tossed it into the trash. "Yeah. I know." She patted the dog on the head. "I'm supposed to take you with me."

She packed the diaper bag with all the essentials, slung it over her shoulder, and then loaded Sammy into the Baby Bjorn. Carrying both the heavy diaper bag and a twelve-pound baby was a workout. Luckily, Sammy was a very good baby. She smiled down at baby Sammy, who was cooing and pounding her little fists against Lexi's boobs.

Lexi snagged her keys off a hook by the door.

Camo sat by the door, guilt-tripping her with those sad brown eyes.

"Okay." She grabbed his leash off another hook and attached it to his collar. "Why not?"

She clutched the pocket on the diaper bag that held her nine-millimeter Glock. After they finished therapy school, maybe she would give Camo some do-it-yourself K9 police training. He could help her fight off PTSD *and* help her fight the bad guys. "Good boy."

It was still dark out. The sun wouldn't be up for another half hour. The morning air was chilly and damp. Her Charger was only six blocks away today. Even so, carrying the baby and the diaper bag, she was out of breath by the time she got there.

She opened the passenger side door and then pulled a blanket out of the diaper bag and laid it on the seat.

"Hop in."

Camo hopped in.

"You ride shotgun."

She opened the back door and fastened Sammy into her car-seat—across from her fresh case of Diet Mountain Dew.

"And you can guard mommy's pop."

———

JESSICA PACED UP and down the hallway. Her FBI badge had gotten her into headquarters, but the marshal hadn't given her a key to the office. She pulled her phone from her pocket. Only ten minutes later than the last time she checked.

The building was nearly deserted. The only sounds were the humming of the air-conditioner and the tapping of her cowboy boots on the tile floor. It even smelled deserted. Usually, it was full of the aroma of various perfumes, colognes, and lunches or popcorn heated up in office microwaves. Now, all she could smell was a hint of stale floor polish.

To distract herself, she read the office numbers and name-plates as she passed. The Art Crimes Division was tiny compared to the Fraud Division. *How is forging a check different from forging a painting… or its provenance?*

She chewed on a ragged fingernail as she paced. *Come on, marshal. Hurry up.*

Unbidden, the memory of watching Nick kiss the marshal came back into her consciousness like a snake striking a rat. Men were untrustworthy. Maybe not all men. But the ones she fell for. Even Nick.

Virtue is just the flip side of vice. Whatever their virtues, there was always the flip side of the coin—their vices. The super-nice ones were disingenuous. *You never know when they're for real.* The super-hot ones were too risky. *Everyone wants a piece of that action.* But the super-smart ones were the worst. *They can really mess with your mind.*

Then, there was Nick. He was nice, hot, and smart. A triple threat. A few months ago, she thought he'd been about to propose to her. Maybe he had. Then he went into witness protection and disappeared…. disappeared into the arms of Marshal Lexington Colt.

The clicking of heels echoed through the hallway and announced the marshal's arrival. *Finally.*

Camo appeared first from around the corner, followed by the marshal. "What's so important I had to get over here in the middle of the damn night?"

Speak of the devil. Wow. She's not wearing her usual navy blazer and skirt. Today it's black slacks, matching pumps, and a black sweater.

The marshal marched to the office door, dropped the baby's diaper bag, and fiddled in her pocket. She pulled out a set of keys and unlocked the door.

"I know who killed Frank Motton." Jessica followed the marshal and the dog into the office.

"Can you hold the baby?" The marshal twisted Sammy free from the Baby Bjorn.

"Hey you, little sweetie." Jessica held the baby up in front of her face. Sammy smiled and kicked her little feet. She was wearing an adorable yellow terrycloth onesie with elephants on it. "You've grown overnight." She cuddled the baby. "She'll be asking for the car keys before you know it."

"That's a scary thought." The marshal dropped the diaper bag next to her desk. "Hit me," she said, hands on her hips. Camo went to her side and licked her hand.

"Dean Braugh." Jessica blew a raspberry on Sammy's chubby cheek. "He killed Frank." The sweet scent of baby powder and drool hit her nostrils.

The marshal squinted. "The Gutenberg bible duffus?"

"He's also Frank's roommate." Jessica sat at the table and bounced the baby on her knee. "I smelled him when we found Frank's body."

"You smelled him?" The marshal raised her eyebrows.

"I have a very sensitive nose." She bristled. Usually, Jessica said her nose was her superpower, but the marshal didn't seem like she went in for superhero movies. "Dean has a distinctive camphor medicine smell. He was there when Frank died. I know it."

"I thought you said the roommate was visiting his mother?" The marshal dropped into her desk chair as if she was holding a fifty-pound weight. Camo sat next to her chair on high alert.

"I think Frank was lying." Jessica kissed the baby's fuzzy head.

"Why would he lie about his roommate?" The marshal tilted her head. Mirroring her gesture, Camo tilted his head.

"Good question." Holding the baby on her lap, Jessica opened her computer. "We've got to interview the mother." She tapped the computer and did a search. "She lives in Middleton. Google says it's thirty minutes away, which means it will take at least forty-five… unless you're driving and then it will take twenty." She glanced at the time. "Probably too early to go now."

"Yeah. It's still dark out, for cripes sake." The marshal rummaged in the diaper bag. "Let me give Sammy a bottle, and then we'll make a plan." Like Mary Poppins, she pulled a baby bottle, a bib, a blanket, and then a bottle of water out of her bag.

"How do you fit all that in there?" Jessica laughed.

"You'd be surprised at what all I've got stuffed into this bag." The marshal poured water into the baby bottle, shook it, and then fetched Sammy. "Come on, my beautiful girl. You must be hungry… again." She sat down, held Sammy close, and fed her. The baby put one tiny hand on either side of the bottle and sucked eagerly. "Okay. Let's review the evidence. What have we got?"

Jessica opened a file on her computer. If there was one thing she'd learned in graduate school, it was how to make detailed notes. "Our suspects are, first, Tick Tock Tommaso, crime lord currently in prison. His lieutenants could have pulled the heist to get a bargaining chip for his release—"

"But no one has come forward to make a deal." With a cloth over her shoulder, the marshal was burping the baby.

"How many times have stolen masterpieces been recovered in drug busts?" It was a rhetorical question. Jessica had learned it was plenty of times.

The marshal shrugged. "You tell me."

"Really?" Didn't the marshal already know?

"Enlighten me." The marshal opened her desk drawer and pulled out a Snickers bar. "Want one?"

Jessica nodded and the marshal lobbed the candy bar. "There's the Caravaggio taken by the Sicilian mafia." She counted on her fingers. "Edvard Munch's The Scream was found during a Norwegian drug bust. The Camorra gang used two stolen Van Goghs to buy cocaine—"

"Okay. I get the picture." The marshal shifted the baby on her lap. "Gangsters like art."

"Our next suspect loves art. Mr. Eggs Benedict, one of the most infamous art thieves." Jessica looked up from her computer. "But he was in prison at the time of the robbery. Could he have orchestrated it from behind bars?" She unwrapped the candy bar.

"If that's a hypothetical question, the answer is yes." The marshal got up and installed Sammy in her baby rocker. "If it's a real question, then the answer is we don't know yet. If he planned the heist, then why was he killed?" Camo followed her and sat next to the rocker, protecting the baby.

"His partners didn't want to share?" She took a bite of the gooey chocolate goodness.

"Could be." The marshal unwrapped her Snickers and devoured it into two bites.

"There's our Dr. No suspect, the rich art collector Rockefeller Vanderbilt." Jessica read her notes. "His lawyer seemed fishy—"

"His lawyer gave us Cobra." The marshal pulled a nailfile

from the diaper bag. "So far, I'd say all roads point to Snake-Eyes."

"True. Cobra was Eggs Benedict's mysterious partner, and now poor Eggs is dead…" Jessica tapped a pencil on the table. "And what a coincidence! Santo Romano, the mob lawyer, works for Cobra."

"I don't believe in coincidences." The marshal filed her nails.

"Could they all be working together?" Jessica looked up from her computer. "Maybe Santo Romano is actually the mastermind."

"Possible." The marshal admired a freshly filed nail. "Where does our dead security guard fit in?"

"Frank was the inside man, and the robbers decided he was too much of a risk." She picked up a pencil from the table and twirled it between her fingers. "So, they killed him."

"You think Dean Braugh was one of the robbers?"

"He has an airtight alibi. He was in jail during the robbery." The pencil flew out of Jessica's hand, and Camo fetched it. She patted Camo on the head. "Your dog is more of a mastermind than Dean Braugh."

"He did fall off a building because he didn't calculate the weight of the bible in his escape plan." The marshal chuckled. She got up, went to the fridge, and grabbed a pop. "Want one?"

Jessica shook her head. She drew the line at Mountain Dew for breakfast. "And Middlestate Mortuary College isn't exactly Harvard." She laughed.

"If Dean is such a duffus, then why do you suspect he is our murderer?"

"He was out on bail when Frank was killed, so he had the opportunity." Jessica chewed a jagged fingernail. "As for motive, maybe Dean found out Frank was the inside man and threatened to blackmail him."

"In that case, why would Dean kill his golden goose?" The marshal shook her head. "It doesn't make sense."

"I know he was there. I smelled him." Jessica scowled. *Come on, Jesse. I smelled him sounds so stupid. No wonder she doesn't believe me.* Camo licked her hand. Jessica clicked her tongue and Camo sat at high alert. What a good dog.

"Even if he was there, that doesn't make him a murderer," Lexi said.

The marshal wound her dark hair into a knot and, like magic, whipped it into a neat bun. "Could be Dean lied to Frank about going to his mother's. Still, if Dean Braugh killed Frank, we need a motive."

"What about means? I don't think Frank overdosed on heroin." Jessica scratched Camo's ears. "I think he was poisoned. When do we get the toxicology report?" There was just something weird about the odor of the syringe. Not that she'd smelled heroin before. But the smell was sour like pickles. *Maybe Frank overdosed on pickles?*

"Is it possible the same person who had Eggs killed in prison, killed Frank?" The marshal narrowed her eyes. "Or do we have two killers on the loose?" Her voice cracked. Camo went back to her side. "With suspects dropping like flies, do we just wait for the last man standing and call him the murderer and thief?"

"Well, we have no shortage of suspects." Jessica scanned her document. They still hadn't discounted the former museum director or the head of Black Cat Security.

"Let's go pay a visit to Dean's mother." The marshal downed her Dew, crushed the can, and then reloaded the diaper bag with baby bottle, water, nail file, and burpy bib. "If you're right and the bible thief is our murderer, then he's at the top of our list."

Jessica searched for any Braughs in Middleton. *Jackpot.* Braugh Blueberry Farm. *The wacky bible thief grew up on a fruit farm?*

The marshal lifted sleeping Sammy from the rocker and slipped her into the baby sling. "Can you get Camo's leash and lead him?"

Jessica fetched the leash from where it was hanging over the back of a chair. "Come on boy." She attached the leash to his collar and clicked her tongue. "Let's go catch a killer."

Chapter 20

In the spring, when rural Massachusetts turned from stick trees to lush green, the countryside reminded Lexi of Tennessee where she grew up. Rolling hills and shades of green as far as you could see.

Row houses and crowded malls gave way to mansions with massive gardens and pick-your-own produce farms. Only a half hour from the city, Middleton, Massachusetts was another world.

"Make the next right." The cowgirl stared down at her phone. "Onto Mulberry Lane."

Oh, for pity's sake. Mulberry Lane was a gravel road. Lexi didn't like to take her Charger off the pavement. She eased up on the accelerator. Rocks flew in her wake. *I'd better not get a crack in my windshield.*

Braugh Blueberry Farm was at the end of the gravel road. About fifty yards off the road, down a dirt driveway, sat an old farmhouse with a wide wrap-around porch and gabled roof. Well-manicured shrubs, a lush green lawn, and flowering trees in full spring bloom decorated the front yard.

On either side of the lawn were blueberry fields

surrounded by wire fencing. A weathered wooden sign marked their arrival.

Lexi pulled up in front of the farmhouse. "You stay here with the baby and the dog."

"No way." The cowgirl opened the passenger door. "I'm going with you. This is my suspect."

"I'm not taking Sammy and Camo along to interview the mother of a murder suspect." Lexi glanced back at the baby, who was sound asleep. A drive was a sure-fire way to put Sammy to sleep. Although it was a wonder that the bumpy gravel road hadn't woken her up.

"Come on." The cowgirl huffed. "She's the mother, not the murderer."

"What if she's hiding her son?"

"If Dean is here, he probably isn't the killer." The cowgirl shut the car door.

"How do you figure?"

"His alibi holds. He was at his mother's last night when Frank was killed."

"Just because he is here now, doesn't mean he didn't kill Frank last night." Lexi took a swig of Dew. "For a Ph.D., your reasoning isn't so good."

"Okay." The cowgirl slumped in her seat. "I'll babysit while you find the killer." She pouted. "But this isn't what I signed up for."

"Me neither." Lexi hopped out of the car and slammed the door, which she immediately regretted. The baby wailed from the backseat.

The cowgirl waved her fist from the front seat.

Camo licked Sammy's tiny hand.

Poor Sammy. Why did she have to get me as her mother? Ignoring her heartstrings, Lexi marched up to the farmhouse.

A short, buxom woman answered the door. "Blueberries aren't ready for another month."

"I'm not here for blueberries," Lexi said. "I'm here to ask you some questions about your son." She flashed her badge.

"My son?" The woman's pupils constricted to tiny dots.

"Are you Edward Dean Braugh's mother?"

"I'm Cora Braugh." She wiped her hands on her apron.

Cora Braugh had close-set, dark eyes and gray-streaked hair pulled tight into a ponytail. She wore a low-cut paisley cotton housedress and high-heeled pink slippers like some forty's movie star. *Who wears heeled slippers?*

"What's Eddie done this time?" Her voice raised an octave. A commotion inside indicated Mrs. Braugh was not alone.

"That's what I'd like to ask you." Lexi peeked around the woman to see inside the house. "Can I come in?"

Cora Braugh glanced around. "My husband's sick. I don't want to disturb him." She rubbed her hands together as if dusting them off. The smell of banana bread baking suggested she'd been cooking.

Lexi's stomach growled. "Was your son here last night?" *Might as well get right to the point.*

"Yes," the woman said tentatively. The exposed skin above her neckline went all red and blotchy.

"When did he arrive?"

"I don't know." She stared up at the corner of the doorframe. "Around four in the afternoon?"

"When did he leave?"

"Leave?" she asked as if she didn't understand the question.

"Is he still here?"

"No." When the woman shook her head, a strand of gray hair fell over her cheek. "He went back to the city this morning." She narrowed her eyes. "Why?"

"Can I speak with your husband?"

"I told you he's sick."

"It won't take long." Lexi tried to push past, but Cora Braugh blocked the doorway.

"No." The woman narrowed her dark eyes. "I don't want him disturbed." She took a step backwards and then shut the door in Lexi's face.

"Well, okay then." Lexi turned on her heels and headed back to the car. If Mrs. Braugh wasn't going to cooperate, they'd have to get a search warrant.

When she opened the driver's side door, Jessica looked up at her expectantly. "What happened?"

"She confirmed Dean's alibi but wouldn't let me talk to her husband. Wouldn't even let me into the house." Lexi turned the ignition. "Guess we'll need a warrant."

"Let me try."

Before she could stop her, the cowgirl opened the passenger door and jumped out of the car. Then she opened the door to the backseat, scooped up Sammy and grabbed Camo's leash. "Drive back out to the main road. Give me five minutes and then come back."

"What do you think you're—" *Dammit.* The upstart intern had snatched her baby and her dog and was halfway to the farmhouse.

▭

JESSICA HELD the baby tight to her chest. She shifted her weight from foot to foot waiting for someone to answer the door.

"I told you…" A stubby woman opened the door and stood staring at her.

"Sorry to bother you—"

"No blueberries for another month." The woman poked her head out the door and looked around.

Jessica followed her gaze to where the car was parked earlier. *Good.* The marshal had done as she'd asked and taken off. "Sorry to bother you," she repeated. "But can we use your bathroom?"

The woman took a step toward her and onto the porch. Jessica took a step backwards and nearly fell off the step.

"Where's your vehicle?" the woman asked, her unblinking eyes trained on baby Sammy.

"It broke down just out on the county road." Jessica blew at her bangs and shifted the baby to her other hip. "I could really use a glass of water."

"Can't you just call someone?" the woman asked. "Don't tell me. Your phone is broken too."

"No reception."

The woman sighed. "We're in a dead zone." She opened her mouth, shut it again, and then shook her head. "Stay right here." She disappeared back inside the house.

The door was ajar just a crack, and Jessica used her foot to open it further. She tiptoed into the entryway. The minty smell of camphor and eucalyptus. *Yup. He's here alright. But how to get to talk to him?*

The woman returned with a glass of water.

"Is Dean here?" Jessica asked. "His daughter wants to see him." She held up the baby.

The woman's eyes flashed, and her neck reddened. The glass slid out of her hand and shattered on the floor. "What game are you playing at, sister?" She balled her long-nailed hands into fists.

Sammy bawled. Camo barked. And Jessica flushed. "Didn't Dean tell you that you're a grandma?"

The goth girlfriend emerged from a bedroom and stood in the hallway. "Dean has a baby?" Her pale face was white against her jet-black hair and black eyeliner. "Dean? Is that your baby?"

The bible thief—and suspected murderer—appeared behind Goth-Girl. "You!" He pushed his girlfriend out of the way and stormed to the front door. "You're lying." He rushed at Jessica. "That's not mine."

Jessica clicked her tongue.

Camo intercepted him and knocked him down.

"Eddie, what's going on here?" Arms akimbo, his mother stood over him.

"Co?" Goth-Girl asked Mrs. Baugh. "Is that really Dean's baby?"

"She's that cop from the hospital." Dean wriggled off the floor and onto his feet. "I stand firm wearing the belt of truth buckled around my waist and the breastplate of righteousness—"

Bible verses again. "I'm not a cop," Jessica said, holding the baby even tighter. "I'm just an intern… for art crimes."

Dean's mother focused her beady eyes on Jessica. "Get out of my house." She rushed toward the door. "I told the other FBI broad to get a warrant or leave us alone." She shook a stubby finger at Jessica. Her nails were almost as long as her fingers. "I'm warning you. I'm going to have you arrested for trespassing if you don't get your boney ass off my property right now."

"Alright. I'm going." Jessica tugged on Camo's leash and stepped outside onto the porch. "Just one question." She turned back to face the trio gathered in the doorway. "Dean, did you kill your roommate, Frank Motton?"

"What?" Dean's face fell. "Frank is dead?"

Crapulence. Doesn't he know Frank is dead? "I know you were there." She couldn't say "because I smelled you."

"I'm calling my lawyer," Mrs. Braugh said.

"Where were you last night?" Jessica asked.

Dean squinted at her. "Playing Dungeons and Dragons at my friend Peter's house, if you must know."

"Shut up." Mrs. Braugh scolded her son. She turned back to Jessica. "Get off my porch before I push you off." She stomped one of her slippered feet. "Scat!"

Jessica trotted down the steps just as the Charger skidded to a stop in front of the farmhouse. Holding the baby tight to her chest, she broke into a gallop with Camo in tow. After installing the baby in its car seat and Camo on his dog blanket, Jessica ran around and hopped in the passenger seat.

"Let's get the heck out of here."

Chapter 21

"How dare you use my daughter as a prop." Lexi threw the Charger into high gear and floored it. "What if she got hurt?"

"But she didn't." The cowgirl bit her lip.

"If anything happens to her—"

"Sorry." The cowgirl stared down at her hands. "I wouldn't do anything to hurt Sammy."

"You'd better not, or I'll mess you up." Lexi glanced in the rearview mirror. Sammy was fast asleep in her car seat. Camo was snoozing next to her. *I really need to find a new babysitter or daycare. I can't keep bringing the baby to work.*

"Dean is there, and so is his goth girlfriend." The cowgirl perked up.

"So, the mother was lying." Lexi merged onto the freeway.

"The mother is a lioness protecting her cub."

"You still think Dean killed Frank?" She glanced over at the cowgirl.

"I don't know." Jessica screwed up her face. "When I flat-out asked him if he did it, he acted like he didn't know Frank was dead."

"Maybe he's just a good actor."

"Maybe." Jessica chuckled. "His mom threatened to call her lawyer."

"Let me guess. Santo Romano." Lexi swerved in and out of traffic.

"Wouldn't that be something?" The cowgirl grabbed the dashboard. "If you're so concerned about your daughter's safety, maybe you should slow down."

"Don't you dare talk to me about my baby's safety." Lexi eased up on the accelerator. "She's my daughter, not yours." She glared over at the cowgirl. Finding a babysitter had just become her top priority.

The cowgirl blanched. "Does Nick know?"

"Does Nick know what?" Lexi tightened her grip on the steering wheel.

"About the baby?"

She could feel the cowgirl's eyes boring a hole in her skull. "Does he know he has a daughter?"

Lexi shrugged.

"The baby is his, isn't she?" The cowgirl's stare was unnerving.

"What business is that of yours?" Lexi knew full well why Jessica was giving her the third degree. The cowgirl had been Nick's girlfriend when he entered WitSec... before Lexi slept with him.

"None, I guess." The cowgirl blew at her bangs. "Sorry I asked."

They rode the rest of the way back to headquarters in silence.

When they got there, Lexi pulled into the parking lot. "You go in and write up a report on our visit to Mrs. Baugh. And while you're at it, finish up the rest of the outstanding paperwork."

"Are you punishing me?"

"Something like that." Lexi waved her away. "From now

on, I give the orders, and you check in every two hours. Got it?"

The cowgirl nodded. "How long do I have to shuffle papers?"

"You'll do paperwork until I say you're done."

"When can I go back into the field?"

"When I say so. Now hand me a pop and then hop to it."

The cowgirl reached around her seat, slipped a can of Dew out of its plastic ring, and handed it to Lexi. "Enjoy." She opened the passenger door, slammed it shut, and then stomped off to the entrance.

Damned cowgirl is going to get us both fired… or worse. Lexi watched until Jessica was inside. She popped the top on her Dew. *Now what?*

She decided to take Sammy and Camo home, feed them both, leave the baby next door, and then visit Black Cat Security.

Not that I don't trust Adrián Garcia…. Yeah. I really don't.

▭

JESSICA FLOPPED into the marshal's chair. At least with the marshal gone, she wouldn't have to sit in the corner like a schoolgirl. You'd think after four years of college and five more years of grad school, she'd be used to shuffling papers. But busy work and creative thought inhabited opposite planes of existence. In fact, busy work was the death of creativity.

The marshal was right. She shouldn't have used baby Sammy as a prop. She didn't blame the marshal for being mad. Really. What if something had happened to Sammy? What if she'd been hurt? Jessica never would have forgiven herself… and the marshal probably would have killed her.

But how could she just sit around filing paperwork with the murderer still out there? She was so close that she could smell it… literally. Eucalyptus and camphor. The smell of

Edward Dean Braugh. And if he was the killer, then he had to be involved with the robbery. If only she could put all the pieces together.

Why would Dean want Frank dead?

Maybe Frank was the inside man and Dean was afraid he'd talk. Frank had been starting to crack the last time she interviewed him. And if Dean was in the apartment at the time, and not at his mother's, then he had heard everything. She thought back to the interview. But what did he hear? Frank had lied and told her that Dean was out in Middleton. *Why?*

Was Frank's death connected to Eggs Benedict's murder? It wasn't possible that the same person had killed them both. Eggs was killed in prison. And Frank was killed in his own apartment. But someone could have hired a hitman—or two hitmen—to kill them. It had to be someone pretty well connected to pull off two murders, with one of them inside a prison.

Obviously, Eggs had told them too much. Someone was afraid he'd spill the beans. Why else kill him? But who? She thought back to their interview.

Eggs had been arrogant and brash, but kind of charming in his own slimy way. He claimed he knew who had pulled the Albertina heist. He'd told them if they got him out, then he would spill his guts. The thief must have found out Eggs was about to make a deal with the FBI and sell him up the river.

But who was the thief? There's no way Dean Braugh had the kind of criminal power it took to command a prison hit.

The marshal was right… again. Dean was a nerdy mortician who didn't have the good sense to consider the heft of his haul. He was one of those stupid smart people Jessica had to put up with in graduate school. Lots of book learning but no real-world common sense. Could he be a cold-blooded murderer? Maybe rounding up business for his funeral home?

Her phone buzzed and interrupted her speculations. She

pulled it out of her jacket pocket. *Adrián. I hope he's got some good intel.*

"What's up?" she asked. "Got any new info on our case?"

"I'm downstairs," he answered. "How about I come up, and we work together?"

"You're here at headquarters?" He had to have something really important since he'd made the trip out to headquarters. *If the marshal comes back and finds Adrián in her office, she'll be livid.* Why, she didn't know. "I'll come down. Be right there." Jessica dropped her phone back into her pocket, grabbed her backpack, and skedaddled down the five flights of stairs to the lobby.

Adrián was standing at the reception desk with a lollipop in his mouth and his fedora tipped back on his head. He looked like a young Antonio Banderas playing Kojack.

"What's new?" she asked.

"Let's go across the street to Starbucks and catch up." He smiled. "If Marshal Colt will let you off the leash."

"I'm nobody's poodle." She winked. "More like Pavlov's dog… when it comes to Caramel Macchiatos."

"My treat." He tipped his fedora.

"You're on." She headed for the exit.

On the way to Starbucks, she filled him in on the visit to Mrs. Braugh. "I smelled Dean in Frank's apartment the night he was killed. I think he's the murderer."

"*No me digas.*" Adrián's eyes got wide. "You think the roommate killed Frank? But why?"

"That's what we need to find out."

"How?" Adrián touched his St. Christopher's medal.

"What do you say to a stake out?"

"I'm in." Adrián smiled. "Let's take my Vespa."

"I guess it is stealthier than my ancient Chevy Vega with its broken muffler."

"You couldn't sneak up on a deaf mole rat in that thing."

Adrián laughed. "And I hate to think what would happen if we needed to make a quick get-away."

"Coronel Mustard Vega has his virtues." She said, opening the door to the coffee shop.

"Name one."

Jessica pursed her lips. "My car will never get stolen."

"Too bad for you," he said, following her inside.

They got their to-go coffees and drank them on the way back to headquarters.

A bright red scooter was parked in front of the building. "Wow! Is that your new Vespa?" The Vespa wasn't as badass as Lolita's red Harley Superlow, but it was pretty darn cool.

"*Sí.*" He pulled a key fob from his jeans pocket and headed for the scooter. "Put this on." He grabbed the helmet that was hanging from the handlebars.

"What about you?" She took the helmet.

"I'll be okay." He threw a long leg over the scooter. "Hop on."

She climbed on behind him. Afraid she'd slide off the back, she put her arms around his waist. He turned the key in the ignition and revved the engine.

Weaving in and out of traffic on the tiny scooter was more exhilarating than riding with the marshal. Obviously, Adrián liked going fast. But he wasn't a crazy driver like the marshal, who always drove like she had a death wish.

Jessica shouted to be heard over the street noise as she gave directions.

Fifteen minutes later, they were leaving the city behind and cruising through the suburbs. Another ten minutes, and they'd reached the farms and orchards of Middleton. Instead of entering the long driveway to Braugh's blueberry farm, Adrián took a hiking path through the hardwood forest adjacent to the farm.

Branches wacked her in the face as they slowly bumped their way along the path toward the edge of the blueberry patch. When they reached the edge of the forest, Adrián killed the bike and then hopped off.

"Jump off, and I'll get the binoculars," Adrián said.

She did as she was told.

Adrián opened a compartment under the seat and pulled out field glasses. He aimed them at Mrs. Braugh's farmhouse. "They're on the move!" He handed her the binoculars. "Take a look."

She held the glasses to her eye and adjusted the lens. Sure enough. The back hatch of a black SUV was open. Dean and his goth girlfriend were loading a large flat cardboard box into the car. *Could it be?*

Adrián unwrapped a lollipop and stuck it in his mouth. "Want one?" he whispered.

She shook her head and reached into her pocket, pulled out an open bag of gummy bears, and stuffed a handful in her mouth. She held the bag out to Adrián.

He raised his eyebrows and grabbed a handful. After rewrapping his sucker, he popped the gummies into his mouth. A moment later, he nodded at her. "These are good," he whispered with his mouth full.

She watched as Dean went back inside and then emerged again carrying a smaller rectangle wrapped in paper. "Paintings," she whispered. "They're loading up the paintings." She handed the binoculars back to Adrián.

Her phone buzzed. Her face went hot, and she nearly jumped out of her skin. She pulled the phone from her pocket. *Crapulence.* It was the marshal. *Double crap.* She was supposed to be back at the office doing paperwork. How was she going to explain her field trip with Adrián?

"I think we've found our robbers," Adrián said, sucker back in his mouth and the field glasses glued to his face.

"Hello," Jessica said softly into the phone. "I'm just out getting a coffee," she lied.

"Get me a pop on your way back to the office," the marshal said. "I have some news." She hung up.

Dang. Now what? She grimaced. "I've got to get back to the office."

"Now?" Adrián lowered the binoculars. "We need to move in and catch those thieves red-handed."

"How about you call the marshal and tell her to get out here on the double?" Maybe the marshal would forgive her for disobeying orders when she got out here and saw what was going on.

"*Qué va.*" Adrián scowled. "And give her all the glory. No way." He handed her the field glasses. "Whistle if you see anyone coming." He handed her his lollipop.

"What am I supposed to do with this?" She blinked.

He took off through the weeds toward the edge of the blueberry patch.

Where does he think he's going? She watched in horror as he skirted the blueberry patch and made his way to the front yard. She lifted the binoculars and homed in on Adrián.

He was crouched at the corner of the fence closest to the driveway. She scanned the area. Dean and the goth girlfriend had gone back inside and hadn't come out again yet. Mrs. Braugh was nowhere in sight.

Her heart was pounding as she watched Adrián dash across the gravel and slide to a stop by the side of the SUV. Kneeling by the car, he opened the driver's side door. *What in the world is he doing?* A few seconds later, he shut the car door.

A creaking sound made her jerk the glasses toward the house. *Oh no!* She dropped Adrián's lollipop in the weeds.

Dean opened the front door and stepped out on the porch.

She pursed her lips and blew, but no sound came out. Adrián said to whistle. She couldn't get the sound to come out. *Adrián. No.* She wanted to scream. Her hands were shaking as she held the binoculars to her eyes. Had Adrián heard Dean come out?

Still on his knees, Adrián looked straight at her and gave her a thumbs up. *Crapulence.* He didn't know he was about to be discovered.

Dean stepped off the porch and began walking to the SUV. He was carrying a large package

Adrián please. Get out of there! She tried whistling again. Nothing.

Dean opened the back of the SUV and deposited the package.

Adrián flattened himself against the side of the vehicle. He'd heard. At least, he knew now he was in trouble.

Her eyes stung with fear. *If Dean is the murderer, what will he do when he finds Adrián?* She bit down on her knuckle to keep from screaming.

Dean slammed the hatchback shut and turned on his heels. He'd only taken a couple of steps when he whirled around and marched back to the car.

"Adrián. Watch out." Jessica screamed at the top of her lungs.

Dean stopped in his tracks, shielded his eyes with his hand, and stared in her direction.

Adrián took off sprinting across the field.

"Hey you." Dean shouted, chasing after Adrián. "Stop!"

"Start the engine." Adrián yelled as he raced toward the forest. "Turn it around first."

Jessica stuffed the binoculars in her jacket pocket and jammed the helmet on her head. She kicked at the kick stand, pushed the scooter in a U-turn on the path, and then threw her leg over the bike. She turned the key in the ignition and the scooter roared to life. "Come on Adrián. Hurry!"

Adrián came crashing through the brush and hopped on behind her. "Go! Go! Go!"

She gunned it. White-knuckling the handlebars, she manhandled the scooter as it bounced along the bumpy trail.

"*Vamos!*" Adrián's arms were clamped around her waist. "Faster."

The scooter skidded off the path and onto the county road. As she turned the bike onto the pavement, she saw Dean in the distance barreling through the trees.

She revved the engine and gunned it all the way back to the pavement. The little red scooter charged onto the freeway like an angry bull.

<hr>

Chapter 22

<hr>

Jessica's heart was still pounding as she slid the scooter into the parking lot at headquarters. She couldn't wait to tell the marshal what they'd seen. Then again, how could she tell the marshal without admitting that she'd disobeyed orders and then lied about it?

As soon as she cut the engine, she heard a crackling sound coming from inside Adrián's coat. He jumped off the back and kicked the kickstand.

She removed the helmet and shook out her hair. "What's that noise?"

"Listen." He removed his cell phone from his inside jacket pocket.

A woman and a man were arguing.

"Who are you calling?" she asked.

"Just listen."

The woman accused the man of cheating on her.

Wait. Is that Dean Braugh and his goth girlfriend? "How did you get that?"

"I planted a bug in their car." Adrián smiled.

Another woman's voice, a deeper voice, joined the conversation. "Why are you such a screwup?"

Dang. It's Dean's mom, Mrs. Braugh.

"Whoever tries to hide his sins will not succeed, but the one who confesses his sins and leaves them behind will find mercy."

Dean, quoting the bible again. The background noise indicated they were on the road.

"Your father may have been a womanizer and a drunk," Dean's mother said. "But he was a genius when it came to hijacking museums… not like you."

"We need to go after them." Jessica pleaded. "If they're in their car, then they're getting away."

"Don't worry." Adrián held up his phone. "Once we find the listening device's signal, we'll know which BTS mobile network it is bouncing off of. Then we can track them down."

"We need to tell the marshal." Jessica pulled at his sleeve. He didn't budge. She took off toward the entrance to head-quarters. "Come on."

"Wait." Adrián caught her up and grabbed her elbow. "Shouldn't we find out what they're up to first, so we can give her a full report?"

Jessica gritted her teeth. Maybe he was right. *Crapulence. The Mountain Dew.* The marshal had asked her to bring a pop. "Okay. We'll listen while we get the marshal her soda. But then we have to tell her." *Whatever the consequences.*

Adrián held the phone up between them as they crossed the street to the convenience store on the corner. *Yikes!* Intent on listening, Jessica almost walked into an oncoming car.

"Cora, where are we going?" It was Goth-Girl. Jessica would have recognized her nasal whine anywhere. *We really need to interview Goth-Girl… alone.*

"Now that they've found us, the FBI will be back," Mrs. Braugh said. "Thanks to you two knuckleheads."

"Nothing I do is ever good enough for you," Dean said. "Judge not, that you be not judged—"

"You got caught trying to steal a bible," his mother interrupted. "And then you led the cops to my door."

Honk. Honk. Honk. Horns honked in the background. *Where are they going?*

"We should be following them." Jessica stopped on the sidewalk in front of the store and leaned her head closer to the phone.

"Don't blame me for you past," Dean said. His voice was barely audible above the road noise. Maybe he was sitting in the backseat. "Fathers—or mothers—shall not be put to death because of their children, nor shall children be put to death because of their fathers. Each one shall be put to death for his own sin—"

More bible verses. Deuteronomy, if I'm not mistaken. All those years of Sunday school came in handy.

"I've flown under their radar for twenty years, and you and Miss shit-for-brains go and mess up what should have been a simple robbery." Brakes squealed in the background.

"Whoa," Jessica said. "Did you hear that?"

"What did she mean?" Adrián asked. "She's flown under the radar?"

"I don't know." Jessica patted his arm. "I'll be right back." Stupid Mountain Dew. She headed into the store.

Her boots slid across the polished floor down the aisle to the cold section in the back. She grabbed the biggest bottle of Diet Dew they had and scooted back to the register.

Coming out with the plastic bottle in a paper bag, she felt like a boozehound getting her afternoon fix.

At least she wouldn't arrive empty-handed when she had to tell the marshal that she and Adrián had gone back out to the blueberry farm.

▭

MIERDA. Think fast, hombre. When Jessica gets back, she'll insist we inform Marshal Colt. Colt will get all the credit. I can't let that happen.

Adrián held the phone up to his ear and listened to the robbers arguing.

Even if he ran back across the street and hopped on his scooter, it wouldn't be long before Marshal Colt and Jessica caught up to him.

He needed to be the one to make the arrest. He needed to get the credit. He needed to show his father he wasn't worthless… that he could make it in the FBI. No way he was ever going to work as a cashier in one of his father's crummy supermarkets.

Ay. He glanced around. *I have an idea.* It had worked before. *What do they say in this country? All is fair in love and war.* His relationship with the intrepid Jessica James was a little bit of both. He liked her… a lot. But he wasn't going to let her beat him, especially when his entire future hung in the balance.

He watched the entrance to the convenience store. Jessica wasn't back yet. He still had time.

Still holding the phone and listening to the robbers, he dashed next door to Starbucks. What was it Jessica drank? Some sickeningly sweet American version of a proper coffee. Caramel macchiato?

He ordered the syrupy drink for Jessica and a flat white for himself. Shifting his weight from foot-to-foot, he waited for the barista to call his name.

When she did, he dropped his phone into his pocket, grabbed the coffees, and took them to a little table in a dark corner. He peeled the lid off the macchiato. *Venga! What's with all the whipped cream?*

He dashed back to the counter and grabbed a stir stick… and a couple of packets of sugar for good measure.

Back at the table, he removed a small vial from his inside jacket pocket. He carefully screwed off the top, inserted the stir stick between the edge of the cup and the whipped cream, and then carefully poured in the Rohypnol.

They handicap horse races, don't they? Why should chasing art robbers be any different?

▭

WHEN JESSICA CAME out of the store, Adrián was nowhere to be seen. *Where the heck is he?* She was just about to cross the street when he came up behind her.

"Hey. Wait for me." Adrián was holding two Starbucks coffees. "I got you a caramel macchiato." He held out one of the cups.

"I don't usually drink caffeine so late in the day," she said, taking the cup. "But thanks."

"It's going to be a long day," he said. "Better fuel up for the chase."

She took a sip and winced. "Needs more sugar."

"Here." He handed her a packet of sugar.

She tucked the can of Dew under her arm and then ripped the packet open with her teeth, popped off the Starbucks lid, and poured it in. "What did I miss?"

"Miss?" Adrián looked like he'd been caught with his hand in the cookie jar.

"Dean Braugh and company. What did they say?" The light changed and she stepped into the crosswalk. "Where are they going?"

"Let's find a place to sit and finish our coffees while I tell you."

She gave him the side-eye. "We should go up and tell the marshal… after I give her the Dew."

"Wouldn't it be best to have our story straight before we talk to Marshal Colt?"

"Maybe you're right." It was going to be tricky to explain everything to the marshal. She stepped up on the curb.

"Where can we sit?" She glanced around the headquarters entrance and the parking lot.

"How about your car?" Adrián strode around the side of the building.

"Okay. Why not?" She followed him to the side lot and then to her car. *How does he know where I parked? Granted, it's the most beat-up car in the lot.*

Her car was so worthless she didn't even bother locking it. She set the Dew and the coffee on the hood, opened the driver's side door, and then fetched the drinks again, and climbed inside.

Adrián got in the passenger side. After settling in, he pulled out his phone and they continued eavesdropping.

"Did the FBI give you those listening devices?" she asked. Why didn't she get any cool gadgets?

"I bought them on E-bay." He sipped his coffee.

"Is this even legal?" Without thinking, she stuck the key in the ignition.

"You want to catch the bad guys, don't you?"

"Yeah. But I don't want to *become* the bad guys."

"What's that supposed to mean?" he asked, narrowing his brows.

"I'm all for bending the rules if the system is broken, but we can't start acting like the criminals." She thought of Jack, her Chicago boyfriend, who'd gone to prison for freeing the lab animals. It was her fault. She'd cried her eyes out over the lab chimps.

"In this case, the end justifies the means." He unwrapped a *Chupa Chups*. "Want one?"

She shook her head. "You might just be screwing up the end if the case is thrown out because you collected evidence illegally."

"Is your coffee sweet enough now?" Adrián asked, obviously changing the subject.

She took a drink and nodded.

He smiled and fiddled with his St. Christopher's Medal.

"I should probably get upstairs before the marshal comes looking for me." She blew at her bangs.

"Listen." Adrián held the phone up.

"If only you were more like your father." Mrs. Braugh was berating Dean again. "He may have been a lousy husband, but he was a great thief. God rest his soul."

"Did she just say thief?" Jessica's mouth fell open. "Holy crap. Could she mean—" All the excitement was making her head spin. She took another sip of the sweet coffee.

Suddenly, she was feeling weird and sleepy. Maybe Adrián was right. She needed more caffeine. She took another slug of macchiato. It didn't help. She gripped the steering wheel.

"Are you okay?" Adrián asked. "You look sleepy."

"Not really," she whispered. *What's happening to me?* She slumped over the wheel, and everything went black.

ADRIÁN GRABBED the keys out of the ignition. "Why don't you take a nap?" He gently pried her off the steering wheel and laid her back in the seat. "It's okay. I can go back out to the blueberry farm on my own."

He found a pen in the cupholder and wrote a quick note on the back of a folded piece of paper that he found in his pants pocket. "I'll be back soon. Don't worry." He dropped a *Chupa Chups* in her pocket along with the note.

After collecting the two incriminating coffee cups, he climbed out of the car. He pressed the button to lock all the doors and shut the passenger door, careful not to wake Jessica.

She was out like a light. He'd given her a few extra drops. Just enough so she wouldn't wake up for hours. Enough time for him to find Dean Braugh and company, recover the paintings, and make the arrests.

He strode over to the trash can near the building entrance

and dropped the cups inside. He glanced back at the beat-up Vega. "Sweet dreams, dear Jessica."

He held his phone to his ear. Nothing. The robbers had obviously arrived at their destination and gotten out of the car. *Where are they now?*

He followed the instructions he'd gotten with the listening device. It worked. He'd triangulated the BTS area where the car had to be parked.

Interesting. They hadn't gone far. In fact, it looked like they were back at the blueberry farm.

His phone buzzed. A text from Stevenson. The results had come back from the forensics report on the fibers he'd collected from Vanderbilt's closet. That would have to wait.

Adrián hopped on his scooter and sped out of the parking lot. Away from FBI headquarters. Away from the meddlesome Marshal Colt. Away from the invincible Jessica James.

Chapter 23

Lexi glanced at her phone. *After four in the afternoon.* The cowgirl should have been back hours ago. *Where the hell is she?*

Dammit. Lexi slammed her computer shut. She needed to get home and pick up the baby from Mrs. Faheem's before her husband got home from work.

Maybe Lexi had been too hard on the cowgirl, and she'd skedaddled. *Nah.*

Maybe she hadn't been hard enough. First, Jessica had used baby Sammy as a prop to interview a murderer and now she'd gone AWOL. The cowgirl didn't have much of a future in art crimes if she kept this up.

She tapped her phone. No answer. *What is that cowgirl up to now?* Lexi had to admit, the cowgirl was clever. But it took more than book smarts to be a good detective.

Guts and glory. No glory without guts. That's what Sargent Durbin used to say as he grabbed his crotch. *And no guts without a bigass gun.* His wasn't as big as he thought it was. The dirtbag. Her palms were sweating, and a wave of nausea made her grab the edge of her desk.

When it subsided, she reached into her purse and took out the pill bottle. She shook out a yellow tablet directly into her mouth and bit down. The bitter taste made her cringe. But eventually it would help chase away the ghosts.

She shook her head hard as if she could shake the army out of her mind. If only it were that easy. The army shrink had told her it would take time. *How much time for cripes sake?* She'd been out for over five years now and still had flashbacks.

She took a deep breath and tried the cowgirl's number one more time. Still no answer. *Where is she?*

Dammit. She punched Stevenson's number.

"Stevenson." Just the sound of his voice turned her stomach.

"Where's your boy, Garcia?" she asked, skipping any pleasantries.

"No clue."

She heard laughing and music in the background. "Where are you?"

"Following a lead in the Bahamas."

She rolled her eyes. "Figures."

"I'll have you know that I found the former museum direc-tor, Jim Johnston." Stevenson scoffed. "He wasn't behind the robbery, but let's just say, he made off with the museum's cashdrawer."

"If you hear from Garcia, have him call me." She hung up.

Time to go home. She'd deal with the renegade cowgirl tomorrow.

Lexi packed up her purse, slung it over her shoulder, and headed out. She hit the light switch and locked the office door. If the cowgirl did come back, she'd be locked out. Too bad for her.

Lexi stepped out of headquarters into long shadows and a warm breeze. Her heels clacked on the concrete as she walked to the parking lot. Once she reached the asphalt, she had to concentrate on the uneven surface to keep from twisting her ankle. Heels weren't practical, but they made her feel powerful. Just the sound they made announcing her arrival gave her courage.

In the distance, two dark figures stood peering into a car. She walked toward them to investigate. Folks loitering in the FBI parking lot must be up to no good.

She squinted as a defense against the ball of sun low in the sky and shielded her eyes with one hand.

Good grief. She recognized the two. They were the cowgirl's friends from Chicago. The same friends she'd met in Wyoming. The ones who'd ambushed her in a freezing parking lot and left her for dead. The gun happy gangster and that poker hostess chick.

Lexi picked up her pace. "Hey! What are you doing?"

They were next to the cowgirl's broken-down Chevy.

"Marshal Ava Gardner." The poker chick's long, shiny black hair blew in the breeze. She was holding a motorcycle helmet.

Who is Ava Gardner? Lexi wasn't even going to ask.

"I'm Lolita Durchenko. Good to see you again." Dressed in black leather from head to toe, she looked like a whip flexed to crack.

"The feeling is not mutual." Lexi approached the car. "What's going on?"

"Our Montana friend is dead to the world." Lolita pointed at the car with her helmet. "You've been working her too hard." She smiled.

Lexi glanced in the car and then narrowed her brows. *What the—*

"I think she *is* dead." The skinny gangster dropped his cigarette and ground it out under his alligator lace-up. "She sold the ranch."

"Bought the farm," the Russian chick corrected. She turned back to Lexi. "You remember my cousin, Vanya?"

"Nothing like being coldcocked to imprint a memory." Lexi touched the back of her head.

"Sorry about that." Vanya shifted his weight from foot to foot like he had to pee. "I thought you was hurting Miss Jesse." He nodded toward the car.

"Speaking of…" Lexi stepped in front of the Russians and rapped on the driver's side window. No response. She leaned her forehead against the glass.

The cowgirl was sprawled across the front seat like a passed out drunk.

"Something's not right here." Lexi tried the door handle. "It's locked."

"She's as comfortable as an insect in a carpet." When Vanya grinned, his gold grill reflected the setting sun.

"Snug as a bug in a rug," the chick said under her breath. "Strange. She never locks her car." She handed her helmet to her gangster cousin. "Enough of this chit-chat." She tapped on Lexi's shoulder. "Excuse me please."

Instinctively, Lexi stepped aside.

Lolita reared back and slammed her boot into the window.

Good Lord. The whip had cracked. The Russian broke the window with one kick. "Was that really necessary?" Lexi pulled a Slim-Jim out of her purse and held it up. "I could have opened the door."

"My friend may be hurt." The poker chick reached inside the car through the broken backseat window. "Every second counts."

This chick is crazy.

"I wouldn't want to meet that foot in a dark alley." Vanya chuckled. "As deadly as she is beautiful."

The sleeve of the Russian chick's motorcycle jacket caught on a shard of glass, and she punched her way through. She pulled up the lock and opened the driver's side door. Gently, she straightened the cowgirl in the seat and said something to her in Russian.

"That's no normal nap," Lexi said. "Move aside."

"Whatever you say, Marshal Colt." The Russian chick slid out of the way.

Good God, please don't let her be dead. Lexi's heart was racing as fast as a Kentucky thoroughbred as she felt for the cowgirl's pulse. "Thank the Lord." The pulse was weak, but it was there.

"She's alive." Lexi dropped her purse by the car and then put her face close to Jessica's and sniffed.

"Awake sleeping beauty with a kiss?" Vanya asked in between puffs on his cigarette.

"She doesn't smell of alcohol." Lexi slapped the cowgirl lightly on the cheek. "Come on. Wake up." She may not have been drunk, but she was definitely on something… either that or she was sick… or maybe in a coma. *Why would she be in a coma?* "Is she diabetic?"

Lexi noticed the green bottle poking out of a paper sack in the cupholder. "She got my pop." She grabbed the Dew. *Just when the cowgirl was starting to grow on me…*

"My Montana friend is healthy as a horse," Lolita said. "But she does have a penchant for strong whiskey and weak men."

"It's not whiskey." If it were, Lexi would smell it. "And there aren't any men." *Wait a second.* An orange wrapper caught her eye. She pushed the button to unlock all the doors. "Keep trying to wake her up." She jogged around the car to the passenger side, opened the door, and knelt next to the car.

Aha! Lexi picked up the colorful lollipop wrapper. *Adrián.* She glanced over at Jessica. *What has he done to you?*

"Call 911." She barked. "Now."

The gangster cousin smiled. "No cops."

"I'm a cop," she said, cracking open the Dew.

The poker chick tapped her phone. "I'll call."

Lexi took a big swig of pop, paper sack and all. She climbed into the passenger seat and took Jessica's hand.

Come on, cowgirl. Don't die on me.

<hr>

Chapter 24

<hr>

Where am I? Jessica's head felt like a pine knot thrown into a bonfire. She opened her eyes a crack. That was as far as they'd go.

The room was spinning. She squeezed her eyes tight and held onto the bedframe. *Whose bed?*

The smell of chemicals mixed with the scent of jasmine. *Lolita?* Her best friend wore jasmine perfume. She had to be hallucinating. When she tried to move her head, a wave of nausea forced her back into the darkness.

"What happened?" she whispered, tears forming in the corners of her eyes. The last thing she remembered was talking to Adrián... they were working on a case together. "What's happening to me?" she asked the universe.

"Your asshole Spanish friend drugged you." A familiar voice came out of the darkness.

What the... "Lolita?" Jessica's eyes flew open. A slim, dark figure moved closer and took her hand. "Lolita? Is that you?" She felt Lolita's long fingernails resting against the back of her hand.

"Yes, my Montana friend." Lolita stroked her head. "It's me. How do you feel?"

She gazed up at her friend. "Like I've been run over by a logging truck." Jessica forced a smile. Her friend's face was a welcome sight. She fought back tears… tears of joy mingled with tears of fear.

"This is what happens when I'm not around." Lolita brushed a lock of hair off Jessica's face. "If I find that Adrián guy, I'm going to kick his ass."

"Why?" Jessica blinked hard, trying to clear her vision. "Where is Adrián? We were working together—"

"I'm with Marshal Hottie on this one." Lolita squeezed her hand. "That dude is bad news."

"Bad news." A deep voice echoed from the corner of the room.

"Vanya?"

"In the skin." Vanya chuckled. When he moved closer, Jessica smelled stale cigarettes.

"Flesh," Lolita corrected.

"What's the difference?" Vanya asked.

"Flesh is thicker," Jessica said. *The thickness of the world.*

"Skin plus meat equals flesh," Lolita said.

"Disgusting." Vanya sniffed.

The screeching of metal on metal made Jessica jerk her head. *Ouch!*

Someone pulled back the curtain… *hospital curtain.*

"Why am I in the hospital?" she asked. The room was coming into view. A table with a pink plastic water pitcher, an old, boxy television hanging from the ceiling, an IV pole attached to her left arm.

"Sorry to interrupt this touching reunion," the marshal said, and marched into the room. She was carrying baby Sammy and had Camo in tow. "I need to ask my partner some questions." The marshal came to the bedside. "If you're up to it."

She called me, partner. It hurt to smile. Jessica nodded. "Okay."

Vanya sauntered across the room to pet Camo. "Nice doggie."

"Don't touch him," the marshal barked. "He's working."

"You think we've got a bomb?" Vanya asked.

"He's not a bomb sniffer," Jessica said. "He's a thera—"

The marshal's stern look stopped her from finishing the sentence.

"I need to talk to Jessica." The marshal glared at Vanya. "In private."

"Let's go get the Presidential Suite ready," Lolita said, letting go of Jessica's hand. "We'll be back in a few hours." She bent down and kissed Jessica's cheek.

"Presidential Suite?" Jessica asked. "You're not—"

"Yes, darling. I am," Lolita purred. "I'm hosting a poker game for some Harvard boys." She smiled. "The Charles Hotel. Saturday night. Ten pm. You should come clean their clocks."

"Why would college dudes need their watches cleaned?" Vanya asked.

Lolita ignored him. "I know you spent all your winnings from the last game on that trip to Italy." She zipped up her leather jacket. "Wouldn't it be fun to show those stuck-up Harvard boys a thing or two?"

Jessica had to admit, cleaning out a bunch of Harvard boys would be fun. *But just because you're good at something doesn't mean you should do it.* "I don't know…"

"You've got a couple of days to think about it." Lolita grabbed her helmet from the window ledge and strapped it on.

Jessica shrugged. *Ouch.* Everything hurt.

"In the meantime, I'm going looking for the dude that did this to you." Lolita had that feminist avenger glint in her sage-green eyes.

"What did he do to me?" Jessica grimaced. Adrián didn't assault her, did he?

"Marshal Colt will fill you in." Lolita headed for the door. "We leave you in her capable hands." She motioned for Vanya to join her. "See you later, *Milaya.*"

At the door, Lolita turned back. "As your mother says, be good. And if you can't be good, be careful." She blew Jessica a kiss.

"Be good and careful," Vanya said, his Italian lace-ups tapping across the polished floor as he followed Lolita out into the hallway.

After her friends had left, Jessica reached for the plastic cup on the side table. Her hand was shaking. She took a sip from the straw and then winced. *Orange juice.* The bittersweet taste surprised her.

"Where did you find those two?" the marshal asked, taking a seat in the chair next to the bed. Camo sat at attention on the floor next to her. "Boris and Natasha." The marshal dropped the monster diaper bag on the floor.

Jessica laughed. *Ouch.* Her head felt like it could explode. *Note to self. Don't laugh.* "Why am I in the hospital? What happened?"

"What's the last thing you remember?"

"Adrián…" *The marshal isn't going to like this.* "Ah, Adrián and I were discussing the case." Jessica fiddled with the hem of the hospital blanket.

The marshal scowled. "Did you eat or drink anything?"

Jessica squinted at her. "Why?"

"What did Adrián give you to drink?" When the marshal bounced Sammy on her knee, the baby cooed.

"Starbucks coffee." Jessica stared down at her hands and then glanced up at the marshal. "So what?"

"You had Rohypnol in your bloodstream." The marshal's piercing glare forced Jessica to avert her gaze again.

"Are you saying that Adrián slipped me a Mickey?" She shook her head. "No way. Why would he?"

"No sign of sexual assault, though." Now the marshal averted her gaze. "You tell me. Why would Adrián want you out of the way?"

She shook her head. "I don't know."

"Are you blind in one eye and can't see out of the other?" The marshal sighed. "Adrián Garcia is competitive to a fault. He wants to win at all costs, even if it means cheating."

The end justifies the means. Adrián's words echoed through her head. But would he drug her just to take credit for solving the case? No. They were working together. They were a team. Just like in Italy.

Wait a second… Just like in Italy. The grappa. She'd passed out after drinking a grappa Adrián bought for her. And it was on the day the final assignment was due. That's why she turned the assignment in late and was bumped from the internship program. If that witchy French curator hadn't been hit by a scooter… *Holy crap!* Did Adrián do that too?

Her head was spinning. No. It was just a coincidence that she'd passed out at the very moment when they were supposed to turn in the final assignment of the art crimes course. Right? It had to be.

"Unless," she whispered to herself. "Adrián drugged me… *Twice.*"

"If your Chicago buddies hadn't found you, who knows what might have happened." The marshal patted Camo on the head. The dog had been frantically licking her hand. The marshal seemed as cool as a cucumber. But Camo obviously thought otherwise. And he should know. He was a trained therapy dog.

"What?" Jessica shook her head. *Ouch!* She put her hands to her temples. Whatever he'd slipped her, it had a terrible kick.

Camo put his paws on the arm of the chair and licked her face.

Wow. The marshal must really be in bad shape if the therapy dog is going for the face.

"Adrián Garcia is guilty of attempted murder." The marshal held her hand up to guard against Camo's kisses. She whispered to the dog. "I'm okay. Chill out."

"I don't think he was trying to kill me." Jessica bit her lip. *Was he?* No way. Adrián wasn't a murderer. The idea was too far-fetched. "He's one of the good guys."

"You'd be surprised how many of the *good guys* are rotten to the core." The marshal made air quotes around "good guys" and added, "Especially when it comes to women."

"That's true." Jessica didn't know why it always surprised her when good people went bad. She always hoped for the best. But she should know better, especially when it came to men.

After five years in a Ph.D. program where she was known by her male professors as the "pasty-faced, dumb blonde" she should have no doubts about misogyny's reach… every freaking corner. "Our whole culture is marinated in sexism."

"Not all men are bad." The marshal bristled.

"I'm not saying they are." Jessica opened her palms to concede the point. "But none of us escape the ideology of our culture."

"The idea-what?" The marshal squinted at her. "No need to impress me with ten-dollar words." She sniffed. "I need to call Stevenson and tell him to call off his dog."

"If Adrián really did drug me, what makes you think Stevenson can control him?" *And what if Adrián is a murderer?* She shuddered. "How much Rohypnol did he give me?"

"Enough." The marshal stood up and tucked Sammy back into the baby sling. "I'll just have to go after the Spanish bastard myself."

"I'm going with you." Jessica sat up in bed. A wave of nausea knocked her back down.

"You're not going anywhere except back to sleep." The marshal's tone reminded her of her mother.

Jessica cringed. What would her mother say about her ending up in the hospital and almost getting killed? She would insist Jessica come back to Whitefish and get a job slinging burgers or dipping soft serve. She shuddered at the thought.

"I'm coming with you," Jessica repeated. She forced herself upright. "I know where to find Adrián." Actually, she didn't have a clue where to find him. She fell back against the pillow. *Where would he be now?* She tried to remember what he'd said before she blacked out. "How long have I been out?"

The marshal reached into an outside pocket of the diaper bag and pulled out her cell. "I found you just after four… and it's almost seven-thirty now."

"Over three hours!" Adrián could be anywhere by now. *Think, Jesse, think.* She closed her eyes. What were they talking about when she blacked out? *Crapulence.* The whole afternoon was a black hole.

"You rest, and I'll come back tomorrow morning, and then we can go looking for Adrián." The marshal slung the diaper bag over one shoulder. "He must have learned something important or found the vital clue. Otherwise, why drug you now?"

"I can't remember." Jessica covered her face with her hands. "I'm sorry."

"Give yourself a break." The marshal shifted the diaper bag. "You're too hard on yourself."

Baby Sammy squealed as if in agreement.

"You're a fine one to talk." Jessica pulled the blanket up to her chin. "Do you ever let anyone penetrate that hard outer shell of yours?"

The marshal frowned. "Doc says you can go home tomorrow. I'll come pick you up." The marshal started for the door.

"Wait." Jessica didn't feel like being alone. "Didn't you say you had some news?" She had a vague memory of the marshal mentioning news last time she talked to her on the phone.

"You need to rest," the marshal said. "I'll tell you tomorrow."

"Please tell me now." Jessica's eyes stung. "Please, don't go."

The marshal sighed. "Okay." She dropped the diaper bag on the floor next to the chair and plopped down. "But then I've got to get the baby home."

"Thanks." Jessica smiled. She wished the baby could stay with her in the hospital bed. Or maybe Camo. She could use a good cuddle. Camo clearly having sensed her distress, came to the side of the bed, and licked her hand. She patted his head. "Good boy."

"The toxicology report came back on Frank Motton."

Jessica sat at attention.

"There were no traces of heroin. Some THC from marijuana, along with toxic levels of Formalin."

"Formalin?" Jessica squinted. "What's that?"

"Formaldehyde, glutaraldehyde, and methanol." The marshal raised her eyebrows. "Embalming fluid."

"Dean Braugh!" When Jessica waved her hand, she nearly ripped out the IV. *Ouch.* She rubbed her arm. "He's a mortician. You've got to arrest him."

"I sent officers to his apartment *and* out to the blueberry farm." The marshal tilted her head and smiled. "They should be making the arrest at this very minute."

The diaper bag chimed. The marshal dug her phone out of a side pocket. "Now what?" She tapped the phone. "Marshal Colt." Her face reddened. "Well, find him!" Her eyes were shooting daggers.

"What happened?"

"No one was at the apartment or the farm." The marshal slumped in the chair. "Our visit to the farm tipped them off." She sighed. "Dean and his mother are on the lam."

"Where would they go?" Jessica's pulse quickened. It was her fault they'd lost them. She should have called the marshal instead of going off with Adrián. If only she could remember…

"Good question."

"Maybe, if you find Adrián, you'll find the Braughs." Jessica thought for a minute. "You can triangulate his cell phone."

"Good idea."

She had to try calling Adrián. *Where's my phone?* She scanned the room. *Darn. My backpack.* It must still be in my car. "Can you fetch my backpack from my car and bring it to me?" *And my jacket. Where's my jacket?*

The marshal got up and went to the closet. "It's here." She lugged the backpack across the room and sat it on the edge of the bed.

"My phone is in my jacket pocket."

The marshal went back and fetched the phone.

Jessica tapped the phone and called Adrián. No answer. "He must have gone after them, right?"

Holy crap. Memories came flooding back to her. *The blueberry farm. Adrián's scooter. The quick getaway. The marshal's diet Dew.*

Jessica remembered bits and pieces. *Whoa. The listening device.* If only she could remember what she'd heard… and seen. Unfortunately, most of the afternoon was still a blur.

The marshal's phone buzzed again.

"Good grief." She pulled the phone back out of the diaper bag. "Colt here." She glanced over at Jessica. "Okay."

Her sour look told Jessica it wasn't good news.

"We'll let you know if we find him." She stuffed the phone back into the outer pocket. "Stevenson says Adrián didn't check in like he usually does."

"Maybe he's in trouble." Jessica grimaced.

"He's in trouble alright." The marshal yanked the diaper

bag off the floor and marched out of the room without another word.

"Wait," Jessica called after her. "You're coming back first thing tomorrow, right?"

She called Adrián again. It went straight to voicemail. *Come on, Adrián, answer.* Where could he be?

Chapter 25

Jessica knew she should be resting, but instead she was wracking her brain for answers. With the flashing lights in the hallway, IVs beeping up and down the hospital floor, and nurses coming in every few hours to take her temperature, it wasn't like she could sleep even if she wanted to.

She grabbed her phone from the bed table and tried Adrián again. When it went to voicemail, this time she left a message. "Where are you? What did you do to me?" She hung up.

She'd been calling him every half hour since the marshal left. If he did drug her, no wonder he wasn't answering her calls.

Thank you, marshal. She smiled over at the military surplus backpack sitting in the chair next to the bed.

Jessica padded over to the chair, pulled out her computer, and then climbed back into bed. Since she couldn't sleep, she might as well do something useful.

If only she could remember what she'd heard on Adrián's listening device. Yes, it must have been something important for him to go to all the trouble of drugging her.

She opened the computer and set it on the bed table.

Maybe if she reviewed her notes on the case, it would jog her memory. She opened the folder called Albertine Carpenter Heist. Inside, she had a file for each suspect.

Edward Dean Braugh was at the top of the list. He was certainly their best suspect in the murder of Frank Motton, especially since that toxicology report came in. But was he clever enough to have planned the heist? He was in jail when it took place, so he couldn't have pulled it off himself. Maybe Goth-Girl helped him.

Dean had bungled the attempt to steal the Guttenberg Bible from the Harvard library. And he seemed a little wacko. Maybe his motive for killing Frank had nothing to do with the museum. Maybe it was a crime of passion. Maybe they were fighting over Goth-Girl.

That would be a weird love-triangle. She smiled to herself.

Jessica's hands flew over the keys as she typed up her theories, such as they were.

She couldn't rule out the Dr. No suspect, Rocky Vanderbilt. He was a tricky one to figure out. His demeanor was smooth and practiced. But behind the façade, something else was going on. *Something sinister?*

Her gut told her she hadn't dug deep enough. She did yet another google search on Rockefeller Vanderbilt.

There were lots of pictures of Vanderbilt at various balls, galas, and benefits. He favored costume balls. She laughed out loud at a picture of Vanderbilt dressed as a cowboy. With his long rider's jacket, pearl studded string-tie, and dust-free, black hat, he didn't look like any other cowboy she'd ever met. She scrolled through headlines like "Boston's Best Catch," and "Girls He's Still Single."

She kept digging. "Wealthy Philanthropist Donates to Local Museum," "Rocky Times for Rocky Vanderbilt," and "Boys, He's Still Single" with a picture of Vanderbilt at Freddie's Toolbox, a local gay bar.

Interesting. Why was Rocky having rocky times? She read on.

Holy Cow. Vanderbilt had a lot of money invested in some hedge fund that bet against GameStop when those nerdy game boys gamed the stock market and GameStop stock went through the roof a few months ago. A margin-call nearly bankrupted him. *Wow. So, Vanderbilt needs money.*

She'd found another motive. In addition to being an art collector, he had a financial motive for knocking off the museum. She went back and read the article on his donation to a local museum. *Could it be? Did he donate to the Albertina?* No. Turned out a friend of his had a foundation, The Carlyle Foundation, which loaned a few paintings to the Albertina. Vanderbilt just posed for the photo-op.

Wait. OMG. One of those paintings was the Rembrandt. *Weird coincidence? Or something more?* Jessica's fingers flew across the keys as she made more notes.

Rockefeller Vanderbilt was quickly moving up the suspect list. He was definitely powerful and rich enough to have Eggs Benedict murdered in prison. *But why? Did Eggs know too much? Was Eggs about to spill the beans?*

Eggs Benedict and Frank Motton were both dead. Which meant they both must have been involved in the robbery, but maybe not the masterminds.

No way that stoner Frank could have been the mastermind. But he could have facilitated the robbery. He was on duty at the museum, and he did open that side door, and he did let the robber or robbers in. He was also mighty nervous when she interviewed him… just before he was murdered. Injected with a syringe of embalming fluid. What a terrible way to go. Poor guy.

Where did Tick Tock Tommaso and his lawyer Santo Romano fit in? Neither was an upstanding citizen. Tick Tock was in prison. But he could have had his guys pull off the heist. *Heck.* Santo Romano could have helped him. Or maybe they were innocent… okay, not innocent, but not the robbers either.

Jessica took a drink from the pink sippy cup sitting next to her computer.

The squeak of the curtain announced the night nurse's arrival. "Hey, girl. Why you still awake?" The full-bodied nurse was wearing baby blue scrubs with cartoon kittens and puppies playing. The childish pattern, along with her spikey, burgundy hair and nose ring, transformed the nurse into an anime cartoon character.

"I couldn't sleep." Jessica opened her mouth for the thermometer and waited for the cuff to tighten around her upper arm.

"Nothing like sleeping in your own bed." The nurse went about her business. "Ugg. I can't wait to get home to mine."

"Me too." Forget about bed. Jessica was chomping at the bit to get out of the hospital and back on the case.

"Get some sleep, Sweets." The punk-kitty nurse disappeared back behind the curtain.

Fat chance of that.

Jessica went back to her computer. *Wait. Speaking of punk… I wonder what I can find out about Goth-Girl.* Jessica googled the homepage of Middlestate Mortuary College.

Her eyes got heavy as she scrolled through page-after-page describing courses in Embalming Theory and Practice, Funeral Directing, Methods of Disposition—*I hate to think—* and Restorative Art… Definitely not the type of restorative art she studied at the Center for Russian Art and Culture.

Young faces smiled at her from the screen. Mostly men, but a few women too. Those future morticians looked happy. Her finger froze on the mouse.

Blue-streaked hair caught her attention. *Goth-Girl.* There she was, *sans* baby bump, wearing goggles and peering down at a table just out of the frame.

Jessica was getting close. She could feel it. Her fingers

tingled. A slug of orange juice revived her and gave her sustenance for the search. She dug deeper into the bowels of the Middlestate Mortuary College website.

Holy moly. Goth-Girl was valedictorian of her class. There she was in all her gothy glory accepting a plaque from some pasty dude in a suit. Gloria Sallow. *Now we're getting somewhere.* Jessica typed Gloria Sallow into her notes on the case.

The sound of metal on metal made her look up. Was the nurse back already?

The sky outside her window had gone from blue-black to burnt orange. *What the heck time is it? Have I been awake all night?*

The curtain opened, and the marshal appeared.

"You're back already?" Jessica shut her computer.

"It's nearly six." The marshal came in and plopped into the chair.

"Where are Sammy and Camo?"

"Sammy is with Mrs. Faheem. Camo is in the car."

"Are you here to spring me?" She smiled.

"As a matter of fact…" The marshal pulled a folded yellow paper from her purse. "Yes." She unfolded the paper and held it out. "I got a search warrant for the blueberry farm."

"Right on." Jessica threw back the blanket and swung her legs over the side of the bed. Wearing nothing but a hospital gown and little hospital booties, she padded across the room to the closet.

"What do you think you're doing?" the marshal asked.

"I'm going with you to search the farm." She grabbed the plastic bag from the bottom of the closet, yanked it open, and pulled out her jeans.

"You need to rest." The marshal gathered up her purse.

"We don't have time to spare. We've got to find the paintings… and Dean while his trail is hot."

She slipped her feet—booties and all—into her cowboy boots. She glanced back at the marshal, and then ripped off the hospital gown, yanked on her undershirt T-shirt and threw her fringe jacket on over it.

She smiled. "I'm back in the saddle."

▭

ON THE WAY to the blueberry farm, Jessica briefed the marshal on Goth-Girl aka Gloria Sallow and on Vanderbilt's financial situation.

"Interesting. Vanderbilt has an added motive," the marshal said. She kept her eyes on the road… which was a good thing because she was driving like a bat out of hell. "What time is it? I don't want to get into rush hour traffic."

Jessica reached in her jacket pocket for her phone. *What's this?* She pulled out a *Chupa Chups. Wait.* A piece of folded paper. She slid the paper out of her pocket. A note from Adrián. *Wow.* He had a lot of nerve.

She unwrapped the sucker and popped it into her mouth. Not quite banana nut pancakes and witch's brew tea from the Blind Faith Café, but it would have to do.

"What's that?" the marshal asked.

"A note from Adrián." Jessica unfolded the paper. "Says he's going out to the blueberry farm, but he'll be back soon." She chuckled. "Yeah, right."

The marshal glanced over at her. "What's on the back? Looks like a forensics requisition."

Jessica turned the paper over. *Whoa.* "It's a requisition for some fibers found at Rocky Vanderbilt's house in a closet."

"What fibers? Why didn't we know about these fibers?"

A weird idea popped into Jessica's head. "Do you think Adrián could be in cahoots with the robbers?"

"Anything is possible." The marshal shook her head. "I told you he was bad news."

"*I told you so* isn't your best look." Jessica gave the marshal the side-eye… not that the marshal noticed. She was too busy white-knuckling the steering wheel.

"Call the lab and find out if they have the report on those fibers."

"Yes, boss." Jessica examined the piece of paper. *Aha.* The lab's number was at the top. She tapped the number into her phone. *Dang.* "It's a recording. They're not open yet."

"Of course, they aren't." The marshal took out her frustrations on the accelerator as the Charger flew onto the freeway.

Camo whimpered from the backseat. Even the dog was nervous.

"We should talk to the head of the Carlyle Foundation," Jessica said. "They own the Rembrandt that was stolen. It was only on loan to the museum."

"Why am I just finding this out now?" The marshal didn't sound happy. Then again, she never did.

"No one has interviewed them yet?" Jessica twisted a piece of fringe around her finger. "FBI oversight?" Or had Adrián already interviewed them and just not bothered to tell anyone?

"You think?"

The marshal was in a foul mood this morning. Had baby Sammy barfed on the lapel of her navy blazer again? Jessica smiled to herself. "I'll make an appointment with the director of the Carlyle Foundation after we search the farm."

The marshal glanced over at her. Her eyes were bloodshot, and she looked like she hadn't slept in a week. Jessica knew full well that the marshal was living on Mountain Dew and Snickers Bars. She was probably seriously deficient in every vitamin and mineral in existence—except for sugar and yellow-dye-number-five.

Jessica tapped her phone again. "I'd do it now, but it's freaking six-thirty in the morning."

The marshal nodded. "I just don't like being out of the loop."

That's because you're a control freak. Jessica bit her tongue.

"Not telling me is dangerous, and it's wrong," the marshal said, as if reading Jessica's mind.

The Charger chewed up the gravel on the county road into the blueberry farm.

The scenery jogged Jessica's memory. "Over there." She pointed to the path she and Adrián had taken yesterday.

OMG. She remembered now. They'd parked the scooter on the edge of the forest and watched as Dean loaded what looked like paintings into a black SUV. "Look. It's Adrián's scooter." She could just see a flash of red through the trees.

The marshal swerved onto the shoulder and stopped the car. "Let's go see if he's with it, shall we?" She hopped out of the car, tugged on the hem of her blazer, and then took off.

Jessica followed her into the forest and down the path. The scooter was lying on its side. Adrián was nowhere in sight. When they got closer, Jessica saw the pile of *Chupa Chups* wrappers. "He must have been staked out here for a while."

"So where is he now?" the marshal asked. "My guys were here last night and didn't see anyone."

"Maybe he followed Dean and his mom?" Jessica shrugged.

"On foot?" The marshal shook her head. "I don't think so."

Unless he's in on it. Jessica pushed the thought from her head. *Anyway, why would Adrián steal paintings?* He studied art crimes so he could join the international art crimes force, or the FBI, or the Spanish equivalent of the FBI. *Unless… he studied art crimes to learn how to commit them. Yikes.* "Maybe he's still around some place."

"Maybe." The marshal turned on her heels and headed back toward the car. "Dead or alive, that's the question."

Crapulence. Jessica hadn't thought of that. What if Dean had killed Adrián too? She shuddered. Even if Adrián had drugged her drink—twice—she didn't wish him dead…

murdered. She cringed. If anyone was going to kill Adrián, it had better be her. "Let's look in the house."

"Yup."

LEXI KNOCKED ON THE DOOR. "Hello. Anyone home?"

No answer.

"FBI. Open up." Lexi yelled.

Still no answer.

The cowgirl tried the doorknob. "It's locked."

"I'll fix that." Lexi marched back to the Charger and returned with a lockpick set. With a few deft moves, she picked the lock and the door popped open. "FBI," she shouted. "Anyone here?"

No answer.

"You stay here." With gun in hand, Lexi moved slowly through the house.

Inside, the old farmhouse was as tidy and neat as it was outside. With its Craftsman cupboards and wide-plank floors, it looked like something out of *Town & Country Magazine*. The fresh sunflowers in a big, bright blue vase on the rough-hewn dining room table completed the picture. Lexi approved.

The master bedroom was as tidy as the rest of the house. Only one back bedroom showed signs of occupancy. Clothes were strewn across the floor. Posters of grunge bands adorned the walls. Lexi shook her head. No doubt that was Dean's room.

After checking the bathrooms and closets, Lexi returned to the entrance. "All clear." She nodded toward the living room. "You start out here, and I'll take the bedrooms."

"No sign of Adrián?"

"None."

"Where could he be?" the cowgirl asked.

"My guess is he's either in on it or he's dead by now." Lexi holstered her gun. "Well, what are you waiting for? An invitation?"

The cowgirl trotted off to the living room. "What are we looking for… besides the paintings?" She turned over cushions on overstuffed chairs and looked under the sofa.

"Anything that might link Dean or his mother to the killings or the robbery." Lexi watched the cowgirl for a few seconds and then headed back to the master bedroom.

The ivory chenille bedspread was neatly tucked around the pillows on the queen-sized bed. Matching Mission style mahogany headboard, dresser, and nightstands gave the room a cozy feel, which helped counteract its sterility.

It didn't seem right to rummage through someone else's underwear drawer, especially when each pair of panties was so neatly folded it looked like the folded flag for a fallen warrior. Lexi would rather take down a mobster than sort through a middle-aged woman's drawers.

The search was slow going. Lexi refolded every item she touched, something she was sure none of her male counter-parts did.

In the back of the closet, behind neat rows of shoes, was a beat-up cardboard box. *What's this?* On all fours, Lexi reached into the darkness. The box was heavy. She had to kneel and use both hands to pull it out into the light. She hauled it over to the bed. No way she was going to sit on the floor in her linen skirt.

The box was stained and covered in cobwebs. On that white bedspread and in that sterile room, it stood out like a scorpion in the Registan desert. As if it might sting her, Lexi hesitated and then carefully pried off the lid. Inside was an oversized, leatherbound scrapbook. "Well, lookie here."

When she opened the engraved cover, yellowed news clip-pings fell out on the bed. She sorted through page after page of news clippings and old photographs. *Lord have mercy.* "Jes-sica, get in here!"

LEXI BROUGHT the album out to the dining room and spread the news clippings across the Shaker table. The big bound album was a catalogue of Eggs Benedict's greatest hits—from a million-dollar collection of swords and daggers taken from the Harry S. Truman library, to a sketch by Peter Paul Rubens stolen from a collector in New Jersey. Then there was the Degas Ballerina, and a Wisteria Tiffany lamp lifted from a hotel lobby in New York.

"Why does Cora Braugh have an album full of clippings from Eggs Benedict's heists?" the cowgirl said, flipping through the photo album. "Look at this."

Lexi came around the table and stared down at the photograph. It was a faded polaroid of a smiling young woman, a long-haired man, and a small boy. She slipped the picture out from under the plastic cellophane and examined it. "I'll be damned. It's a young Eggs Benedict." She held the picture out to Jessica. "And I'll bet my last dollar that's Cora Braugh with him."

"You'd win that bet." The cowgirl took the photo and squinted at it. "Who's the kid?"

"Good grief." Lexi let out a gasp. "You don't think Eggs and Cora had a kid?"

"Dean." The cowgirl's face lit up. "Edward Dean Braugh… Eddie Braugh… Edward Eggs Junior."

"The rotten apple doesn't fall far from the tree." Lexi gathered up the clippings and slid them back into the album. "I'm going to get a team out here to go through this place with a fine-toothed comb." She headed for the door. "I'm going to put out an APB on Dean and his mother… and get a warrant to search Gloria Sallow's place."

"Goth-Girl?"

"Come on." Lexi marched toward the Charger. "We've got to get ahead of this case before someone else dies."

Chapter 26

While they waited for approval to search Goth-Girl's apartment in Dorchester Heights, Jessica was supposed to follow up with the Carlyle Foundation, and the marshal had gone to interview Rocky Vanderbilt again. Since finding out about his financial troubles, he was once again a person of interest.

Jessica sat at the marshal's desk, raiding the Snickers drawer, and snooping in the other drawers. She pulled open the second drawer. *Wow. Everything is so neat.* A stapler, a roll of tape, three pens, a tiny tray of paperclips, another tiny tray of rubber bands, all lined up in rows.

The bottom drawer was reserved for personal items, but it was just as organized as the office supplies—a hairbrush, dental floss, a travel-sized mouthwash, toothpaste and toothbrush set, and a pacifier neatly tucked into a baggie.

What's this? Jessica slid the small wallet out from behind the travel sized mouthwash and opened it. Inside, she found a military ID badge with a picture of a young Lexi with big hair and a bigger smile, a photograph of Lexi in army fatigues with her arm around a handsome army guy whose smile was even bigger than hers, and a folded piece of card stock paper.

Jessica unfolded the paper. Holy Moly. A wedding invitation. Together with their families, Lexington Arlie Colt and Gabriel Miguel Lopez, request your presence…*Whoa. Almost six years ago.* Was the marshal married? *What happened?*

A noise in the hallway startled her. She folded the invitation, slid it back into the wallet, and put everything back exactly as it was. She'd better call the Carlyle Foundation before the marshal got back. She looked up the phone number and called on the office landline.

"Thank you for calling the Carlyle Foundation. Please hold." The woman put her on hold before she could say a word.

Jessica drummed a pencil on the marshal's desk in time with the Muzak version of "Hey Jude."

Might as well parallel process. Jessica tapped the marshal's computer awake and entered the marshal's security code. Finally, she'd trusted Jessica enough to give it to her. *Partners. In the hospital she called me her partner.* Jessica smiled to herself.

She put her phone on speaker and laid it on the desk. The Muzak version of "Let it Be" floated through the room.

I wonder if the forensic report on the fibers Adrián found in Vanderbilt's closet are in yet. The marshal had asked the forensics department to send the report to her instead of to Adrián or Stevenson.

Jessica looked up the request on the computer.

Bingo! The results were in. She read the report. *Wow.* The fibers contained residue from 17th century wood. So, it could have been Rembrandt's *Storm on the Sea of Galilee.* This was big news. She had to call the marshal.

Jessica had the marshal's cell number on speed dial on her phone. *Crapulence.* No answer. She texted the marshal. "Results from forensics on fibers consistent with Rembrandt."

The marshal texted back with a thumb's up emoji. *She must be in the middle of the interview. I wonder what she's getting out of Vanderbilt?*

Another Beatle's greatest hit later, the foundation woman

came back on the line. "Carlyle Foundation. My name is Ginger. How can I help you?"

"May I speak to the director?" Jessica used her most official voice.

"May I ask who is calling?"

"Jessica James from the FBI." She got butterflies in her stomach just saying that. She wasn't really from the FBI, at least not yet. If she cracked this case though, maybe they'd hire her. *Please. Please. Please…*

There was a pause at the other end.

"I just have a quick question about Rembrandt's *Christ in the Storm on the Sea of Galilee*." Jessica waited for a response. Nothing. "The painting on loan to the Albertina Carpenter Museum?"

"Yes. Please hold."

More Muzak. More pencil tapping. Jessica leaned back in the chair and took another bite off the Snickers.

"This is Caroline Geer. How can I help you, Ms. James?"

Jessica swallowed hard and the pencil froze in mid-tap.

With her practiced tone, the director sounded slick. No wonder she was the head of the foundation.

Through the lump in her throat, Jessica finally got the words out. "I'm calling to confirm that the Carlyle Foundation has loaned the Rembrandt, *Christ on the Sea of Galilee*, to the Albertina Museum."

"That's correct."

"Can you tell me who owns the painting?"

"The foundation."

"And who owns the foundation?" She held her breath.

"Mr. Rockefeller Vanderbilt."

Jessica nearly fell off the chair. "Mr. Vanderbilt owns the Rembrandt?"

"That's right." She dropped the pencil. *Holy moly.* "And he loaned it to the museum?"

"Yes. That's correct."

Crapulence. That would explain why Vanderbilt had the Rembrandt in his closet. The painting belonged to him. Why didn't he mention that he owned it when they interviewed him? Why did he suggest it might be for sale on the black market? What was he playing at?

Unless… he was trying to sell it on the black market to pay his bills. Why do that when he could just auction it off at Sotheby's for a whole lot more than he'd ever get on the black market? Her mind was whirling with questions.

"He's a trustee of the museum," Caroline Geer said, impatiently.

"A trustee," Jessica repeated.

"If that's all, I should get back to my meeting." The woman's voice was all business.

"Oh sorry. Yes, thank you—" The line went dead. "For your time." The director of the Carlyle Foundation had already hung up.

She texted the marshal again. "Vanderbilt owns the Rembrandt!"

Why would Rocky Vanderbilt steal his own painting? And then sell it on the black market? It didn't make sense. Something was off.

Jessica was about to cross his name off the list of suspects.

Wait a sec. She hit redial on her phone.

"Carlyle Foundation, please hold."

The Muzak version of "Twist and Shout" was making her eyes bug out. She wanted to shout alright. *Hurry up and answer the dang phone.*

"Can I help you?"

Finally! "Jessica James again. May I speak to Ms. Geer, please?"

"I'm sorry. She's in a meeting. Please call back in an hour." The phone went dead.

Jessica hit redial again. Busy signal. *Dang.*

This time, she called the marshal. Thank God. The

marshal answered. Jessica explained her theory about Vanderbilt.

"Get over to the Albertina on the double." The marshal barked the order. "Then, get back to headquarters." She sounded like she was commanding a battalion. "We should have our search warrant by then."

"What about lunch?" Jessica's stomach growled at the mention of lunch.

The marshal had already hung up.

What a day… and it was just getting started. A day without food.

Jessica gathered up her backpack. On the way out of the office, she stopped at the little refrigerator. *Maybe the marshal has some real food. Figures.* Two six-packs of Diet Mountain Dew, a half-empty box of Reese's Peanut Butter Cups, and a giant crumpled bag of Cheetos.

Who puts Cheetos in the refrigerator? She grabbed the bag along with a can of Dew.

When in Rome…

WOULDN'T YOU KNOW IT. The museum director, Ms. Finch, was on holiday in the Bahamas and no one else knew anything about the Rembrandt.

Crapulence. Now what? Jessica sat in her Chevy in the parking lot munching on Cheetos and washing them down with nasty florescent-green soda pop. Regular green soda was bad enough, but did it have to be diet too? The saccharin aftertaste forced her back into the Cheetos bag. Then the salty, dusty Cheetos made her thirsty. It was a dialectic of tastes. One nasty flavor counteracted the other in a never-ending loop.

She glanced at her phone. It wasn't quite an hour yet, but what the heck. She redialed the Carlyle Foundation.

She'd finished the bag of Cheetos and was down to the last drops of Dew by the time Caroline Geer graced the other end of the line.

"Yes, can I help you?" Caroline Geer's voice was impatient.

"Is *The Storm on the Sea of Galilee* insured?" Jessica asked, wiping her orange Cheeto-fingers on her jeans.

"As I recall," Caroline Geer paused for a moment. "The loan agreement stipulated that the Albertina insure the painting for ten million dollars."

She recalls alright.

"Ten million bucks," she blurted out. *I call that a motive.*

"It's worth at least four times that much." The director bristled.

"When will Mr. Vanderbilt collect the insurance money?"

"I don't know. You'll have to ask the folks at the Albertina."

"Thanks." She had to track down the director, Ms. Finch, in the Bahamas.

"My pleasure. Feel free to call again if I can be of any more assistance." Caroline Geer's voice was totally disingenuous.

"I will." Jessica echoed her fake tone and then hung up.

Ten million smackers. She whistled.

Pretty nice *coincidence* for Rocky Vanderbilt.

Clever plan. He could steal his own painting, collect the insurance money, and *still* sell the painting on the black market.

That's what I call double-dipping.

Chapter 27

It was already four in the afternoon. Time to pick up the baby from Mrs. Faheem's. *Just great.* Lexi sighed. The search warrant for Gloria Sallow's apartment had finally come through. "The warrant." She glanced over at the cowgirl, who was munching on a Reese's Peanut Butter Cup from Lexi's stash. "We got it. But I've got to collect Sammy."

"I'll go search Goth-Girl's apartment," the cowgirl said with her mouth full. "You go get baby Sammy."

Lexi scowled. No way she'd let the cowgirl go by herself and screw it up. "No." Anyway, it could be dangerous. "You're not authorized to carry a weapon, and we're talking about a possible murderer."

"I grew up shooting—"

Lexi stopped her. "Hunting animals and shooting people are not the same."

"I'll bet they're more the same than you'd like to admit." The cowgirl wiped her hands on her jeans.

Disgusting. No wonder she always looks like she's just slopped the pigs. "Put it this way, your Montana deer tag isn't going to cut it with the bureau." Lexi gathered up her purse.

She didn't want to bring Sammy along to search Gloria

Sallow's apartment. But it looked like she didn't have a choice. She needed to find Dean and his mother… and Gloria's place was their best lead. "We'll go together." *As soon as this case is solved, I'm finding a new babysitter.*

ON THE WAY to Dorchester Heights, Camo rode shotgun while the cowgirl and Sammy napped in the backseat. Lexi fueled up with Dew, slapped the blue light on the top of her car, and sped across town.

It was called *the heights* for a reason. From the top of Telegraph Hill, you could see downtown and the harbor. The view was one of the best in the city. Apart from the monuments to the Revolutionary War, the brick apartment buildings, mom-and-pop stores, and hole-in-the-wall eateries, it looked like the ones in Lexi's neighborhood.

Lexi parked and woke up the cowgirl. "You stay here with Sammy and Camo. If I'm not back in twenty minutes, then call for backup."

"Why don't you stay here, and I go search?" the cowgirl asked, rubbing the sleep from her eyes.

Lexi scowled.

"Okay. Okay." Jessica unclipped the car seat and slid the baby onto her lap. "Little love bug." She snuggled Sammy. The baby gurgled.

"At least, let me Facetime with you." The cowgirl pulled her cell from her jacket pocket. "Let me see what you see."

Lexi reached into the backseat and grabbed her phone from the side pocket of the diaper bag. "Okay." She hopped out of the car before the cowgirl could protest anymore.

GLORIA SALLOW'S apartment was the third floor of a row house. The owner was none too happy about "the feds" showing up to search her tenant's rooms. Begrudgingly—and slowly—the elderly woman led her upstairs. "Gloria is a good girl," the woman kept repeating. She insisted on standing in the doorway and watching as Lexi searched Gloria's rooms.

The third floor was more of an attic than an actual apartment. Lexi got the feeling of being in a doll's house. All the frilly lamps, crocheted doilies, and chair skirts contributed to the effect. Seemed more like an old lady lived here than a twenty-something punk.

The entire apartment was furnished with vintage furniture and retro accessories. The sofa was an orange number with big blue circles. The small kitchen table had a boomerang pattern with thick, steel legs and matching vinyl chairs. A vintage pig cookie jar sat on the counter taunting her to look inside.

Who knows? There could be evidence inside. She lifted the pig's head. The jar was full of Oreos. She grabbed one and popped it into her mouth. She opened all the drawers and cupboards in the kitchen. Nothing but thick ceramic dishes and blue glass tumblers. Nothing unusual, except for the punk's taste.

Lexi stopped at the threshold to the bedroom. *Wow.* It was like entering another country. The entire matching bedroom set looked like Ikea. Nothing old in this room. Except. *What in the—* Tacked on the wall was a large painting of a woman in white holding a baby and a lamb.

Good Lord. Is that the missing Bouguereau? Lexi held up her phone. "Are you there?"

"I'm here," the cowgirl replied.

"Is this the missing Bouguereau? The Innocent, or whatever it was called." She pointed the phone at the canvas.

"Holy cow!" The cowgirl's voice went up an octave. "Can I come in and see it?"

"No." Lexi took a few pictures. "Is it the missing painting or not?"

"Yikes. Is it tacked onto the wall?"

"Yes." Lexi stood admiring the painting. The pink skin of

the woman and the baby were luminous. And you could almost feel the folds of the flowing dress and shawl. It was the most beautiful painting she'd ever seen. The baby reminded her of little Sammy. So sweet and innocent.

"Are you still there?" The cowgirl's voice brought her out of her daydream.

"I'm going to look around a bit more."

"Can I come up?"

"No. Stay with Sammy."

"I'll bring Sammy with me."

"Absolutely not." *The cowgirl better not bring my daughter up here, or I'll skin her alive.*

"Maybe I'll see something you missed." The cowgirl was persistent.

"Unlikely." After spending the last week with the cowgirl, Lexi knew she was probably right. But no way in hell was Lexi going to admit it. She turned off the Facetime, and the cowgirl's perplexed face disappeared from the screen.

Lexi called headquarters. Vereen was going to want to know she'd found the missing Bouguereau. Now, if they could only locate Dean, his mother, and the punk girlfriend, no doubt they'd find the rest of the plunder.

The director would be pleased. Lexi could use all the brownie points she could get. She made the call. Got the brownie points. Smiled to herself. And then continued searching the apartment. *Sure, Vereen was sending over a team, but why should they have all the fun?*

She opened every drawer of the dresser and looked under the bed. She picked up the book on the nightstand. *Embalming for Dummies.* When she opened it, a brochure dropped onto the floor. She bent down and picked it up. Wallis Cove. *Why does that sound familiar?*

She folded the brochure and slipped it into the pocket of her blazer.

She checked every closet and cubbyhole in the bedroom.

One last look around the kitchenette and she'd call it done. The kitchenette was small, but neat and clean. *Wow.* Even the inside of the oven was spotless. Either Gloria Sallow didn't actually live here, or she ate out for every meal.

Lexi was a fine one to talk. She hadn't eaten a proper meal in her apartment since she moved in over a month ago.

The miniature refrigerator was stocked with Diet Pepsi and individually wrapped string cheese. *A girl after my own heart.* If only it had been Mountain Dew, she'd be tempted.

Next to the refrigerator was a full-sized door. *A cupboard or pantry?* Lexi opened the door, and the smell about knocked her backwards. Strong vinegary chemicals. She flipped the light switch on and gasped. "Lord have mercy."

At the back of the closet was a small table with several trays sitting on top of it. Along one wall was a set of floor-to-ceiling shelves. The bottom shelf held neat rows of bottles and a tray laid out with medical instruments. The middle shelves had an assortment of small animals—rats, mice, squirrels, and an opossum.

Good Lord. It looked like a miniature natural history museum. Gloria Sallow had an embalming studio in her kitchen. Lexi shuddered. *Downright ghoulish.* She took a series of pictures of the creepy closet. *What kind of girl keeps pickled rodents in her kitchen?*

Lexi couldn't wait to get out of that creepy place.

The old woman was standing in the doorway wringing her hands. "Gloria is a good girl."

"Define good." Lexi scooted around the old woman.

"What?" the woman held her hand to her ear.

"Thank you." Lexi ran down the stairs and back out to the car as fast as her short heels would allow.

Thank the Lord. The cowgirl was still in the car. She'd traded places with the dog. Now, she was in the front and Camo and Sammy were both in the back snoozing.

Lexi opened the driver's door and climbed in. "You won't believe what I saw."

"What?"

Lexi tapped her phone and passed it to Jessica. "Look."

"Stuffed animals?" The cowgirl's mouth fell open. "What does it mean?"

"That girl is sick. She has pickled rodents in a closet." Lexi shook her head and turned the key in the ignition.

"What else did you find?" The cowgirl passed her phone back.

Lexi pulled the brochure from her blazer pocket. "Wallis Cove. Sound familiar?" She unfolded the flyer and handed it to the cowgirl.

"Holy crap!" Jessica snatched it out of her hands. "Wallis Cove. Isn't that where Eggs Benedict had a cabin? The one his ex-wife took."

"His ex-wife, Cora Braugh." Lexi revved the engine. "Get me directions to Wallis Cove."

The cowgirl pulled her phone from her jacket pocket.

"Call Mrs. Faheem and tell her I'm bringing Sammy." She maneuvered out of the parking spot.

"One order at a time." The cowgirl frantically poked at her phone.

"And call for backup." Lexi stomped on the accelerator.

Chapter 28

Adrián tried to reach the back of his head. It hurt like hell. He couldn't reach. *Mierda.* His wrists were taped together behind his back. His eyes. He couldn't see. He could barely breathe. *Qué pasó?*

When he became fully conscious, he realized there was tape over his eyes and his mouth. He was lying on a cold floor somewhere.

Joder. Now he remembered. Cora Braugh had coldcocked him with a pistol.

He tried to yell. The sound came out muffled by the duct tape.

Mierda. Mierda. Mierda. Where have they taken me?

He screamed again. *Maldito* tape.

"Shut up." The voice was a woman's. A smoker. *Cora Braugh?*

Someone kicked him in the stomach. He grunted. By the feel of it, it wasn't the first time. He felt like he'd been run over by a semi-truck… and his pants were wet.

He lay as still as possible. Playing dead was his best option.

Thud. Another kick to the stomach. He held his breath and

didn't react. Someone grabbed him by the hair and lifted his head. He did his best to relax and not resist. *Ouch! Joder.* The *maldito* thug dropped his head, and it hit a hard surface.

"He's passed out again." It was Dean's voice. "Come to me, all you who are weary and burdened, and I will give you rest."

Adrián braced himself for another kick. *Gracias a Dios*, it never came. He tried not to move a muscle. He concentrated on his happy place. He imagined he was sitting on the Persian rug in his grandmother's morning room watching the Muppets. She'd just baked his favorite almond cookies, *almendrados*, and they were still warm. The house was filled with the sweet aroma of almonds and his grandmother's rose petal soap.

"If you weren't so incompetent, we wouldn't be in this situation."

Cora Braugh's gravelly voice knocked him out of his happy place and back into the nightmare that was his current reality.

"Now I can go to Harvard like *I* wanted all along," Dean said. "Mr. Vanderbilt will pay my tuition. That's the deal."

"Don't you want to be a mortician?" The younger woman's voice was high and whiney. *Must be the girlfriend.* "I thought we were opening a funeral home together."

"We can still do that on the side," Dean said. "While I get my degree at Harvard Divinity School."

"You're a dreamer," Cora said. "You always have been. You must get that from your father. That's what landed him in prison. Grand plans. Always with the grand plans."

"Open my eyes, that I may behold wondrous things." Dean started quoting the bible again.

Adrián listened and took it all in. Was Vanderbilt behind the heist? Was that the deal? Vanderbilt would pay Dean's tuition if he robbed the Albertina? But how could Dean have pulled off the robbery? He was in jail. Was it his mother or the girlfriend? Did they do it?

"A couple decades in prison will bring you closer to God," Cora said. "We've got to clear out before the Feds find us."

"What about him?" Dean asked.

Adrián felt a kick to his shoe.

"Kill him," Cora said.

Dios ayúdame. God help me. Adrián silently pleaded with God for his life. Instead of comforting him, the St. Christopher's medal around his neck was choking him.

"I'm hungry," the girl said. "Can we eat first?"

"Yeah," Dean said. "I can't think on an empty stomach."

Cora scoffed. "You can't think, period."

Why was she so hard on her son? Adrián thought of his father. Would his father mourn his death? He imagined his parents at his funeral. His mother weeping and his father looking at his watch.

"Let's go to The Picket Fence," Dean said. "They serve breakfast all day. I could go for a big plate of home fries."

"Me too," the girl said.

Adrián's stomach growled. If he wasn't so nauseous, he'd be famished.

"Should we kill him now?" Dean asked, kicking Adrián's foot again.

"Put him in the closet," Cora said.

Someone grabbed his feet and dragged him across the floor. Must have been Dean. *Be careful, Pendejo!* Adrián grimaced when his head hit the sharp edge of a piece of furniture.

Dean dragged him up some stairs and then stuffed him inside a small space, maybe a closet. Dean leaned him up against a wall. He fell sideways. Dean propped him up again.

Click. The distinctive sound of someone cocking a gun.

This was it. His life would end in a closet. He would go

straight to hell, unloved and unmourned, except by his dear mother.

"Mama." Adrián held his breath and prayed for forgiveness.

Chapter 29

After they dropped off the baby, Jessica, the marshal, and Camo loaded back into the Charger and headed for Wallis Cove.

The marshal chugged two Diet Mountain Dews and was out-doing herself for reckless driving. *That woman definitely has a death-wish.*

Jessica knew better than to say anything. Instead, she gripped the handhold like her life depended on it and prayed the airbags worked.

Wallis Cove was on seventeen-mile-long Lake Chaubunagungamaug, sixty miles from Boston at the Connecticut border. *Geez. The name is longer than the lake.* Jessica tried to read about the lake on her phone but spent most of the drive white-knuckling it as usual. By the time they got to the lake, she had cramps in her right hand.

The Charger bumped along a gravel road that took them around the lake. The water was dirty green and as flat as glass. Lush, leafy trees formed a canopy over the one-lane road. When in full leaf, these deciduous trees gave her favorite pine trees a run for their money… if trees had money.

At the end of the bumpy road, they finally reached Wallis

Cove, a peaceful inlet with sandy beaches, grassy lawns, and—thankfully—only a handful of cabins.

"Why don't we split up?" Jessica asked. "You take that half, and I'll take this one." She unbuckled her seatbelt and pointed toward the cabins to her left.

"You'll stay in the car." The marshal's voice was firm. "With the dog."

Sometimes, you treat me like a dog. "I'm coming with you." Jessica turned and reached into the back seat to pat Camo on the head. "Good boy."

"You don't have a weapon, and these people are armed and dangerous." The marshal dropped her key fob into her purse and then must have thought better of it. She retrieved it and stuffed it into her pants pocket instead.

Jessica looked around the car. She reached past Camo and hauled the diaper bag into the front. The thing weighed a ton. "What have you got in here?" She dug through the bag. *There must be something I can use as a weapon.*

"Dammit. I forgot to leave the diaper bag with Mrs. Faheem." The marshal snorted like a horse late for dinner. "What do you think you're doing?"

"Finding a weapon." Jessica pulled a can of aerosol baby powder out of the bag. "Aha. What's this?" She fingered a heavy metallic object. "Come to mama." She yanked the taser out of the bag. "I'm armed and dangerous too." Holding up the baby powder in one hand and the taser in the other, she smiled at the marshal. "See?"

"Oh alright." The marshal shook her head. "But stay behind me." When she opened the driver's door, Camo whimpered. "Alright. You, too. But be careful." She sighed. Camo jumped over the seat and followed the marshal up the dirt drive toward the cluster of cabins.

Jessica hopped out of the car and hurried to catch up.

Most of the cabins were small two-story wooden structures with porches or decks. And most of them seemed empty.

Summer season was probably not in full swing yet. Next week after the fourth of July, would be another story.

After hiking through the park-like forest between cabins, they finally found one that was occupied. An elderly couple answered the door. They looked like they were glued together.

"Can you direct us to the Braugh's cabin?" the marshal asked. "A middle-aged woman and her son?"

"Check the burgundy-colored cabin, two-doors down," the old woman said. "The weirdo son and his crabby mother live there in the summer." She pointed her boney finger into the distance.

"They live there in the summer," the old man repeated in a whispery voice. His cataracted gaze followed his wife's finger into the distance.

Jessica trailed the marshal across the lawn and then through another small stand of trees. When they emerged from the forest, they stood in front of the porch of the burgundy cabin.

Except for the color, the cabin was like the others, a modest two-story wooden house with a small porch on the ground level and a balcony on the second level. Jessica hung back with Camo while the marshal knocked on the door.

"FBI. Open up," the marshal shouted, her gun drawn. "I have a search warrant. We're coming in." She tried the door-knob. "Locked." She shoved her shoulder into the wooden door. It didn't budge.

The marshal holstered her gun and removed the lock-picking set from her blazer pocket. She jiggled the pick in the lock. The door popped open. "Easy-peasy."

"Badass." Jessica smiled.

The marshal drew her sidearm again. "Stay here until I make sure we're clear." She opened the door, and then turned back. "Stay!"

Jessica and Camo both straightened to attention.

A few minutes later, the marshal came back. She holstered

her gun. "All clear. You can come in now." She pulled a copy of the search warrant from her pocket, wedged it into the doorframe, and then held the door open.

"Camo. Stay here and warn us if anyone approaches." The marshal reached down and patted his head. Camo made a weird almost human sound.

Dang. "He understands." Jessica stuffed the taser under her arm and petted him as she passed.

"He's a smart dog," the marshal said, beaming.

"Wow. Nice place." Jessica surveyed the interior.

With its natural wood walls, ceilings and floors, it reminded her of cabins in Glacier Park where she'd stayed as a kid. Her mom hated the "God-forsaken wilderness," so she and her dad would go for horse-packing trips in the mountains, just the two of them. Those were some of her best memories. Just her and her dad riding and singing off-key. "My home's in Montana, I wear a bandana."

"You take upstairs," the marshal said, pointing to the staircase. "And I'll take down. Rip the place apart if you have to."

The wooden stairs creaked as Jessica climbed to the second floor. On either side of the hallway was a bedroom. She tiptoed to one of the bedrooms and peeked inside.

Matching craftsman bedroom set. Ivory chenille bedspread. Antique comb and brush set laid out in perfect alignment on a dressing table. *Geez. Am I the only person in the world whose room looks like a cyclone hit it?*

She took a step into the room and glanced around. The marshal had said it was all clear, but still, her heart was racing at the thought of running into a murderer hiding in a closet.

Three small, framed ballerina sketches hung over the bed.

No way. Jessica trotted to the bedside and leaned on the bed for a closer look. *Well, I'll be darned.* "Marshal," she yelled. "You're going to want to see this."

She whistled. They were Edgar Degas sketches, alright… the three missing drawings never recovered from one of

Eggs Benedict's heists. *What are they doing in Cora Braugh's bedroom?*

"What's up?" The marshal's heels clacked as she climbed the staircase. "Find something?" She poked her head in the bedroom.

"I'd say." Jessica pointed to the sketches with the taser.

"Ballerinas. So what?" The marshal squinted at the sketches.

"*Degas* ballerinas." Jessica raised her eyebrows. "Only the most famous ballerinas in art history."

"Good Lord." The marshal rushed to her side and stared up at the drawings. "The missing Degas sketches from the Benedict heist."

Jessica nodded. "Why are they hanging above Cora Braugh's bed?"

"She is Eggs Benedict's ex-wife." The marshal shrugged. "Maybe he gave them to her as an anniversary gift."

"Before she kicked him out." Jessica dropped down onto the bed. An image from yesterday came into focus in her mind. "I heard something yesterday."

"Go on." The marshal stood next to the bed looking down at her. "Are you okay?"

"Fine," she answered, not sure if it was true. She swallowed the bile building in her throat. "Remember I told you that Adrián placed a listening device in Cora Braugh's SUV?" She dropped the can of baby powder and the taser onto the bed.

"Did you remember something else?" The marshal sat on the bed next to her.

"We heard everything." Jessica's mind was galloping back through the events of yesterday. "Yes."

"What?"

"We saw them carrying paintings to their car." Jessica rubbed her temples. "At least, I think they were paintings. They were wrapped in cardboard." She closed her eyes and replayed the scene in her mind. "Adrián ran across the yard and put the listening device in the car." Her eyes flew open. "Dean saw him. Adrián ran back to the scooter, and I drove us back to headquarters." She glanced over at the marshal. "He didn't want me to tell you… not until we had more information."

The marshal sighed. "And you didn't think that was a tiny bit odd?"

"It made sense at the time." She shrugged.

"From now on, you tell me everything, and you tell me first." The marshal looked her straight in the eye. "Got it?" She stood up and stared down at her.

She nodded. At least, the marshal was a straight shooter. "I think they killed Frank… and Eggs." Her mind was buzzing. For the first time since she came-to yesterday, her thoughts were crystal clear.

Dean carrying paintings. His goth girlfriend whining. Adrián insisting they drink coffee and eavesdrop instead of reporting to the marshal.

"Cora." Jessica sucked in air.

"Cor, what?" The marshal put her hand on Jessica's shoulder. "What's going on in that noggin of yours?"

Holy crap! Jessica jumped up off the bed and nearly knocked the marshal over. "Cora Braugh is not just Eggs Benedict's ex-wife." She grabbed the marshal's elbow to keep her from tumbling backwards. "I think she's his ex-partner."

"You've got to be kidding me." The marshal rolled her eyes. "How did you come up with that gem?"

"If only you were more like your father." Jessica paced the length of the bedroom. "That's what Dean's mom said." *Concentrate, Jesse.* She stopped in her tracks. "Eggs may have been a lousy husband, but he was a great thief."

"Cora said that?" the marshal's mouth dropped open. "Great thief? She used those words?"

"Edward Dean Braugh." Jessica started pacing again. "His

mom calls him Eddie. He's named after his father, Edward Eggs Benedict."

"We already knew that… remember the scrap book… the photograph of Cora, Eggs, and the baby? The marshal tucked her hair behind her ear.

"Right." Jessica made another lap. "What I heard confirms it. Eggs is Dean's father."

"Okay. And why does that make Cora his ex-partner?" The marshal put her hands on her hips. "Cobra is a man… at least that's what the bureau—"

"Cobra." Jessica gasped. "Cora Braugh."

"No." The marshal shook her head and then just stood there with her mouth hanging open, gawking.

"Cora Braugh is Cobra, Eggs Benedict's partner in crime." Jessica poked the air with her index finger for emphasis.

"Lordie." Now, the marshal started pacing. "Lordie. Lordie. Lordie." She shook her head and kept repeating "Lordie."

"That would explain why she has the missing Degas sketches in her bedroom." The sound of Jessica's cowboy boots tapping across the wood floor helped her concentrate. "And…" Her eyes went wide. She stopped, whirled around, and stared at the marshal. "And that's why she had Eggs killed. She couldn't let us find her after all these years."

"Dammit. I should have seen it. I knew Cobra had mob connections and was well connected." The marshal pounded her fist into her palm. "Eggs told us his partner would kill him if he—she—found out."

"Looks like he was right." Jessica bit her lip. "Could Cora Braugh be the mastermind behind the Albertina heist?"

"If Cora Braugh is Cobra, then she definitely could have planned and executed the robbery. She's a pro."

Thump. Thump.

"Do you hear something?" Jessica asked.

Thump. Thump.

"Where's it coming from?" Jessica strained to hear.

More thumping.

"The closet," the marshal said, drawing her gun. She motioned toward the closet with her sidearm, and mouthed, "Open the door slowly."

Jessica went to the closet and stood in front of the door. Her heart was racing faster than a pony on the way back to the barn. She put her hand around the doorknob and turned it in slow motion. Taking a deep breath, she looked back at the marshal and mouthed, "one, two, three." She yanked the door open.

"Oh my God." Jessica rushed into the closet. "It's Adrián." She looked back at the marshal.

"Is he okay?" the marshal asked.

"I don't know." Jessica was paralyzed. "I think he's unconscious." She just stood there staring at the marshal, afraid to look over at Adrián. "What if he's dead?" His limp body was propped in the corner.

"He was just making that pounding noise," the marshal said. "So, he can't be dead… unless that was his last act." The marshal pulled her phone out of her blazer pocket and tapped it awake. "Agent down in Wallis Cove. Send an ambulance." She dropped her phone back in her pocket. "Well? Is he dead or alive, for Pete's sake?"

Jessica knelt next to him. He stunk of urine. Dried blood crusted in his hair and over one ear. "He looks like he was rode hard and put up wet."

"What's that mean?"

"Horses," Jessica answered. "Not good." She felt Adrián's neck for a pulse. "He's alive!" She tugged at the duct tape covering his eyes. *Yikes.* The sound it made when she ripped it off made her skin crawl.

Adrián convulsed. One of his eyes was bruised and swollen shut, and he had a split lip. His hair and clothes were damp with sweat and pee. The chain on his St. Christopher's Medal had left raw red marks on his neck. The perps must have used it to try and strangle him.

"We're going to get you out of here," Jessica said. She looked up at the marshal. "Help me get this tape off him."

"Move aside." The marshal pulled a tiny pen knife out of her pants pocket. She knelt and cut the tape around his wrists, ankles, and head. "Good Lord. What did they do to him?"

"We got to get him out of here." Jessica wiped her eyes with the backs of her hands.

"Do you think it's safe to move him?"

"We can't just leave him here." Jessica sniffed.

Adrián groaned.

"Let's at least get him out of this closet." Jessica took his arms.

"Oh, alright." The marshal lifted his feet and took a few steps backwards out of the closet.

Struggling not to drop him, and to keep up with the marshal, Jessica gritted her teeth and used all her strength to carry him. *Come on, Jesse. You can do it.*

Adrián yelped when his head hit the bedpost.

"Sorry about that," Jessica said, panting. "Can we rest a second?" She lowered Adrián's arms. She put her hands on her knees and bent over trying to catch her breath. "He weighs a ton."

"More like one-hundred and sixty-five pounds." The marshal was winded too. "You need to get to the gym more often."

Jessica blew out a big breath. "Yeah." She bent down and lifted Adrián's arms again. "Shall we?"

Camo barked. Not his normal comforting therapy-dog bark. But a ferocious attack-dog bark.

Crapulence. "Oh no." A knot in Jessica's stomach turned a somersault. "They're back."

"Leave him," the marshal said as she dropped Adrián's feet and drew her gun.

I need a gun. Jessica lunged at the bed and grabbed the taser and baby powder. Her heart was racing as she galloped down the stairs after the marshal.

The marshal was creeping across the living room like a cat about to pounce on a mouse.

Camo stopped barking. *Oh no. They wouldn't.* Armed with the baby powder and taser, Jessica tore past the marshal, jerked the door open, and burst out on the porch.

Dean knelt in the yard petting Camo. Cora—aka Cobra—stood feet apart on the porch pointing a shotgun at Jessica's gut. Behind her, Goth-Girl struggled with a stack of white carryout boxes.

Jessica surveyed the scene, and then made a clicking sound with her tongue. Camo knocked Dean to the ground. Cora took her eyes off Jessica for a split second. Jessica lunged forward, dropped the taser and aimed the can. She sprayed baby powder right into Cora's eyes.

Cora screamed and stumbled backwards. She lost her balance and fell off the porch.

The shotgun flew through the air. It landed on the porch.

Jessica dropped the baby powder and grabbed the gun. *That's better!* She had no clue how to use a taser. From the porch she had the drop on Cora. She cocked the gun.

Dean made a run for it.

"Stop!" Jessica kept the rifle trained on Cora.

"But Gloria and the baby..." Dean skidded to a stop in front of Goth-Girl. "Let me take those," he said, reaching for the take-out boxes.

The marshal marched out holding her sidearm in front of her with both hands. "Hands in the air, all of you," she shouted, waving her gun. "Now!"

Goth-Girl dropped the boxes. Hash browns, scrambled

eggs, and little pig sausages danced across the lawn. Camo went to investigate.

"Has anyone seen my hat?" Adrián staggered out onto the porch holding his head. "What's going on?" He looked around.

"We cracked the case," Jessica said, never taking her eyes off Cora.

"Nicely done, partner," Adrián said. "We make a good team."

"You mean me and my partner." The marshal jerked her head in Jessica's direction. "*We* make the good team."

"Right," Adrián said, and promptly collapsed.

"Don't forget Camo." Jessica kept her aim steady, not letting Cobra out of her gunsight.

Camo was busy cleaning up the mess on the lawn.

A red Harley Davidson roared into the driveway. The bike skidded to a stop in front of the porch. After the gravel and dust settled, Vanya hopped off the back of the motorcycle. "We missed all the fun?"

The marshal holstered her gun and pulled a set of handcuffs from the back of her pants. She snapped a cuff around Dean's wrist and another around Goth-Girl's.

"You started the party without us?" Lolita said, killing the engine.

"Never," Jessica winked.

"What are Boris and Natasha doing here?" The marshal used a plastic zip tie to fasten Cora's wrists together behind her back.

Jessica cracked a smile but still didn't take her eyes off Cobra. "You said to call for backup."

Chapter 30

Early the next morning, Jessica went to visit Adrián in the hospital. She had to know why he'd roofied her. Why was it so important for him to solve the case and get all the credit?

The marshal was hassling her to press charges. But she wasn't convinced.

If Adrián was guilty, hadn't he been punished enough already? He had three broken ribs, a broken eye socket, and two missing teeth… not to mention a nasty gash on the back of his head that required seven stitches, and so many bruises to his torso that he looked like a purple potato.

"Knock. Knock." She knocked on the door of his room and then poked her head in. The room smelled of rubbing alcohol and a cafeteria, open-faced turkey sandwich.

"Come in," he said weakly.

She tiptoed into the room to keep her boots from clicking on the polished floor. "How are you feeling?" Stupid question. It was obvious the dude was in a lot of pain.

He was lying in the hospital bed, his St. Christopher's Medal resting in the notch between his collar bones. For the first time since she met him, Adrián looked small. It didn't help that he was hooked up to a morphine pump and various other IVs and monitors. "I'll live." He cracked a smile and then grimaced.

"I brought you a Tootsie Pop." She handed him the sucker. "The American version of *Chupa Chups*."

"Thanks." He took the lollipop and tore off its orange wrapper. When he licked it, he made a sour face. "Sorry. Just off food right now." He rewrapped it and laid it on the bedside table next to his uneaten lunch. "I'll save it for later."

"Would you rather have some gummies?" She pulled a bag of gummies from her pocket.

His eyes lit up as he ripped the bag open.

She smiled and took a seat in the chair next to the bed. "You know, I was in the hospital two days ago with enough Rohypnol in my system to knock out a horse."

He stared down at the blanket and troubled its edge between his fingers.

"*Someone* slipped me a Mickey." She kept her eyes trained on him.

He didn't say a word. He just stared down at the blanket.

"Why?" She sat on the edge of the chair and leaned closer. "Why did you do it?"

He glanced up at her and then averted his gaze. "I don't know."

Did a tear just drop onto the blanket?

"I'm sorry. I get so competitive sometimes… it makes me crazy." He turned on the waterworks.

She got up and fetched a box of Kleenex from the side table. "Here." She handed him a tissue. "Stop blubbering."

"Sorry." His shoulders shook. "Must be the drugs. I never cry."

"You're still in shock." She stood next to the bed, looking down at him. He looked so vulnerable. "Get some rest. I'll come back tomorrow." She turned on her heels.

"Wait!" He wiped his blotchy face with the tissue. "Wait. Please."

She stopped in her tracks and turned to face him.

"Did you see the Muppets movie where Miss Piggy poses as Lady Holiday and then the real Lady Holiday's necklace is stolen, and Kermit gets kidnapped?"

What the heck? What's in that IV drip?

"Gonzo overhears the thieves plotting to steal the Baseball Diamond from the Mallory Gallery—"

"Are you alright?" Jessica narrowed her eyes. "How badly did you get hit in the head?"

"I'm Gonzo."

"Okay." She took a few steps closer to the bed. "You're Gonzo."

"I overheard them talking. Dean and Cora. They thought I was unconscious." With all the tubes attached to his arms, when he waved his hands around, he looked like a marionette. "I think Vanderbilt is involved."

"How so?" Jessica sat down in the chair next to the bed.

"Vanderbilt is paying for Dean to go to Harvard."

"Is that the morphine talking?" She scoffed. "Dean, go to Harvard?" First, the Muppets and now Harvard. "You're delusional."

"What if Vanderbilt was behind the heist? What if he's like the Muppets criminal mastermind, Constantine."

"What in the heck are you talking about?" She was starting to feel sorry for him. He was seriously messed up in the head.

"What if Vanderbilt planned the heist and paid Dean to pull it off?"

"First off, Vanderbilt owns the Rembrandt." She held up one finger. "Why would he steal his own painting? It wasn't even insured."

"So, the carpet fibers matched." He poured water from a pink plastic pitcher on the bedside table into a pink plastic cup.

"Yeah. When were you going to tell me about that?" She glared at him.

"I was waiting to get the results from forensics." He fiddled with the St. Christopher's Medal around his neck.

Aha. Another tell. She was good at poker because she could always spot the tell and knew when her opponent was bluffing. "Whatever." She held up two fingers. "Second, Dean was in jail at the time of the heist. So how could he rob the museum?"

"I don't know." Adrián took a sip of water from the pink plastic cup. "And I'm in no position to find out. But you can." His cheeks flushed. "Don't let Vanderbilt get away with it." He went from semi-immobile to highly animated. "I've known his types all my life. I grew up with them." He was directing an imaginary symphony. "They think they can do anything they want, that they're above the law. Like my father—"

"If Vanderbilt's behind it, then he stole his own painting." She interrupted his rant. "For the insurance money?"

"Ms. Finch told us it wasn't insured." Adrián shrugged, unwrapped the sucker and popped it into his mouth. "You probably found out about Vanderbilt's financial trouble."

It isn't insured? She didn't want to admit she'd forgotten that little tidbit. Who was right? The museum director? Or the director of Vanderbilt's foundation? *If it's true, there goes Vanderbilt's motive.* "I found out a lot of things, no thanks to you." She blew at her bangs. She would have to settle the insurance issue ASAP.

"I'm really sorry." He closed his eyes. "I'm a terrible person."

"Sometimes, good people do bad things." Although in his case, maybe he was right. *What kind of person pretends to be your friend and teammate, and then withholds information… and drugs you to boot?* She really should know better than to trust men, especially overly competitive men who feel challenged by smart women.

"What can I do to make it up to you?" he pleaded.

Go back to Madrid and never come back? Jump in the Charles River? "Help me solve the case and recover the Rembrandt." Maybe she could guilt trip him into telling her everything he knew.

"In case you haven't noticed, I'm laid up in the hospital with three broken ribs, an eye-patch and an annoying catheter—"

"Alright, alright." She didn't want to hear about his catheter. "Did you overhear anything else besides the Harvard thing?"

"Dean's mother constantly berates him for not being as good as his father… who, I gather, must be dead."

Ha! There was something she knew that he didn't. "Edward Dean Braugh is Edward Eggs Benedict's son."

"*No me digas.*" His eyes went wide.

"Yup." She couldn't help but smile… not that she was gloating or anything. "Cora Braugh is Eggs Benedict's ex-wife."

"No way." He pushed the control to bring the head of the bed up, grimaced, and fell back against the pillows with a yelp. "Ouch."

"But Cora Braugh is not just Eggs Benedict's ex-wife, she's his—"

"His ex-partner!" He put his hand to his mouth. "*No me digas.* Cora Braugh is the notorious art thief who alluded the FBI for the last twenty years."

"Yup." Jessica smiled.

"Cobra is a she, not a he." He whistled and then winced. "Ouch."

"The FBI obviously didn't consider that a woman could be that clever." She shook her finger at him. "It wouldn't be the first time men underestimated a woman."

He hung his head. "True."

"I'd better get back to it." She stood up. "And you need to rest."

"Will you come back later?"

"Sure." She nodded. *And I'll bring some hemlock laced gummies.*

He smiled and popped the lollipop back into his mouth.

At the doorway, she turned back. "Can I ask you a question?"

"Shoot."

"Simone Bernard was run down by a scooter in Italy." She took a deep breath. "Did you do it?"

"Are you joking?"

"Did you run her down?"

"She was run down by a Honda scooter." He smirked. "I wouldn't be caught dead on one of those hunks of junk."

Smartass.

"Didn't you hear?" He threw his tethered hands in the air. "She's back at the Louvre with her snooty nose in the air."

"That's a relief."

"Snobbery isn't a capital offense."

"Not yet." She waved. "See you later."

"What's your next move?"

Is he trying to keep me here? The hospital is a lonely place. "I guess I'll visit Rocky Vanderbilt and find out if his Rembrandt was insured."

"Good girl."

As she stepped into the corridor, she realized that, once again, she'd told him more than he'd told her.

———

ADRIÁN FELL BACK against the pillow. *Mierda. I should be the one visiting Vanderbilt. I should be solving the case. Instead, I'm strung up like a ham in this hospital bed.*

He pounded the bed with his fist. What had he done? If only he hadn't been so competitive, so set on beating the unimpeachable Jessica James… then maybe they'd still be working together.

When he wiped his eyes with the backs of his hands, the tubes attached to all those machines tugged back. He was just trying to impress her… her and his father.

My inglorious father. Now I'll have to go back to Madrid. Unless, of course, Jessica presses charges. In that case, I'll go to jail.

He closed his eyes. He would never hear the end of his failed career. His father would hold it over him forever.

I'd rather go to jail than work for him and his grocery stores.

El Superadela was named after Adrián's mother, Adela. His father always bragged that he'd turned a small butcher shop in Madrid into a national supermarket chain. Now, his father was one of the wealthiest men in Spain, infamous for firing managers on the spot whenever they spoke against him.

Adrián would be expected to keep his head down and his mouth shut.

He could hear his father's voice in his head, "You have to start at the bottom to appreciate the top." *Whatever you say, pops.*

A college degree and a certificate from the most prestigious art crimes institute in the world, and Adrián would be bagging groceries and sweeping floors for a living.

He depressed the button to administer the next dose of morphine.

Just thinking about going home made his head hurt.

▭

PATIENTS IN WHEELCHAIRS or holding onto their IV poles gathered to smoke under the awning outside the hospital. Visitors sat on benches, soaking up the June sunshine and taking a break from whatever desolation waited for them inside. Whatever their troubles, at least they could shed the frigid winter of clenched teeth and the twenty extra pounds of clothing.

Jessica stepped out from under the hospital awning and into the sunshine. Relieved to get away from the hospital, she inhaled the warm scent of spring turning into summer.

As she walked across the parking lot, she contemplated her next move. They'd caught the notorious Cobra, after twenty years. That was a big deal. But they still hadn't recovered the Rembrandt. And they still didn't know who was behind the heist.

Maybe Adrián was right and Rocky Vanderbilt was the mastermind. After all, the Rembrandt hadn't been found at the lake cabin. But why pay someone to steal his own painting? The answer had to be for the insurance money. The foundation director told her the painting was on loan on the condition that it was insured for millions. But like Adrián said, the museum director told us it wasn't insured. *What gives?*

Colonel Mustard was right where she'd left him. With plastic taped over the backseat window, the beat-up Chevy looked even worse than before. *Thanks a lot, Lolita.*

She climbed into the driver's seat and then pulled her phone from her pocket. She needed to confirm that the museum hadn't insured the Rembrandt.

"Albertina Carpenter Museum." A woman answered. "Can I help you?"

"May I speak to Eliza Finch?" Jessica asked. "The director."

"May I ask who is calling?"

"Jessica James from the FBI Art Crimes Division."

"One moment please." *Aha. She's back from her vacation. Good.*

Jessica was beginning to wonder if Ms. Finch had skipped town with the Rembrandt, and they'd been on the wrong track all along.

Jessica James from the FBI Art Crimes Division. She could get used to saying that. What would folks in Whitefish think? She imagined her mother bragging to the church group.

"Eliza Finch." The director's voice startled her.

"Jessica James here."

"What can I do for you, Ms. James?" The director sounded chipper. The vacation must have done her good.

"Can you confirm that the stolen paintings were not insured?"

There was silence at the other end. "Unfortunately, we hadn't finalized the insurance policy yet."

"They were going to be insured?" *Aha.* Maybe Vanderbilt *thought* his Rembrandt was insured. Maybe he thought the museum had kept its part of the bargain and insured it.

"The loan agreement from the Carlyle Foundation stipulated a ten-million-dollar insurance policy on the Rembrandt." Another pause. "I'm afraid we hadn't yet paid for the insurance policy at the time of the robbery."

Holy moly. "So, the Rembrandt was *supposed* to be insured?"

"Yes." The director exhaled into the phone. "I'm so sorry."

"Does Mr. Vanderbilt know?"

"It's complicated." Another pause. "We're in conversation with Mr. Romano, his lawyer."

It's complicated, alright.

Rocky Vanderbilt probably thought he was going to collect ten million bucks. *If he did mastermind the heist, then going bankrupt will be the least of his worries.*

———

GOOD GRIEF. My office is starting to look like a nursery. Playpen, stuffed bears, teething rings, diaper pail, baby swing, and a Costco-sized box of dog treats. It was getting ridiculous. Lexi really needed to find a new babysitter and fast.

Sammy was fussing in the playpen. When Lexi bent down to pick her up, the baby reached her little arms in the air. So adorable. Lexi's life before Sammy was nothing but a recurring nightmare. Now, she couldn't imagine life without the little mite. When she cuddled the baby to her chest, Sammy nestled her fuzzy little head into Lexi's neck.

Lexi sang in a whisper. "Robed in garlands soaked in brine… you are gone and lost forever, oh my darlin' Sammy mine." She kissed the fuzzy little head.

Bang. Lexi's heart leaped into her throat, and she broke out in a cold sweat. Camo came to her side and frantically licked her hand.

"Hey, Marshal." *Damn cowgirl.* It was just Jessica slamming the office door.

"Where in Sam Hill have you been?" Lexi laid the baby down in the playpen.

"Visiting Adrián in the hospital." The cowgirl dropped her backpack on the floor.

"I wouldn't give that dog a drink if he were dying in the desert."

"Don't you believe in second chances?" Jessica plopped into one of the plastic chairs at the table she'd been using as a desk.

"Try three strikes and you're out." Lexi tapped her keyboard. "I suppose he's going to live."

"I thought maybe I could get some information out of him." She sighed.

"If there's one thing I learned in the army, it's that the future is always like the past." Lexi opened the file on the Albertina heist. She'd already started writing up the report and hoped she could wrap it up after the interviews. "Stevenson, Garcia…"

"People can change."

"A snake may shed its skin, but it's still a snake." She glanced over at the cowgirl. "What info did you get from the snake?"

Jessica grimaced. "Nothing."

"Figures." She shook her head. "We are set to interview Dean and Cora Braugh in about an hour."

"Actually…" The cowgirl twisted the fringe on her jacket. "Adrián did tell me that Rocky Vanderbilt is paying for Dean to go to Harvard." She raised her eyebrows. "Does Harvard offer degree programs in prison?"

"How does Vanderbilt know Dean?" Lexi wound her ponytail into a bun and stuck a pencil through it to hold it up. "Unless…"

"Exactly." The cowgirl grinned. "Unless he hired Dean to hit the museum."

"Dean has an ironclad alibi, remember?" Sammy gurgled in agreement.

"Maybe Dean delegated the job after he got caught trying to steal the Gutenberg Bible." She unwrapped a Tootsie Pop and stuck it in her mouth. The cowgirl had picked up some of Adrián's bad habits. "Afterall, Dean didn't know he would get caught."

"Delegated to who?"

"To whom."

"Okay college girl." Lexi rolled her eyes. "To whom."

"How about his mother or his girlfriend?" Jessica squinted like she was trying to make out something in the distance.

Lexi had learned that the cowgirl squinted like that when she was concentrating. "You think Vanderbilt planned the heist and hired Cora and the girlfriend to carry it out?"

"It's possible." The cowgirl stood up and paced the length of the room.

"Stop pacing." Lexi gritted her teeth. "You're making me nervous."

Jessica froze in mid-step. "Let's not forget about poor Frank Motton, Dean's roommate, and most likely the inside man." She stood there with her leg in the air.

"Come on." Lexi shut down her computer. "Let's go put the squeeze on Dean and see what we can get out of the little turnip." She gathered up the diaper bag. *Now what to do about the baby?*

Mr. Faheem had taken Mrs. Faheem for a long weekend on the cape to celebrate their thirtieth wedding anniversary. Thirty years. *How in heaven's name could you live with a man that long without strangling him?*

Lexi thought of Nick's beautiful neck. She'd tried hard not to think of Nick. Where is he? WitSec had moved him for his own protection. They'd moved her too… demoted to art crimes. She had to admit, art crimes were more challenging than she'd expected.

"How about after squeezing Dean, we pay a visit to Rocky Vanderbilt and squeeze him too?" Jessica grabbed her backpack and heaved it over her shoulder. "Want me to get Sammy?"

Lexi snapped out of her daydreams. "I'll get her." She gathered up Sammy's paraphernalia and loaded it in the diaper bag. The Baby Bjorn was next. She slipped it on, picked up Sammy, and slid her into the sling. "Come on, Camo." She fetched the dog's leash from the hook by the door. He waited patiently while she clipped it onto his collar. "Good boy."

"Are we dropping Sammy off at Mrs. Faheem's?"

Lexi shook her head. "Nope." At least Jessica didn't seem to mind having a baby and a dog in tow. Any other partner wouldn't take too kindly to Lexi's entourage. Maybe the cowgirl wasn't so bad after all. They did make a darned good team.

"Shall we saddle up?" Jessica kicked up a cowboy boot.

Lexi shook her head. The cowgirl did have a certain charm.

Chapter 31

Awesome. Since the marshal had the baby with her, Jessica got to question Dean. Of course, the marshal was watching from the other side of the one-way glass. Jessica felt like a TV cop going into the booth to crack the bad guy and get a confession. If only Dean would cooperate and give her one.

Dean's chin rested against the chest of his orange jumpsuit.

When she sat across the table from him, Dean raised his head just high enough to glare at her. Even his cowlick—which was standing straight up on the top of his head—seemed to flip her off.

"Looks like you'll be doing correspondence courses at Harvard from prison." Jessica glanced over at the one-way glass. She wished she could see the marshal's face. No matter what the marshal said, her true thoughts were written on her face. She liked that about the marshal. She always knew where she stood.

"Very funny." Dean sat up in his chair. "I was in jail at the time of the Albertina heist, remember?"

"And why is that?" Jessica pushed the record button on a

tiny tape-recorder the marshal had given her as a backup since the recorder in the interrogation room was on the fritz.

"I told you, I took the bible for research." Dean clenched his jaw. "Dear children, let us not love with words or speech but with actions and in truth."

More bible verses. John 3:18. "You'll have plenty of time for bible study in prison." She wished the marshal was inside the booth instead of outside. Then they could tag-team Dean with the good-cop-bad-cop routine. Jessica preferred to be the good cop. And the marshal was dang good at being the bad cop. They were good compliments to each other.

"What about the night Frank was killed?"

"I already told you. I was playing Dungeons and Dragons at Peter Zelton's house." Dean scowled. "If you'd done your job, you'd have confirmed my alibi."

She had done her job. Unfortunately, his alibi had checked out. Still, that smell. Camphor and eucalyptus... and pickles. He was there. She knew it. "How do you explain the fact that Frank was killed with embalming fluid?" The embalming fluid accounted for the pickles. But what about the minty camphor and eucalyptus?

Dean's eyes went wide. He tilted his head and then opened his mouth to say something. He obviously thought better of it because he closed his mouth again.

What's going on with him? Dean had looked surprised the other day when he heard Frank had been killed, and now he looked surprised to hear the murder weapon was embalming fluid. Maybe he wasn't the murderer, after all.

The disbelief on his face was replaced with distress. "I didn't kill Frank."

"Then who did?"

He shrugged. "How should I know?" His smug smile reappeared.

She changed tactics. "Do you know anything about the

stolen Bouguereau we found hanging in your girlfriend's apartment?"

"She's not my girlfriend."

Wait. "What?"

"She's my fiancé."

"Okay." Jessica sighed. "Why did your fiancé have the stolen painting? Did she steal it?"

"Beautiful painting, isn't it?" He smiled. "You're an art critic. What do you think it means?"

How does he know I studied art? She shifted in her seat. "I'm asking the questions." *Because I work for the art crimes division?*

"I read your dissertation on Nietzsche and the Blue Riders." His steely stare was unnerving.

Holy crap. Is he serious? "You and three others," she said under her breath. *Come on, Jesse, don't let the bible-quoting maniac get to you.* "I'm asking the—"

"Science has drained all the mystery out of life." He cut her off. "What about divinity and transcendence?"

"Science is full of mysteries." She couldn't believe she was having a philosophical debate with a thief and suspected killer. "Mysteries are its bread and butter. There can be divinity in a forest. Or mystery in a blade of grass. Just because—"

"Now, now. We're not in the classroom, Dr. James." He opened both palms and gestured to the ceiling. "Look around. It's just you and me."

And the marshal and whoever else is watching from the other side of the glass. Crapulence. What must the marshal think of this conversation? It was a wonder that the marshal hadn't burst into the room to redirect this derailed interview. "Back to the Bouguereau." Jessica blew at her bangs. "What do you know about the stolen painting?"

"The Virgin Mary holding Jesus in one arm and a little lamb in the other. Innocence personified. Her ivory-pink skin was translucent, the folds of her simple peasant's robe almost tactile. The perfection of her hands and bare feet—"

With a huff, she cut him off. "I'm not asking for a description. I'm asking how your girlfriend got it. Did she steal it?" She resisted the urge to bite her fingernail.

"I told you. She's not my girlfriend." He yelled. "Reproductions of that painting have hung in nurseries for over a century." His tone had changed as fast as the Boston weather. "The perfect gift for a mother-to-be."

"Did someone give it to your girl—fiancé—as a gift?" She sat on her hands. Instead of the direct approach, she was trying to be sneaky. "Because she's…expecting?"

"He chose to give us birth through the word of truth. You're obsessed by death while I'm fascinated by birth." He raised his eyebrows. "Which of us is the morbid one?"

She wasn't going to take the bait. "How long have you known Gloria?"

"Four months." He smiled. "We got engaged after I started at Middle State."

"Your girlfriend was already at mortuary school, and you joined her there?"

"Fiancé. We're going to open a funeral home together. Right after the wedding."

"Your wedding will be in prison if you don't cooperate."

"You're only an intern… and a student of death, whereas Gloria and I celebrate life."

"You two are the morticians. Not me." She shook her head to get back on track. "Just answer my questions, please." *Geez, Jesse. Stop being so polite to this jerk.*

"Do not grieve the Holy Spirit of God, with whom you were sealed for the day of redemption." Dean paused and then looked up to the ceiling. "We help spirits leave this world for the next. Eternal life—"

As much as she loved a good metaphysical debate, this life and death stuff was getting old. "Where did your *fiancé* get the stolen painting?" She held his gaze. "If you really didn't have anything to do with the robbery or Frank's murder, you're only in for the botched bible theft. Cut your losses and tell me what you know, and we'll go easy on you." Of course, she didn't have any authority to go easy or hard or anything else.

"I'm a student of life. *Innocence* represents life. Meditate on that image long enough and God speaks to you just as he did to Mary."

Nut job. "The painting is your means of communicating with God?"

He nodded. "And it will protect my unborn child."

Goth-Girl's baby bump. "Did you convince Frank to help Vanderbilt rob the museum?" A light bulb went off in her brain. "Did Frank open the side door and give your girlfriend the Bouguereau?"

"Fiancé!" He raised both hands to the sky. "She will give birth to transcendence personified."

Cuckoo. "Is that why you had Frank slip it to her out the side door?"

"The patrons of the Albertina don't appreciate the meaning of that sacred painting—"

"And you do?"

"As a matter of fact, yes." He leaned back in the chair and glared across the table at her. "I am God's servant. Where I am, there will my servant be also—"

"Did God tell you to steal that painting?" She was losing her patience. "Did God tell you to recruit your roommate to help Rocky Vanderbilt rob the Albertina?"

"Mr. Vanderbilt appreciates my gifts. He is going to pay my tuition to Harvard Divinity School—"

"Cut the crap." She wanted to wipe the smug look off his face. "You just said you're opening a funeral parlor. Now you're going to Harvard?"

"The funeral home is our backup plan—"

"Prison is your backup plan."

The door opened and the marshal sauntered in. "I'm taking over."

"But I'm just—"

"Switch places with me." The marshal winked, as if to say, "move over, and I'll show you how it's done."

Jessica ceded her chair and slinked into the hallway to watch from the other side of the one-way glass.

A burly uniformed cop cradled the baby. Jessica joined him and then cooed at Sammy. The baby gave her a slobbery toothless grin. She rubbed the baby's fuzzy, little head. "Sweet-pea."

"Marshal says you're to interview the girl in the next room," the cop said, pointing at a door. "Take this." The cop handed her another tiny recorder.

Dang. I guess the marshal isn't going to show me how it's done. The girl in the next room. No one would call Cora Braugh a girl. Must be Dean's girlfriend—fiancé—Goth-Girl.

Jessica opened the door and peeked inside. *Yup.* Goth-Girl was sitting at the table with her head in her hands.

Jessica went inside and closed the door behind her.

Goth-Girl looked up. She had rivulets of mascara running down her cheeks. Her lips were cracked and bright red. *Is that blood or lipstick? Dang. Must suck to be pregnant and in jail.*

"Ms. Sallow, where did you get the painting of Mary and baby Jesus hanging in your apartment?" Might as well get straight to the point.

"From Frank." She teared up.

"Frank Motton, the security guard at the Albertina?" Jessica sat down in the chair across from her and laid the recorder on the table. "Did he bring it to you through the side door the night of the robbery?" She pressed the record button.

Goth-Girl nodded. "Frank and I were… close."

"Did you rob the Albertina Museum?" Jessica held her breath. If Vanderbilt was the mastermind, was Goth-Girl the executioner?

"No." She shook her head. "I just drove the car."

"You must have gotten out of the car to take *Innocence* from Frank through the side-door." Jessica narrowed her eyes. "If not you, then who was the robber?"

"Cora said we were doing it for Dean… so he could marry me." A tear rolled down her cheek. "Am I going to have my baby in jail?"

"That depends." On what, Jessica didn't know… but it sounded like the right thing to say. "On whether you cooperate. Tell me about the robbery and I'll put in a good word for you." A good word with whom, she also didn't know.

"Mr. Vanderbilt asked Dean to get that painting for him… the one with the ship in the storm. Said he'd pay for Dean to go to Harvard."

So far, her story matched Dean's.

Goth-Girl wiped her nose on the sleeve of her jumpsuit. "Dean wanted to get that special bible to divine the truth—that's what he said anyway." She paused. "But he fell and got caught, so he couldn't get Mr. Vanderbilt's painting."

"Who pulled off the heist in his place? You?"

"Not me." Her blue hair flew into her face when she shook her head. "Co, Dean's mom."

"Co? You mean Cora?" Jessica winced. "Or should I say Cobra? Cobra did the robbery for her son."

Goth-Girl gave her a quizzical look. "That ship painting was being moved. We had to take it that night or not at all."

"We?"

"We were just doing it for Dean." She bit her lip. "So, he could go to Harvard… so we could get married… for the baby, since Frank wouldn't…" She stopped herself.

"Frank wouldn't what?"

Goth-Girl shrugged. "Frank and I are, were… really… good friends."

Say what? "How good?"

She glanced around the room and then whispered. "We were engaged."

Wait! What? "You were engaged to Frank Motton?" Jessica's brain was about to explode. "Not Dean Braugh?"

Goth-Girl put both feet on the edge of her chair and hugged her knees to her chest—no mean feat with the baby bump. "Before Dean, I was engaged to Frank."

What the… Goth-Girl was engaged to Frank *and* Dean? "When did you and Dean get together?" Jessica squinted at her, trying to make sense of the love-triangle.

"Right after Frank's death," Goth-Girl whispered.

"What?" Jessica jolted forward in the chair. "You were engaged to Frank when he died?" Her mind was reeling. "And you just got engaged to Dean last week?"

Goth-Girl nodded.

"When is the baby due?" Jessica was trying to work out who was the father…

"November 13th."

Jessica counted the months in her mind. *June to November, five months. That makes Goth-Girl four months pregnant. But Dean said they just got together four months ago.* "Who is the father?"

Goth-Girl's lip trembled. "Frank didn't want a baby because it would ruin his music career."

Crapulence. Frank didn't want the baby. "Frank broke up with you when he found out you were pregnant?" Jessica blinked. The pieces were falling into place.

Tears ran down her goth cheeks.

"And Dean stepped in to raise Frank's baby." *How chivalrous of him.*

Goth-Girl's feet dropped to the floor. "Dean doesn't know the baby is Frank's" She put a hand to each side of her face like she was holding her head together. "Please don't tell him. He thinks it's his."

"Dean thinks you got four months pregnant in a week?" *Dean may be bonkers, but he couldn't be that stupid.*

Goth-Girl bit her cracked lip. "There was a party at

school. We drank too much." She shrugged. "I slept with Dean before Frank broke up with me."

"When was that?"

She shrugged again. "Like, maybe two months ago…" She grimaced. "And maybe again a month later?"

"Another mortician's party?" *Whatever turns you on.*

Goth-Girl smiled sheepishly. "Dean wants to marry me."

"Yeah. I know." Jessica rolled her mind's eye. "So, you can give birth to his divine baby." She leaned into the table. "Let me get this straight. You were engaged to Frank but sleeping with his roommate, Dean. You got pregnant… and Frank refused to marry you….and…" *Holy crap!* "You killed him."

"I'm going to be sick." Goth-Girl put her hand over her mouth.

Jessica glanced around the room and spotted a trash can. She jumped up and fetched it just in the nick of time.

Does puking count as a confession?

▭

JESSICA KISSED Sammy's head as she watched through the one-way window.

The marshal was still questioning Dean. She leaned over the table, her face just inches from Dean's. "Tell me who stole that painting, or I'll make sure you go to prison and don't come out until you need Viagra to get up in the morning."

Dean sputtered. "I prefer to talk to Dr. James."

"Tough cookies." The marshal stared him down. "Tell me what you know about the robbery and about Frank Motton's death, or I'm sending you so far up the river you'll need gills."

Cookies, Viagra, fish? Mixing metaphors. Is this how she roughs up a perp?

"Let me know when you're ready to talk." The marshal stood up straight and adjusted her blazer. "Until then, be careful in jail or you might meet the same fate as your dear-old-dad, Eggs."

Dean furrowed his brows. "Are you threatening me, Marshal Colt?"

"Just stating facts. Prison is a rough place." She looked him up and down. "And unless you're tougher than you look, I'd say you aren't cut out for it." She turned on her heels. When she reached the door, she turned back. "I guess your kid will grow up without a daddy, just like you did."

Dean shivered like he'd been hit by a cold wind.

"If your mother lets you take the rap and walks, then she can raise your kid for you." The marshal opened the door and stepped into the hallway.

"Wait!" Dean lurched out of his chair. "Ms. Colt, come back."

"Yeah, I thought so." The marshal's heels tapped against the concrete floor. "If you ever want to see this divine baby of yours, you'd better cut a deal and tell us who committed the robbery *and* who murdered your roommate." She sat down in the chair across from Dean. "If you didn't do it, who did?"

"Do you promise I'll see my baby?"

Very clever, Marshal. The look of fear and consternation on Dean's face almost made Jessica feel sorry for him. Poor sap didn't even know it wasn't his baby.

"I'll do my best." The marshal's tone softened. "My very best."

"Mr. Vanderbilt paid me and Frank to commit the robbery for him. He wanted us to take that Rembrandt." Dean stared down at his hands.

"And the Bouguereau? Was that your idea?"

Dean nodded. "I wanted Gloria to have it… for her and our baby."

"How did you get it?" The marshal never took her eyes off him. "Explain exactly how it went down."

"Mr. Vanderbilt knew Frank worked at the museum. At

first, Frank wouldn't do it. Then one afternoon, Mr. Vanderbilt came to our apartment and asked me to help him. He said
he'd pay me. When I told him I just wanted to go to Harvard
Divinity School, he offered to pay my tuition." Dean exhaled
a shaky breath. "I talked Frank into helping me."

"How'd you do that?"

"Frank wanted to be a rock star. I told him he'd have
enough money to make his dream come true… we all would."

"Did you kill Frank to shut him up?"

"No!" Dean shook his head. His face darkened. "No. No. I
couldn't…"

Geez. He's not going to start crying, is he? Jessica had already
watched Adrián blubbering earlier this morning.

"Who did? Who killed Frank?" The marshal's tone was
fierce.

Sammy started shrieking. "There, there," Jessica whispered to the baby. "Your mommy is just interrogating the bad
guy."

The uniformed cop bounced Sammy up and down. When
he sang *Bye Bye Blackbird*, the baby calmed down.

Jessica went back to watching through the glass as the
marshal questioned Dean.

"I don't know." Dean was shaking like he was having a
seizure. "I don't—"

"How do you explain that he was killed with Formalin?"
The marshal leaned her elbows on the table. "What about
that nifty embalming room in your girlfriend's kitchen closet?
Just a coincidence?"

"She's my fiancé," he yelled. "You've got to believe me."
He lifted his palms to the sky. "I didn't kill Frank."

"Who did?" The marshal was rattling off rapid-fire questions like a machine gun.

"I don't know." Dean pounded his fist into his palm.
"Please believe me."

"Let me try out a theory." The marshal leaned back in her

chair. "You—or your girlfriend—killed Frank to keep him from talking."

"Gloria's my fiancé." Dean slumped in his chair. The marshal was getting to him. Maybe a one-two punch would finish him off.

Jessica took her chances with the marshal and entered the booth.

"Speaking of your fiancé," Jessica said, walking over to the table. "Gloria says the baby is Frank's and not yours."

Dean jumped up from his chair. "You're lying."

"You killed him when you found out the baby wasn't yours…" Jessica paused for effect.

"No!" Dean shouted.

The marshal looked up at Jessica with a question on her lips.

"Or your *girlfriend* killed Frank when he refused to marry her." Jessica sat on the edge of the table. "Maybe Frank threatened to tell you the baby is his."

The marshal nodded. "Which is it, Dean?"

"The baby is mine." Dean put his hands together in prayer. "Gloria—"

"Gloria lied to you." Jessica pressed rewind on the tiny recorder.

"You're the liar!" Dean's face was beet red. He looked downright apoplectic.

Jessica pressed play and waited.

"Frank didn't want a baby. Said it would ruin his music career." Goth-Girl's voice was shaky, but loud and clear.

Jessica had found the exact moment on the recording.

Dean's mouth fell open, and his lips trembled.

"So, Frank broke up with you when he found out you were pregnant? And Dean stepped in to raise Frank's baby." Jessica cringed at the sound of her own voice on the recording.

"Dean doesn't know the baby is Frank's. Please don't tell him. He thinks it's his."

Bingo. Jessica clicked off the recorder. "Now what do you think of your divine baby and transcendent girlfriend?"

Dean dropped back into the chair and buried his head in his hands. He murmured. "God will be the judge."

The marshal tutted and said, "From what I've read of the good book, even all-merciful God doesn't take kindly to murderers."

"Did you say Frank was killed with Formalin?" Dean's voice cracked.

"Premeditated murder," the marshal said.

"Gloria always carries Formalin in her purse." Dean shrunk like a deflated balloon.

"Of course." Jessica raised her eyebrows. "You never know when you might have to embalm someone."

———————————

Chapter 32

———————————

Three days later, Lexi hand-delivered the report on the Albertina Carpenter heist.

The head of the FBI, Gerald Vereen, shook her hand. "Well done, Colt."

"Thank you, sir." Lexi beamed. "I couldn't have done it without the cow—without my intern, Jessica."

"Excellent." Vereen shuffled some papers on his desk.

His office was the "penthouse" of headquarters. Spacious and well appointed, instead of having a scratched-up metal desk, his was mahogany. He even had paintings on his walls and potted plants on either side of the doorway.

Lexi felt like she was in the Oval Office.

"Glad that internship program is working out for you. Too bad about Stevenson's intern."

"Yes, too bad." She bit her tongue.

Vereen pulled a file from the pile on his desk and opened it. "Anything else?" Obviously, the meeting was over.

"No, sir." She tugged at the hem of her blazer.

"That's all." He looked up and flashed a practiced smiled. "Good work."

As she left his office, she felt lighter than she had in a long,

long time… like a huge weight had been lifted from her shoulders. Maybe Art Crimes Division wasn't so bad, after all. In fact, as her daddy would say, "It was finer than a frog's hair split four ways." Especially with the cowgirl working beside her.

Like a mushroom emerging after a devastating fire, the cowgirl was beginning to grow on her. To Lexi's surprise, she had to admit they did make a good team.

When Lexi got back to her own office, she found the cowgirl lying on the floor. Sammy was lying next to her, eyes wide and drooling on the carpet.

"What in the Sam Hill?" Lexi asked, staring down at Jessica. "What are you doing on the floor?"

The cowgirl rolled over on her own stomach and then came up to all fours. "Giving Sammy crawling lessons." She blew a raspberry on Sammy's tummy and the baby gurgled. "Look." She tickled the baby and then turned her over. "She's getting the hang of it."

Sammy tried to pull herself up to her hands and knees but collapsed back onto the carpet.

The cowgirl clapped and cheered. "Go, Sammy, go."

"You must have pretty low standards if Sammy waving her arms around like a bug on its back counts as crawling for you."

"Teachers must always be encouraging first and challenging second." The cowgirl nodded for emphasis.

"Don't teach her to crawl." *Good Lord.* "How will I keep up with her?"

"Just wait until she's got the keys to your Charger." The cowgirl mouthed, "ha, ha ha, ha."

"That will never happen."

"Did you turn in the report?" The cowgirl got up off the floor and brushed off the knees of her jeans. *As if my office floor is dirtier than her pants.*

"Yes. How about we celebrate?" Lexi picked Sammy off

the floor… just in case it was dirtier. "I'll take you to that Taste of Haiti place you were swooning over." Lexi couldn't believe she was offering to go to a Haitian restaurant, let alone treat. A good rib-eye with thick-cut fries were more her speed. "What do they eat in Haiti, anyway?"

"It's kind of a cross between African and Caribbean food." Jessica shrugged.

"Whatever that means." Lexi had never had either. The bravest she'd gotten was Taco Bell. Even in Afghanistan, she never ventured beyond the mess hall's hamburgers, pizza, and corndogs with chili.

"Lots of yummy veggie stews—"

"Oh boy." Lexi rolled her eyes. The thought of over-cooked spinach made her gag.

"And lots of deep-fried meat." The cowgirl screwed up her face and stuck her tongue out. "Disgusting."

"Now you're talkin'." Lexi gave a thumbs up. As long as she didn't have to go vegetarian—or God forbid, vegan—she would cope.

A knock at the door startled her. She laid Sammy in the playpen and then went to the door. *Great. The Spanish skunk.* "Come to poison Jessica again?"

Adrián ran his hand through his hair. "I came to say good-bye. I'm going home to Madrid." He stepped inside.

"If I had my way, you'd be going to prison." Lexi shut the door a bit too hard. The bang made Sammy whimper. Lexi snatched her up before it turned into a full-blown gale, and walked the length of the office, gently bouncing Sammy to calm the baby… and to calm herself too.

"Not that I'm ungrateful." Adrián removed his hat and glanced at Jessica. "But, going home to work with my father will be punishment, believe me."

"Poor little rich kid going home to eat daddy's caviar and drink his champagne." Lexi scoffed. "You're not going to get any sympathy from me."

Adrián shrugged and took a few steps closer to the table where Jessica was sitting. "I've come to apologize." He fiddled with his hat. "I don't know what got into me. You're just so smart, and I—"

"And you just can't stand to have a woman beat you." Lexi felt like socking him in the kisser. Why wouldn't the cowgirl press charges? What was wrong with her? Lexi would have charged him so hard he wouldn't know what hit him.

"I'm really sorry, Jessica." Adrián shifted from one foot to the other. "It was great working with you… I mean you truly are the best… and I wish—"

"Never mind," Jessica said, putting him out of his misery.

I would have made him squirm. Why is she so forgiving? Lexi shook her head but bit her tongue. *Best stay out of it.*

"I've got a going away present for you." The cowgirl lifted her bookbag off the floor. She reached inside and pulled out a small gift bag.

"No way!" Lexi rolled her eyes. "This takes the cake."

"Wow. Thanks." Adrián grabbed the bag. "A whole bag of gummies." He held up a cellophane-wrapped package of purple gummy candies. "Snacks for the plane." He bent down and kissed Jessica on the cheek. "You're quite a girl."

"Good luck with your dad." The cowgirl smiled.

What is wrong with that girl? Why is she being so nice to this creep? Lexi swiveled her desk chair around so her back was to the sickening good-bye scene. Sammy spit up on Lexi's blazer in agreement. Camo sauntered over and sat next to Lexi's chair. He licked her hand. "It's okay, buddy," she whispered. *I'm not going to have a meltdown.*

"Tell me what happened with Vanderbilt," Adrián said.

Lexi swiveled back around. She wanted to rub it in that they'd solved the case and he hadn't.

"I heard you busted him." Adrián sat on the edge of the table, swinging his legs, and stuffing gummies into his mouth.

"You should have seen the look on his face when we told

him the museum hadn't gotten around to insuring the Rembrandt." Jessica laughed. "When it sunk in, he went white and collapsed onto his Persian rug."

"So, I was right." Adrián held up his hand for a high-five. "Vanderbilt was the mastermind."

"No," Lexi said. "*We* were right. *We* recovered the paintings. *We* caught the bad guys. All you did was drug my partner and get your ass kicked."

Adrián grimaced but ignored her. "Tell me what happened. How did you apprehend Cobra and Dean? And who killed Frank?" He grabbed another handful of gummies and popped them into his mouth. "Want some?"

"No, thanks." The cowgirl had a sly smile on her face. "I'll enjoy them vicariously."

Vicariously. Hmmm. The cowgirl never turns down sweets.

"Tell me all the gory details," Adrián said, his mouth full of candy.

"*We* tracked Dean, his mother, and girlfriend—"

"Fiancé." Jessica interrupted in an imitation of Dean.

Lexi chuckled. "We tracked them to a cabin in Wallis Cove." She wiped Sammy's mouth with a nursing cloth. "Which, by the way, belonged to Edward Eggs Benedict—"

"Who, as you know, turned out to be Dean's dad," Jessica interrupted again. "Cora Braugh was Egg Benedict's ex-wife *and* his ex-partner in crime, Cobra."

"I still can't believe it," Adrián said.

"No one had seen Cobra's face," Lexi said. "And we'd always assumed Cobra was a man."

"Sexism strikes again." The cowgirl stabbed the air with her finger.

"Cobra punches like a heavy-weight," Adrián said, touching his bruised forehead. "When she got done with me, I felt like I'd been hit by a lorry." He hugged himself. His shirt bulged from the bandage underneath.

"Cora Braugh looks like a cookie-baking den mother," Jessica said. "But she's one tough cookie."

"The cover's not the book," Lexi said. "And to think Cobra's been hiding out on that blueberry farm for the last twenty years." She shook her head. "Right under our noses."

"Did Cobra pull off the heist for Vanderbilt?" Adrián asked, popping another handful of gummies in his mouth.

"I thought you were saving those for the airplane," Lexi said.

"If he eats them all, I've got more." Jessica pointed to her bookbag. "Despite all her sniping at Dean, she did it for him. To pay his tuition to Harvard." She scoffed.

"Turns out, he got in but couldn't afford tuition." Lexi shook her head. "Not everyone can be a scholarship student and go to a fancy school and get a fancy degree." She wagged her finger at the cowgirl. "Miss fancy-pants."

"That's doctor fancy-pants to you." Jessica winked.

"I thought Cobra was known for his—her—surgical strikes," Adrián said. "How do you account for that horrible mess at the museum?"

"She did that to throw us off the scent." Lexi kissed the baby's fuzzy head. "Isn't that right, little mite?"

"After twenty years in hiding, Cobra came out of retirement to send her son to college." The cowgirl sighed. "Now, that's unconditional love." She pointed at the baby. "You'd do the same for Sammy, right?"

Lexi laughed.

"Did you ever figure out why that crappy security system didn't show Cobra in the French Gallery?" Adrián had almost finished the entire bag of gummies.

"Get this," Jessica said. "Dean wanted his pregnant girl-friend to have it for some incomprehensible spiritual thing he's got going on." She raised her eyebrows. "Goth-Girlfriend didn't want to marry Dean. She wanted to marry Frank."

"What?" Adrián asked with his mouth full. "A threesome?"

"When Frank found out Gloria was pregnant and refused to marry her, she killed him." Lexi narrowed her eyes. "Almost serves him right." She thought of Nick. *Will Nick want to marry me when he finds out he has a daughter?* She held Sammy closer.

"Want the rest?" Adrián held out the last of the bag of gummies. "You could use some sweetening up."

"I gave those to Adrián." The cowgirl intercepted the bag and gave it back to him. "You have a whole drawer full of Snickers." She pointed at the desk.

Lexi yanked open the top desk drawer. "I *used to* have a drawer full of Snickers." She held up two candy bars and a handful of empty wrappers. "We must have rats."

The cowgirl sucked her front teeth.

"Pretty good rat impersonation." Lexi laughed.

"Wait. Explain it to me." Adrián polished off the last of the gummies. "That punk girlfriend killed Frank? How?" He pulled a handkerchief out of his jacket pocket and wiped his fingers.

"Goth-Girl is a budding mortician." Jessica raised her eyebrows. "Apparently, she carries formaldehyde with her in her purse just in case she has to embalm someone—or something."

"You should have seen her kitchen closet." The marshal laid the sleeping baby back in the playpen. "Every critter who crossed the threshold was embalmed."

"You're lucky they didn't embalm *you*," the cowgirl said.

"I guess so." Adrián crumpled up the cellophane and threw it in the trash. He glanced at his phone. "I'd better be going. My plane leaves in less than three hours." He dug in his pants pocket and pulled out the key to the Vespa. "I want you to have Bella." He held the key out to Jessica.

"You're giving me your Vespa?" Her eyes went wide. "No. I can't take that."

"Why not?" He dangled the key. "It won't exactly fit in the overhead bin." He shoved the key at her. "Come on. It's the least I can do." He smiled.

"No—"

"Take the damn motorbike," Lexi said. "It is the least he can do. If you don't take it, I will."

The cowgirl took the key. "Thanks." She blushed.

"Thanks for the candy." Adrián flipped his hat back onto his head. "Look me up if you're ever in Madrid. I'll be mopping the floor in the produce section." He sighed and unwrapped a *Chupa Chups*. He held it out to the marshal. "Peace offering?"

She scowled. "You're not getting off that easy." She snatched the lollipop out of his hand.

"Goodbye, ladies." Adrián stopped at the threshold and blew Jessica a kiss. "*Adios Linda. Te extrañaré.* I'll miss you."

The minute he was out of sight, Lexi threw up her hands. "What's wrong with you? The guy drugged you and put you in the hospital, and you give him candy?"

"You were right. He's all hat and no cattle. But…" The cowgirl rifled in her book bag and pulled out a Costco-sized bottle. She held it up and waved it around.

"Holy shit!" Lexi laughed.

"Exactly." She unscrewed the cap and turned the bottle upside down. It was empty. "Adrián just ate an entire bottle of gummy laxatives."

Lexi slammed her computer shut. "Serves him right." She grabbed the diaper bag off the floor. "I hope the seat-belt sign is on for his entire flight to Spain."

Chapter 33

As usual, Jessica held on for dear life as the marshal sped through downtown. One stop more before dinner at Taste of Haiti. The presidential suite at the Charles Hotel.

It was Saturday. Later that night, Lolita was hosting the high stakes poker game for the rich Harvard boys. As much as Jessica dreaded playing poker, she dreaded disappointing her friend even more.

"I'll just be a few minutes," Jessica said as she hopped out of the Charger.

"Sammy, Camo, and I will be here waiting." The marshal cut the engine. "Take your time. I'm in no hurry for soggy vegetables."

"Don't forget the deep-fried meat!" Jessica shut the car door and trotted across the parking lot.

Instead of a luxury hotel, the Charles looked like a a dorm, since it was practically on the Harvard campus. Not the typical place Lolita picked for her poker parties.

With its square chairs, low ceilings, and geometrical carpet, the lobby was more fern corporate than ivy league. On the registration desk, a plaque read: *Come for the IQ, stay for the adventure.* Jessica glanced around at the buttoned-up décor. The

Harvard idea of adventure had to be wiping dust off leather-bound books or using the fax machine in the business center.

She asked directions to the presidential suite, hightailed it across the lobby, and waited for the elevator. Of course, it was on the very top floor. Nothing but the best for Lolita's poker players.

Lolita answered the penthouse door wearing her trademark leather pants, pink cashmere sweater, and strappy five-inch platforms. On her kung-fu feet, those Jimmy Choos should be registered as weapons. "*Milaya*. You're early." Lolita kissed her on both cheeks. "You can help us set up."

"Actually, I can't stay." Jessica grimaced. "Sorry."

"You solved the case." Lolita tilted her head. "What more does the hot marshal want from you?" She winked.

"I might have a shot at getting a permanent job with the Art Crimes Division." Just saying it out loud made her stomach buzz.

"Excellent." Lolita gestured for her to come inside. "Given how little the government pays, you'll need some of tonight's trust-fund cash."

Curious about the setup, Jessica went in and looked around. "I like what you've done with the place." Like a magician, Lolita had turned the stuffy living room into a high-class poker lounge, complete with green felt tablecloth, weighted poker chips, and a bar full of top shelf liquor. No doubt, the hippest restaurant in Boston would be delivering dinner at midnight.

"Playing poker makes me nervous." Jessica grabbed a handful of potato chips from a large bowl on the coffee table and munched on it.

"Hey Miss Jesse." Vanya came out of the kitchen carrying a tray with real crystal wine glasses and whiskey tumblers.

"This hotel is fancier than I thought." Jessica whistled.

"Rented," Lolita said. "Everything, except the furniture."

"And Vanya." Jessica smiled.

"No, I'm renting him too." Lolita raised her eyebrows. "And he's not cheap."

"I'm not a cheap fig." Vanya smiled his gold-plated grin.

"Date," Lolita corrected. "He's dealing tonight. I hope those Harvard boys have a sense of humor."

"Yeah, Vanya's a real card." Jessica mouthed *ha, ha, ha.*

"Very funny." Vanya arranged the crystal on the bar. "Want a drink? We have Jack Daniels, your favorite." He picked up a family-sized bottle of Jack.

"No thanks." It was tempting. And she did deserve it. "I'm going out to dinner with the marshal."

"Be back by ten." Lolita put her arm around Jessica's shoulders. "I promise. You'll make more tonight than your entire year's salary."

"You know what they say." Vanya poured himself a whiskey. "Money can't buy scrappiness."

Jessica turned to her friend "Did he say scrappiness?" She turned back to Vanya. "I'm scrappy enough."

"Money may not buy happiness." Lolita winked. "But it can buy your preferred misery. Anyway, I'm staking you, as usual."

"You don't need to do that." Jessica pulled the Vespa key out of her jeans pocket. "How about you take this as my buy-in."

"A key." Lolita examined it. "A Vespa." She laughed. "My Harley Superlow could eat that thing for lunch." She handed the key back to Jessica.

"It's worth ten grand."

"Tonight's buy-in is fifteen." Lolita rearranged the snacks on the coffee table. "I'll stake you. You keep the toy scooter."

"I'll take it," Vanya said. "I always wanted a toy scooter."

Lolita raised her eyebrows and then plucked the key out of Jessica's hand. "Whatever floats your boat." She held the key out to Vanya. "Your payment for dealing tonight."

"Really, *chuvak?*" His face lit up like a kid's on Christmas morning. "*Kruto.*"

"Really, dude." Lolita placed a fresh cellophane-wrapped deck of cards on the table. "Yes, very cool."

Jessica's phone buzzed. She pulled it out of her jacket pocket. "It's Jack."

"*Milaya.*" Lolita took her by the shoulders. "Maybe you should sit down."

"Why?" Jessica looked down at her phone. It was still ringing.

"I didn't want to tell you." Lolita led her to the sofa and sat her down. "But Jack—."

Jessica tapped the green button on her phone. "Hey Jack."

"Cowgirl. Finally." Jack's voice was as smooth as top-shelf scotch whiskey. "I've been calling you."

"Sorry." She glanced over at Lolita, who grimaced.

"You've been gone so long. And I.. well, I don't know what to say." Jack's voice changed. Now, he sounded nervous. She could imagine him pacing the room as he talked.

Wait. She heard a familiar woman's voice in the background. "Is Amber there?" Amber was one of Jessica's best friends and one of Jack's former girlfriends.

"I need to tell you about me and Amber." Jack paused.

"That's okay." Jessica stood up. "I've got to go. The marshal is waiting."

"I didn't mean to—"

"I know." She sighed. "Really. It's okay." Was it okay? She didn't know what to think… or to feel. She hung up. Suddenly she was exhausted.

"I'm sorry, *milaya.*" Lolita took her hand. "I wanted to tell you."

"I'd better go," Jessica said. "The marshal is waiting outside."

"Forget about Jackass." Lolita squeezed her hand.

"There are more sharks in the sea," Vanya said.

"That's for sure." Jessica laughed. She hugged her friend, and then headed for the door.

"Until tonight." Lolita blew her a kiss. "When you clean out those Harvard boys."

"Clock-cleaning time." Vanya flashed his gold-grilled grin.

"I'm glad you're here." Jessica waved from the threshold and then took off at a gallop.

The marshal had said to take her time, but Federal Marshal Lexington Colt wasn't one to wait.

A TASTE of Haiti was a tiny mom-and-pop joint with a steamtable and an aproned dude wearing a plastic shower cap dolloping grub onto plates. The smell of garlic and spices made Jessica's mouth water.

She chose an assortment of all vegetarian options. Her plate was heaped with *diri ak djon djon* black mushroom rice, *zepina* stewed spinach, and *kalalou* stewed okra. *Yummy*. She couldn't wait to dig in.

The marshal got the opposite, which was the *fritay* plate, basically deep-fried everything—potatoes, plantains, pork, and chicken.

Jessica carried her plate and plasticware to the only open table. There were only three of them.

The table and chairs were scuffed but clean and smelled of bleach water. The linoleum floor was dull, but there was not a spot on it. The bleach must have eaten the shiny top layer off.

"They don't have Diet Mountain Dew," the marshal said as she plopped down on a chair across from Jessica. Mr. Faheem was visiting his sister, so Mrs. Faheem had agreed to watch the baby for an hour while they grabbed dinner. The marshal had left Camo at home too.

Since she started on the Albertina case, Jessica hadn't had

a decent hot sit-down meal. She wolfed down the rice and spinach like she hadn't eaten in a month. Her tongue exploded with spice and a hint of heat. *Ummm. Delicious.*

The marshal pushed a plantain around her plate with a plastic fork. "You did a good job on the case." She stabbed a fried potato. "I'm going to recommend that the bureau take you on full time."

Jessica beamed. "Really?" *Maybe I won't be unemployed, after all. Wait until I tell mom. Mom's bingo friends will never hear the end of it. Mom can finally quit lying about me doing something important back east.*

The marshal's phone chimed.

Jessica's pocket buzzed. *What the heck?* They both got text messages at the same time. *Weird.* She pulled her phone from her jacket pocket. *OMG.* She reread the text. "I'm in MT & Wit-Sec OK'd me to contact you." She glanced over at the marshal and felt the uncanny sensation of looking in a mirror. *He's in Montana? Where? Western Montana? My old stomping grounds.*

The marshal's cheeks were flushed.

"What is it?" Jessica asked.

"You go first," the marshal said, holding her phone to her chest.

"No, that's okay." Jessica took a swig of her coke to wash down the bitter taste in her mouth. "You go."

"Nick," the marshal whispered.

"What?" Jessica's breath caught. "Me too."

"He's in Montana." The marshal closed her eyes.

Is the marshal really in love with Nick? Jessica got a sinking feeling in her stomach. Was she jealous? *No. I'm over Nick. Right?* "Why is he texting us?"

"I can't believe Wit-Sec let him send this." The marshal held up her phone. "He's risking his life... and ours." She grimaced.

"They must have a reason." Jessica fiddled with the fringe on her jacket. "Right?"

"Damned if I know." The marshal shrugged.

"Should we text him back?"

"I have only two words for him." The marshal punched the letters into her phone. "Get lost."

Holy cow. She is *in love with him. He* is *Sammy's dad after all.* Jessica wrote back. "Good to hear from you. Be safe."

Immediately her phone buzzed again. Nick had texted back a heart emoji. *What's he playing at? Texting me and the marshal?*

"He's a two-timing snake." The marshal pushed her plate into the center of the table. "I wonder if he sent this text out in bulk to all the women on his contact list." She tightened her lips. Her dark eyes were on fire with rage.

"Don't let him ruin our dinner." Jessica took a big bite of rice.

The marshal crossed her arms over her chest and just sat there pouting.

Dang. She's really mad. "Can I have your plantain?" She pointed at the marshal's plate with her fork.

"Be my guest." The marshal glared at her.

"Aren't you going to eat your dinner?"

"I lost my appetite."

"Forget about Nick." Jessica stabbed a plantain. "Men are overrated."

"Can't live with 'em..." The marshal forced a smile. "Can't kill 'em."

"How many men does it take to wallpaper a room?" Jessica winked.

"I give up." The marshal pierced a fried potato and popped it into her mouth. "How many?"

"Depends on how thin you slice them." Jessica bit her lip to keep from laughing. She thought of Jack and suddenly the joke wasn't so funny.

The marshal burst out laughing and spewed potato across

the table. Her phone jangled again. This time it was ringing. *Was Nick calling her now?*

"Good Lord. Now what?" The marshal wiped her mouth with her napkin and then picked up her phone. "Marshal Lexington Colt." She glanced over at Jessica. "Right. Okay. Got it." She nodded. "Yes, sir. Thank you, sir."

It's not Nick… not unless she calls him sir. So, who is it?

More nodding. "Six AM. Got it, sir." Her cheeks were even redder than when Nick texted earlier. "Got it. You'll send the terms. I understand. I have one week to give you my decision."

Jessica's chest tightened. The look on the marshal's face gave her an uneasy feeling. *Something has happened.*

"Yes, sir. Thank you, sir." The marshal dropped her phone on the table. Even her sigh had a southern drawl. "You want the good news or the bad news?"

"Is that a trick question?"

"Good news. We've both been promoted." The marshal puffed out her chest and held her hand up.

"Awesome." Jessica gave her a tongue-in-cheek-making-fun-of-Adrián-high-five. "Promoted to what?"

"I'm the new director of the Art Crimes Division in Salt Lake City." The marshal lifted her bottle of coke in a salute.

"Utah?" *Wait.* "You're leaving?" *Just when we were starting to hit it off.*

"And you're my assistant…" The marshal tilted her head. "That is if you want the job."

"Is that the bad news?" Jessica asked.

"No." The marshal chuckled.

"In that case, heck yeah." Jessica clinked coke bottles with the marshal. "A toast. To the FBI's hottest art crimes team."

They both took a swig of coke.

"How can you drink this crap?" The marshal wrinkled her nose. "I need a Dew."

"Gotta monkey on your back?" Jessica smirked.

"Say another word about my choice of beverage, and I'll rescind the job offer."

Jessica made a zipping gestured over her mouth. "So, what's the bad news?"

"There's been a robbery at the Charles Russell Museum in Great Falls, and we're flying out there tomorrow… before dawn." She shook her head. "What am I going to do with Sammy and Camo?"

"Bring them along," Jessica said. "They're part of the team." She smiled.

The marshal exhaled. "I guess, I have no choice."

"The Charles Russell Museum," she repeated. She'd been there once with her dad when she was a kid. "Great Falls, Montana." Only four hours from home. She didn't dare tell her mom, or she'd have to visit Alpine Vista Trailer Park. "I wonder what they took."

"I wonder who the hell is this Charles Russell?"

"Only the most famous Western artist in the history of the United States."

"It would have to be back in Montana." The marshal made a hissing sound. "I nearly froze my ass off in Wyoming. Then I did freeze my ass off in Boston." She sighed. "Why can't the bureau transfer me someplace warm?"

"Summer in Montana is glorious." Jessica cleaned her plate and then hovered her fork over the marshal's. "Don't you want that last potato?"

"Have at it." The marshal pushed her plate across the table. "We'd better go to our respective homes, pack, and then hit the sack."

Jessica glanced at her phone. "It's only seven," she said with her mouth full of potato.

"We're not in Podunk, Montana yet. This is Boston. Our flight leaves at six so we have to be to the airport by four in the freaking morning." She threw her napkin on the table.

"Which means we have to leave by three… or maybe three-fifteen."

"Dang. I might as well go to the airport directly from the poker game." She drained her coke.

"Don't go staying out all night and showing up hung over." The marshal scowled. "If you puke on the plane, you're fired."

"I haven't even started yet, and you've already threatened to fire me twice!" Jessica reached across the table and grabbed the marshal's coke. "Okay, off to bed it is." She finished the marshal's coke. *What the marshal doesn't know won't hurt her.*

"I'm going to take you home and stake out your apartment to make sure you don't sneak out to that poker game." The marshal stood up. "Let's go."

Dang. The marshal must be a mind-reader. "Yes, Mom."

Actually, the marshal was nothing like her mother. Jessica's mom was just a tad crazy and lived in a cloud of cigarette smoke. The marshal was as down-to-earth as they come. The no-nonsense cop had her feet firmly dragging on the ground.

"It's going to take me half the night to pack for Sammy." The marshal held the door open. "It's amazing how much gear that kid needs."

"You go pack the kid, and I'll go make us some Montana spending money." Jessica rubbed her hands together. She didn't really like poker, but she was good at it. Anyway, Lolita would never forgive her if she didn't show.

"You'll go home and go to bed." Now the marshal really did sound like her mom. "Otherwise, I'm going to reconsider my offer."

"Again. Really?" *Crapulence. She's serious.* "Are you really giving me an ultimatum?" Jessica stepped out onto the side-walk and into a warm breeze.

"Just some friendly advice." The marshal fished her car fob out of her purse. "As my daddy always said, discipline is choosing between what you want *now* and what you want *most.*"

"You want me to ghost my best friend?" *It's no wonder the marshal has no friends.*

"With friends like those…" The marshal unlocked the car, slid into the driver's seat, and reached around the back for a Diet Dew. "Boris and Natasha. No surprise you're so good at catching criminals."

"No. *We're* good at catching criminals." Jessica hopped in the passenger seat. Riding shotgun for the marshal was like riding a bucking bronco, but it sure beat going back to Alpine Vista Trailor Park and her mom's vodka-soaked sulking.

"I suppose you're right." The marshal revved the engine. "We do make a pretty good team."

"Darn tootin'." Jessica white-knuckled the hand hold. "The best."

Let the rodeo begin.

The End

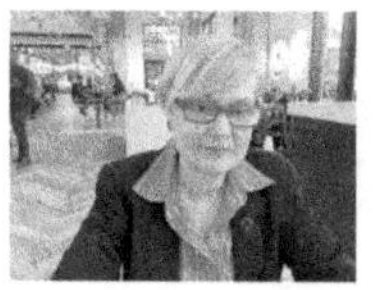

About the Author

Kelly Oliver is the award-winning, bestselling author of three mysteries series: *The Jessica James Mysteries*, the middle grade *Kassy O'Roarke, Pet Detective Mysteries*, and historical cozies *The Fiona Fig Mysteries*.

When she's not writing mysteries, Kelly is Distinguished Professor of Philosophy at Vanderbilt University.

To learn more about Kelly and her books, please visit her website at www.kellyoliverbooks.com.

Also by By Kelly Oliver

The Jesica James Mysteries

The Fiona Figg Mysteries

The Pet Detective Mysteries